GW01605740
Picasso

Distributors in U. K.

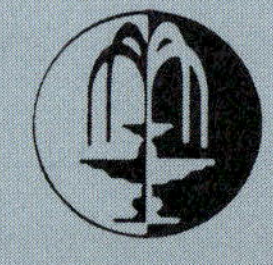

FOUNTAIN PRESS LTD.
45 The Broadway, Tolworth, Surrey KT6 7DW.
Tel: 01-3907768 (3 lines)

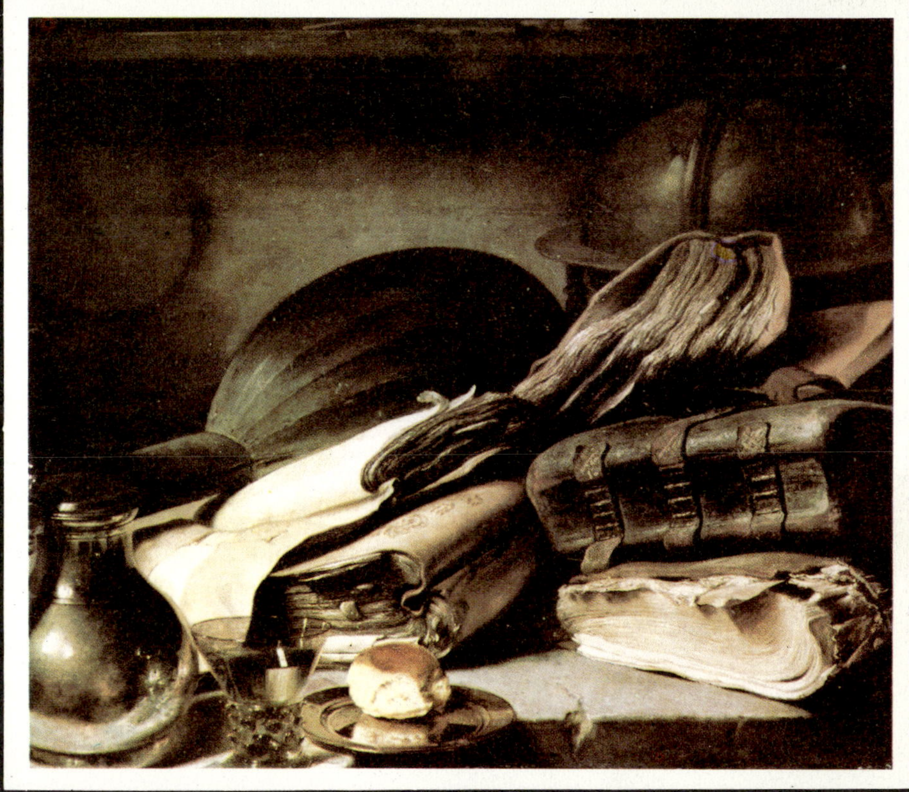

STILL LIFE
IN OILS

JOSE M. PARRAMON

A guide to the technique
and art of oil painting

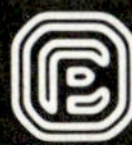

Parramón editions

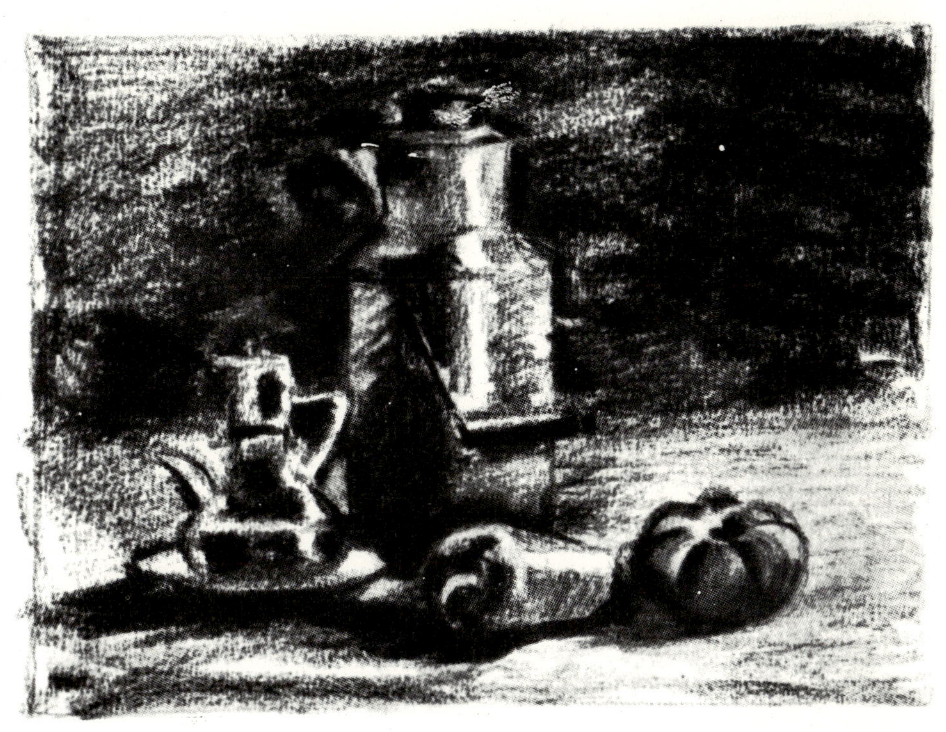

contents

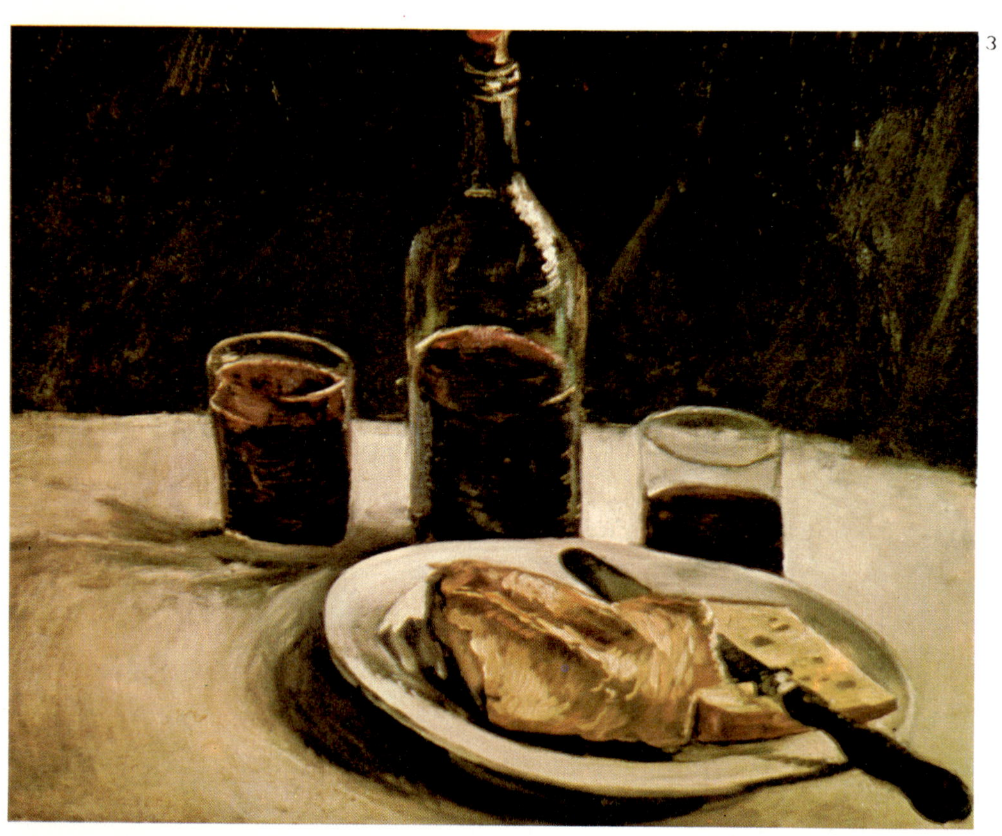
3

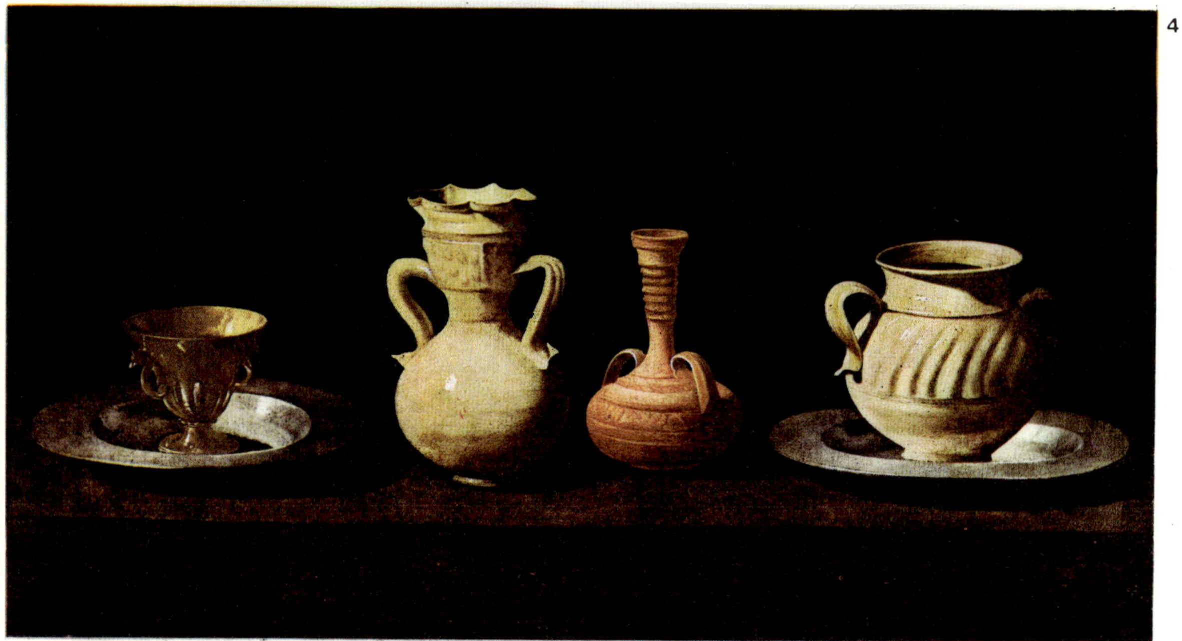
4

introduction

The famous painter Vincent van Gogh wrote one day to his brother Théo about the problem of hiring models. He needed models for his painting, but they had to be paid and he was very short of money. He told Théo: "I've thought about the different ways of earning a living by painting and I've decided to teach. I am going to try to teach still-life painting. I really believe that my method would be better than that used by art teachers in general."

The still life is a very good subject for teaching and learning how to paint; many artists through the centuries have used it. Pacheco recommended it to his pupils Velazquez and Zurbarán as the ideal way of learning how to paint the ordinary things of everyday life - food, fruit, pots and pans, wine carafes and so on. Many such objects can be found in Velasquez's earlier works, the theme continuing right through the ages to Paul Cézanne, who deemed the still life an ideal subject to study: "This is the best way to work, using the still life as a laboratory specimen for trying out new ideas, for combining and composing, developing the visual sense or "feeling", the growing ability to work and the way to arrange different components into one integrated piece of art".

Finally, we know that the still life has been a favourite subject in schools and art colleges because, in the first place, painting a still life calls for the careful selection of each single object. The student can then get away from his predetermined idea of colour and shape. He can choose objects for himself, arranging them on a suitable base and using this like a background, trying to create an original and pleasing unity and learning to work at the composition of a picture. This involves a careful study of light and shade, contrasts and colour harmony in the same subject. Then he can switch objects around, altering the arrangement, the colours and the intensity of light.

Because the still life artist in painting indoors, in a studio or workshop without someone peering over his shoulder and with all his equipment and everything needed at hand, he has an advantage. It's really necessary for the painter to concentrate hard on his work, experimenting and using all the effects of colour, form, technique; in one word: *style,* developing his talent as a painter. Then he won't be like the painter who works exclusively with still life, but he'll become an artist who can paint any subject he likes.

So I've written and illustrated this book: it's meant for anyone who wants to learn and practise with oils —for anyone who wants to paint any subject in oils.

Let's start with a brief look at the origins of the still life in oils, followed by a few illustrated points on its development right up to the present day. Let's have a look now at where, and how, and

Figs. 3 and 4. From a Zurbarán dating from 1600, a 19th-century Van Gogh and up to the present day, the artist has painted "dead nature" or, as we call it, *still life*. Sometimes he has used it for a studio theme. As Van Gogh used to say: "I believe that this is the best subject to copy." But, at other times the still life is painted for its own sake —for a picture of a still life as such.

with what to paint, sorting out an arrangement, organizing the individual parts of the whole and setting out a few basic rules about form and construction. Then we'll move on to the importance of mixing paints and some different techniques of oil painting. Finally, we'll paint some still life studies ourselves, showing through pictures the best way to set about it.

If you have the ambition and want to practise, I hope that you'll be eager to paint at home for your own benefit. If I can help by teaching painting in general, and with oils in particular, then I hope that this book will help you to improve your techniques and teach you to paint better in oils. If it does, I shall not have written in vain.

J. M. Parramon

Fig. 5. Cézanne's *Still life with apples and oranges,* Paris, Louvre. Paul Cézanne painted this in 1900, when he was 61 and had already painted an impressive number of still lifes which he felt expressed his theory that if you "paint from nature, you will find that its forms are based on the cylinder, the sphere and the cube". In this way he had predicted cubism and, with that, modern art.

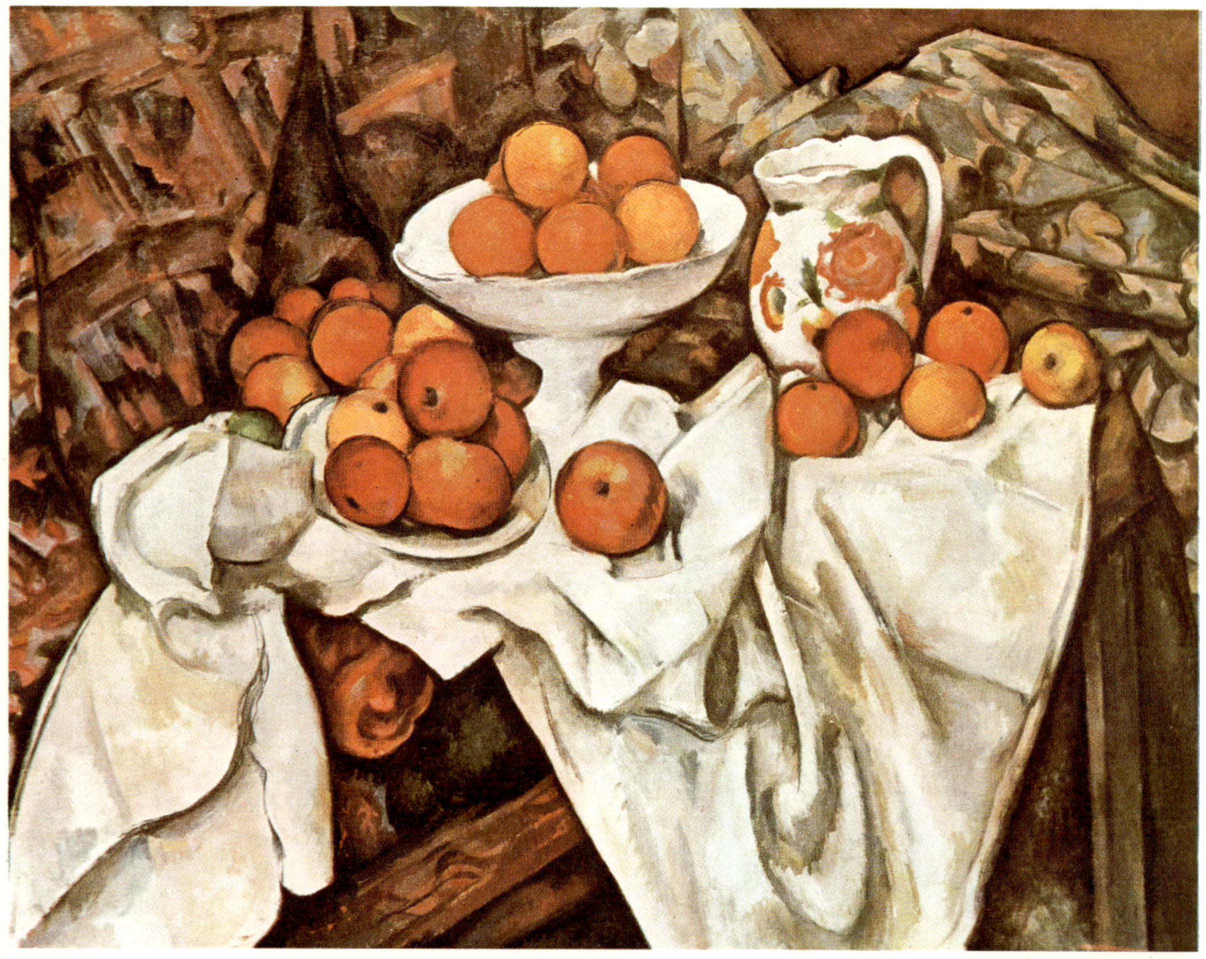

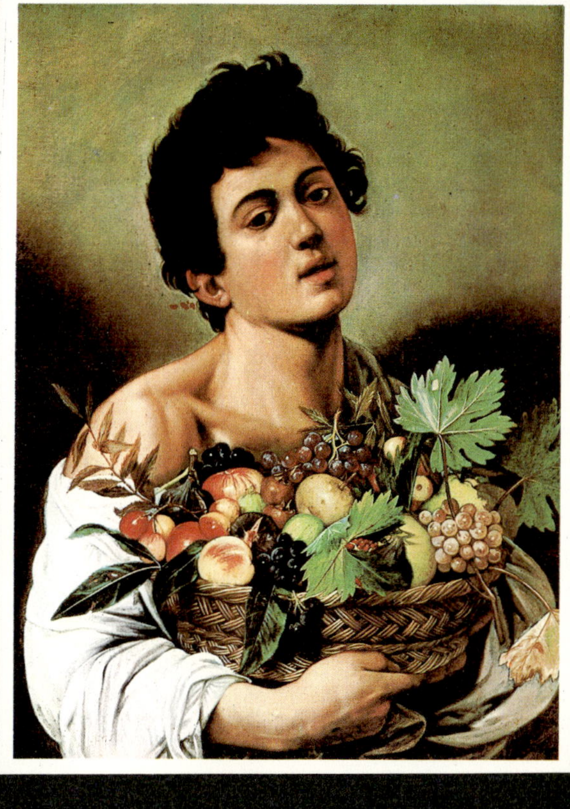

caravaggio: the history of

caravaggio - a zest for life

He was born four hundred years ago in a village called Caravaggio, not far from the northern Italian city of Milan.

His name was Michelangelo Merisi but, by the time he was twelve and apprenticed to a local painter, people were already beginning to refer to him as "Michelangelo from Caravaggio". By the time he arrived in Rome a little later, producing some of the most intense and controversial pictures that had yet been seen, he was known simply as Caravaggio.

He was born in 1573 and died in 1610. A short life indeed —37 years, like Van Gogh— but long enough to exert a profound influence on the work of the greatest artists of seventeenth century Europe: from Velazquez to Rembrandt, from Rubens to La Tour, from Ribera, Zurbarán, Louis Le Nain, Frans Hals and Guido Reni to Murillo, Jordaens and Vermeer —his genius touched them all.

Just what was it that provoked comment like this: "He came into the world to destroy painting" (Poussin). While others considered him the greatest master of all, even going to the extent —in the case of Rubens— of copying his paintings.

Caravaggio changed the basic style of Baroque art, introducing a new dimension into the theory of painting.

The end of the 1600s had seen the Baroque style firmly established. It was sentimental, fantastic and theatrical, to be sure, but at the same time harmonious and beautiful, conforming to certain rules. The Carracci family in Bologna, for example, had laid down principles for the composition of religious works: soft lighting, pastel colours... lilies and clouds, figures gazing heavenwards with rapt expression and, somewhere or other, the obligatory skull. The Church had given its seal of approval to this idealized Baroque fantasy to counter the Reformation movement. And then - Caravaggio burst upon the scene: "this painter who depicts life as it really is, choosing as his subjects the halt and the maimed; who, if he were painting a suit of armour, would choose the rustiest; who clothes his models in the caps, breeches and boots of the commoner, and who delights in reproducing every last wrinkle and wart on the skin" (Bellori, The lives of the painters, 1672).

So why did he choose this style?

Caravaggio was orphaned when he was ten. As a ten-year-old he was apprenticed to Simone Peterzano's workshop in Milan where he studied for four years. History relates that he went to Rome at the age of eighteen and, "being of great

Fig. 6. At the beginning of this chapter, on page 9, we show Caravaggio's painting **Boy with a basket of fruit,** Rome, Borghese Gallery. The figure in this picture is that of Caravaggio himself - a self-portrait. Caravaggio was then twenty, and even at that age the shape and colour of a basket overflowing with fruit really went to his head.

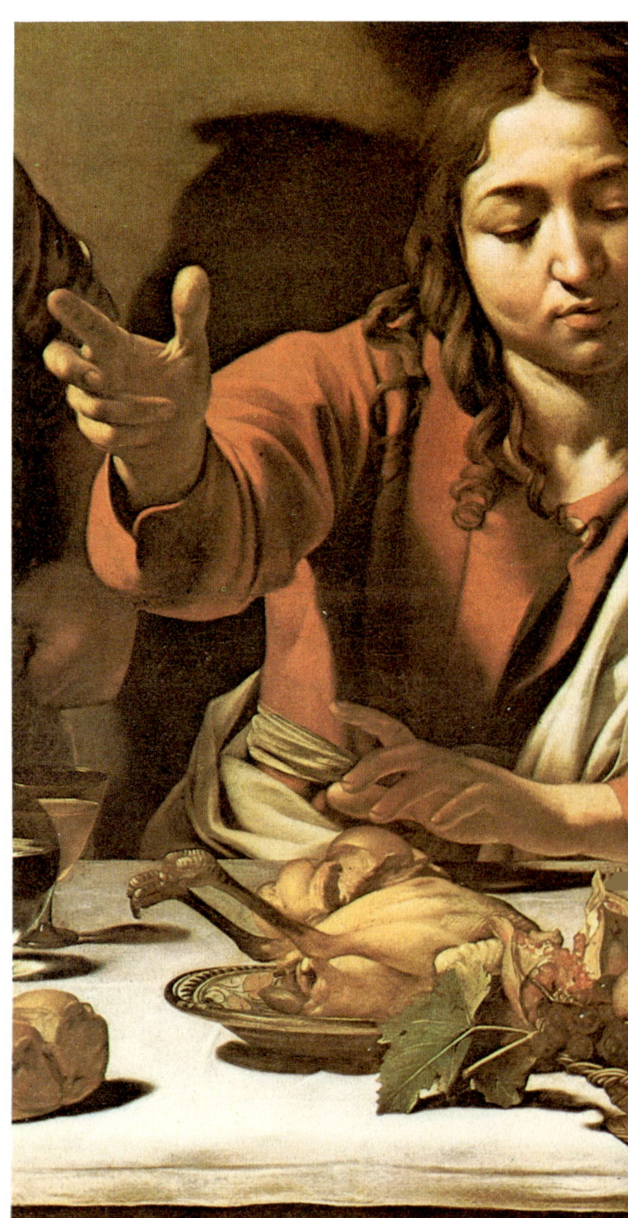

Figs. 7 and 8. Right: Caravaggio's *Entombment of Christ,* Rome, Vatican Gallery. Right: Rubens' copy of this picture, Ottawa, National Gallery of Canada. Note that in Rubens' copy there is no trace of Mary of Cleophas, whose figure, arms extended, appears in the background of the original. It is said that this figure was not shown in Caravaggio's painting at the time that Rubens made his copy, but that it was added later. The perfection of this famous picture is proved by the fact that it has been copied by Rubens, Fragonard, Géricault, Cézanne and even by Baburen and Valentin.

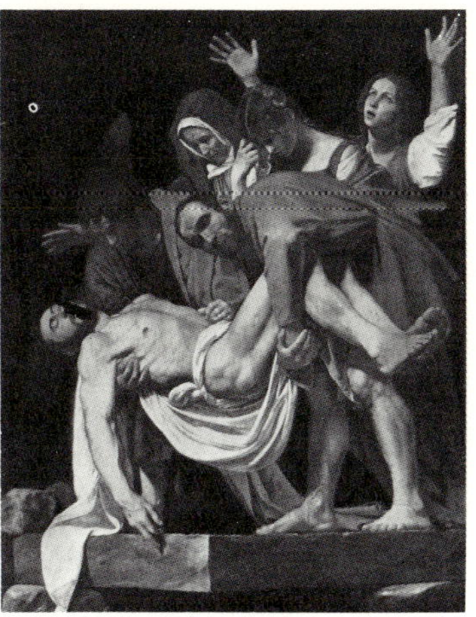

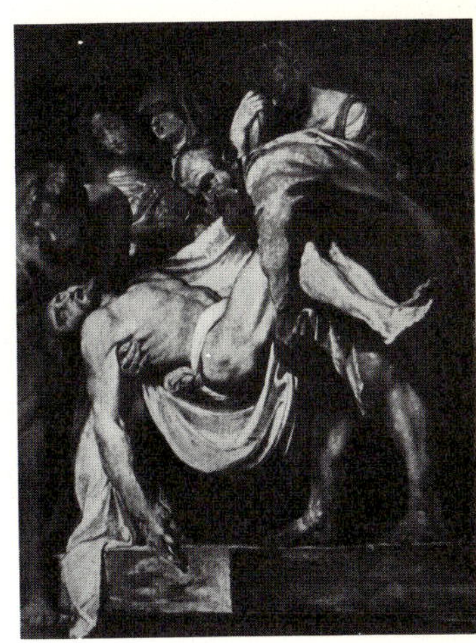

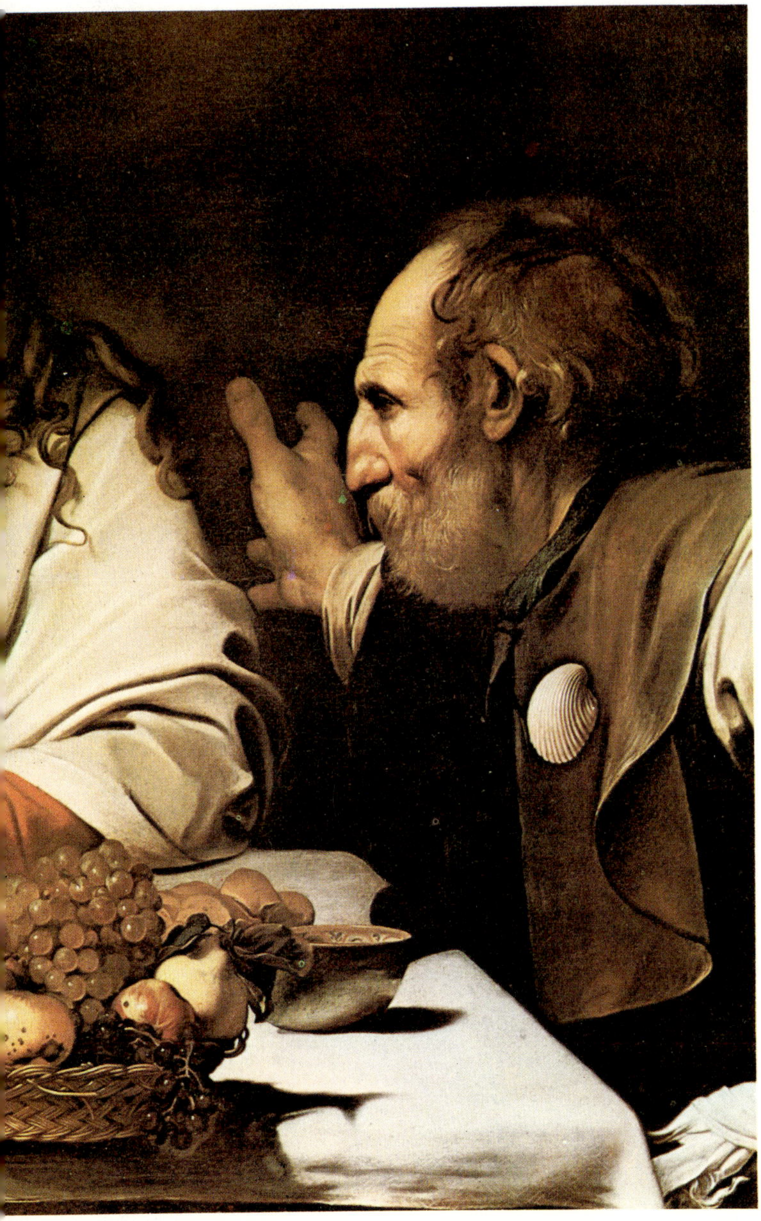

Fig. 9. In this fragment of *The supper at Emmaus,* London, National Gallery, the still life has taken on a natural look. In this marvellous work one's eyes are immediately focused on the figure of Christ, the protagonist. The rest of the painting is seen a fraction later. In Spain, Velazquez, in France, Le Nain followed in Caravaggio's path, using terrific energy to paint these studies of "dead nature", which have come to be called still life. (Caravaggio was 24 when he painted this wonderful picture.)

poverty and low in spirit, worked in Lorenzo Siciliano's studio painting heads - so many heads for an absolute pittance each day, and often three heads a day". (Baglione, 1642). He soon grew ill and was taken to a hospice run by a religious order, but he went on painting. "While he was recovering, he painted many pictures for the Prior." (Mancini, 1619). But what could he paint? For a man who had suffered from hunger since he was ten years old, a man who had often slept rough, sometimes in dirty inns and taverns, spending his time with humble people, beggars and scroungers, what could such a man take as his subject? The answer: "The people themselves, these peasants, these lowly people — precisely these. He took them into his pictures; he portrayed them as they were, grubby, wrinkled, deformed, using them to represent Jesus, St Matthew, St Paul, St Peter! Indeed, did Caravaggio himself not say that Christ, the Virgin Mary and Mary Magdalen were ordinary village people?"

To this complete turnabout, Caravaggio introduced an element which was to change the whole art of painting: *light*. Until then, light had been unimportant. But Caravaggio used light to emphasize, to clarify, to explain, to draw attention to the most important part of his picture. Caravaggio was the true creator of Naturalism within Baroque art.

One day, Caravaggio took a little basket and filled it with a bunch of grapes, a rotten apple, some figs, pears and a peach. Then he painted the first still life in the history of art. This was in 1596, when he was twenty-three. It was not the first time Caravaggio had painted baskets of fruit, jugs, glasses of wine, flowers and even books, musical scores and instruments. In fact, most of Caravaggio's early works include things like these with a mixture of subjects — usually with an element of the secular, or with mythological beings like Bacchus. But he also painted Biblical subjects such as *The Supper at Emmaus.* And it seems as if Caravaggio usually chose to paint real or imaginary settings of taverns and bars or kitchens — places where so often he had spent his time. And with all this, without realizing it, he painted the kind of subjects which were soon to be popular in Spain and France.

Fig. 10. *Basket of fruit,* Milan, Ambrosiana Gallery. Here we have the first still life in the history of art. It's true that there had been earlier trials and errors, as we can see on the next few pages. But the still life as a subject in its own right, i.e. the result of an artist's conscious decision to depict these objects *for their own sake,* did not exist before Caravaggio.

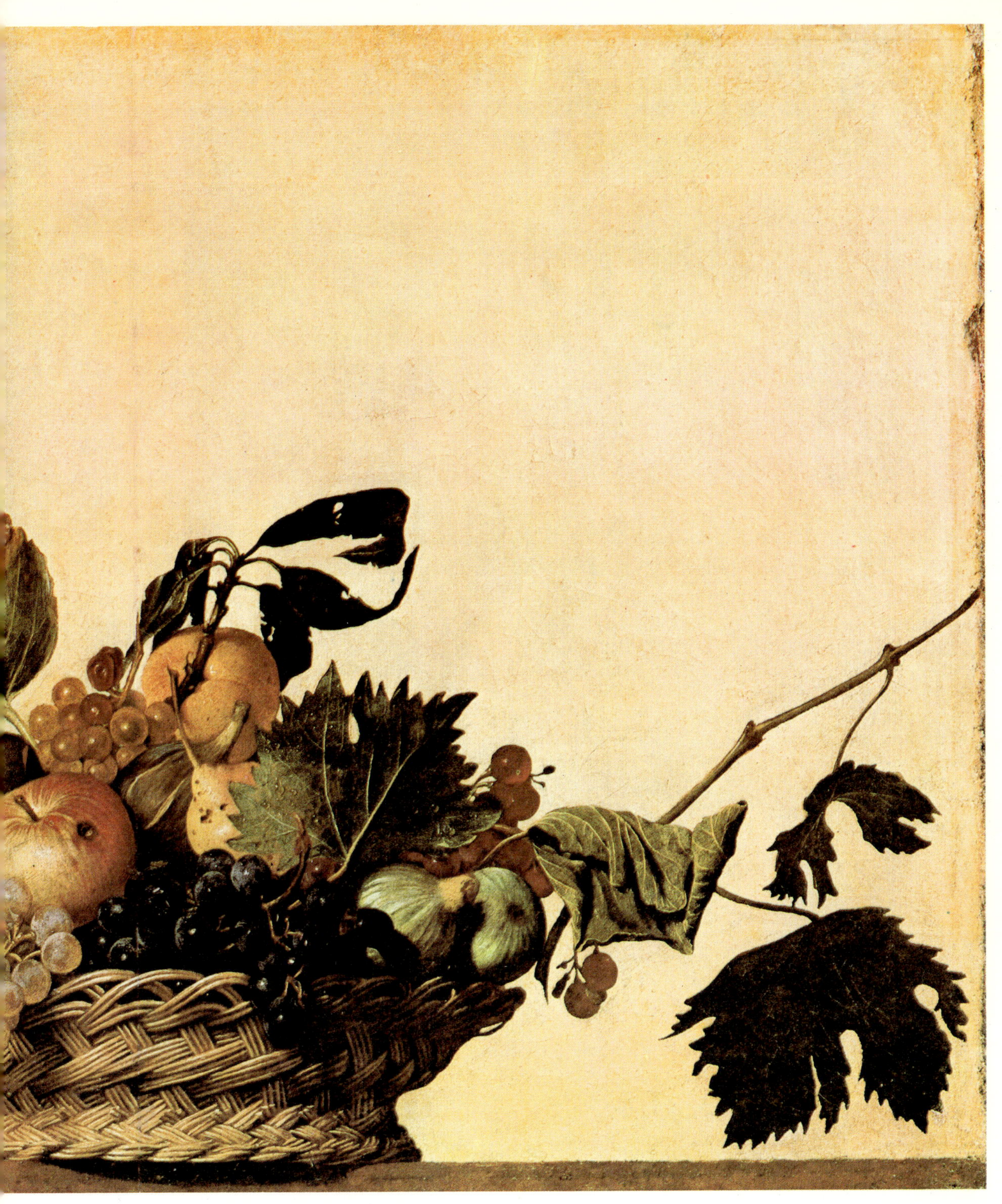

velazquez discovers the still life

HISTORY OF STILL LIFE
VELAZQUEZ DISCOVERS THE STILL LIFE

Caravaggio's strange style —painting the peasant, showing little dark corners of an inn, fruit and foodstuffs with rich light and unexpected contrasts— arrived in Spain, in Seville, to be precise, around 1592. This was at exactly the same time as Caravaggio's stay at the hospice in Rome, where he was painting, as Mancini wrote: "a great number of pictures for the Prior, who took them to Spain, his fatherland". Seven years later, in Seville, Diego Velazquez de Silva was born. Velasquez' early paintings bear witness to the impact of Caravaggio. Velazquez began painting men and women of the street, the village peasants, setting them in inns and rowdy, boisterous taverns, kitchen scenes showing tables spread with food and drink, as in the paintings called *Breakfast, The guests, Two boys eating,* or even in a corner of a simple kitchen, as in the *Old woman cooking eggs, The servant,* or *Christ in the house of Martha.* Velazquez was about twenty when he produced these works, which the critics and the academics called "bodegones". The Spanish word "bodegón" has at other times had a very different meaning —it was once used to describe hack art or canvases which were just daubed with paint.

In order to understand the shock and the scorn that was engendered by the paintings of Caravaggio and Velazquez, together with those of all their young followers, one must remember that in the seventeenth century painting was a most vital medium, more important than any other means of communication. This applied to the upper classes and the scholars, and it was, in its own time, the right type of medium for society in general. What could the State and the seventeenth-century Establishment say about the kind of art which portrayed heroes, gods and saints as simple village people? In Italy, Caravaggio, in Spain, Velazquez, in France, Louis Le Nain were the "lower classes" who "degraded" art, annoying the conservatives and academics.

But, as in other times, the artist had rediscovered truth. And this was the right time for the simplicity of lowliness, "dead nature", the Still Life.

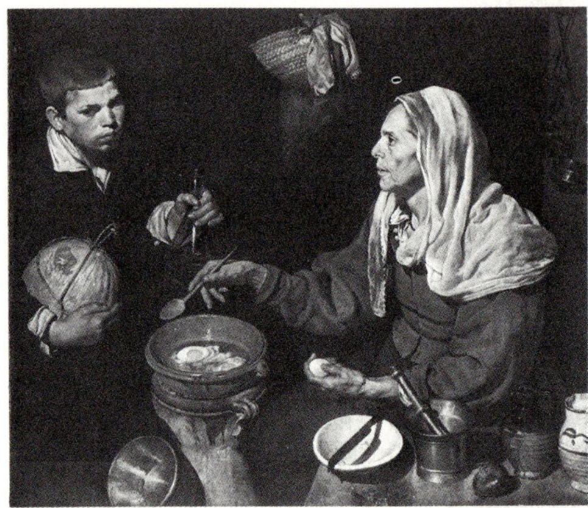

Figs. 11 and 12. Above: Velazquez' *Old woman cooking eggs,* Edinburgh, National Gallery. Below: his *The Water-carrier of Seville,* London, Apsley House. Both were painted in the so-called Velazquez Seville' period (1617-1622), i.e. when Velazquez was between eighteen and twenty-three.

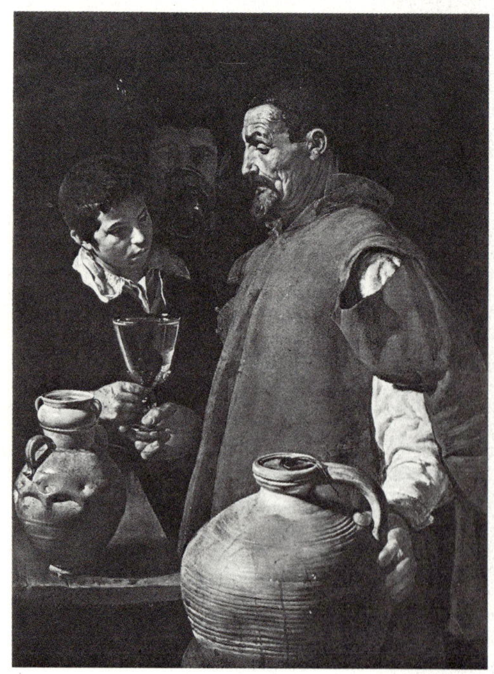

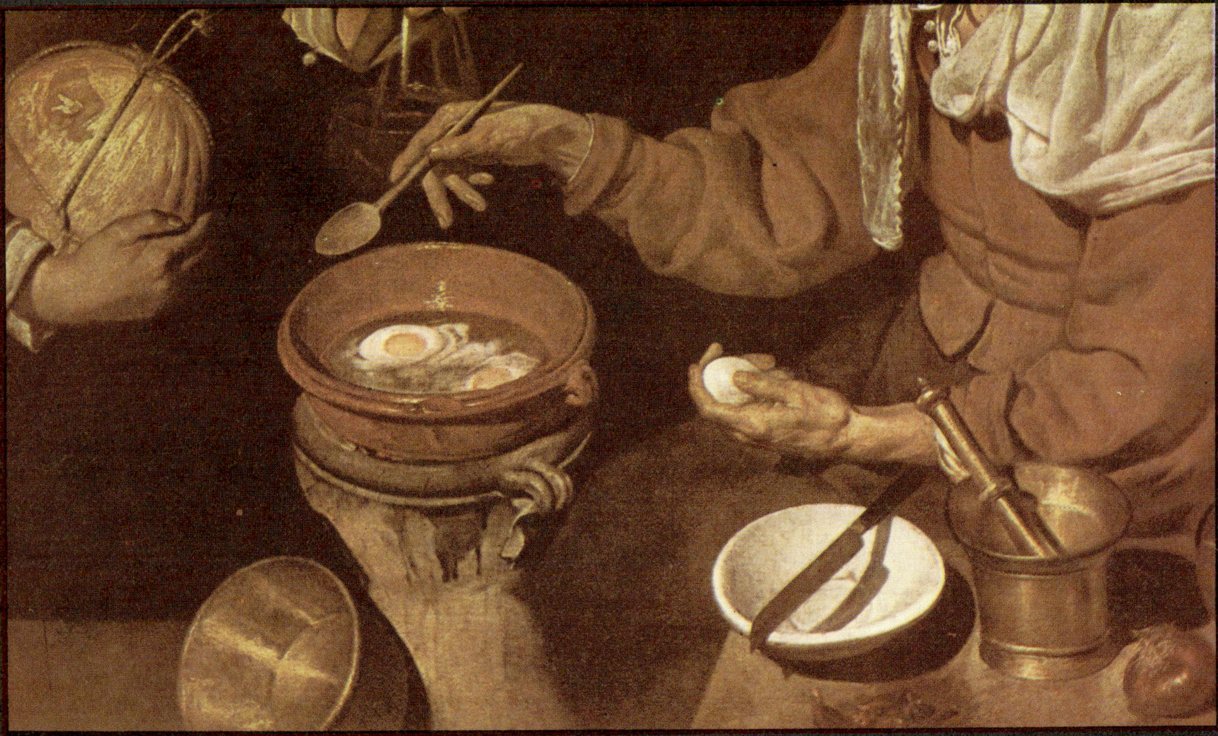

Figs. 13 and 14. Details from Velazquez paintings *Old woman cooking eggs* and *The water-carrier of Seville.* These two amazing examples of still life include a human figure. Velazquez painted them in Seville and they are the contemporaries of pictures by Zurbarán, Alonso Cano and others. Velazquez studied under Pacheco and Caravaggio influenced them all.

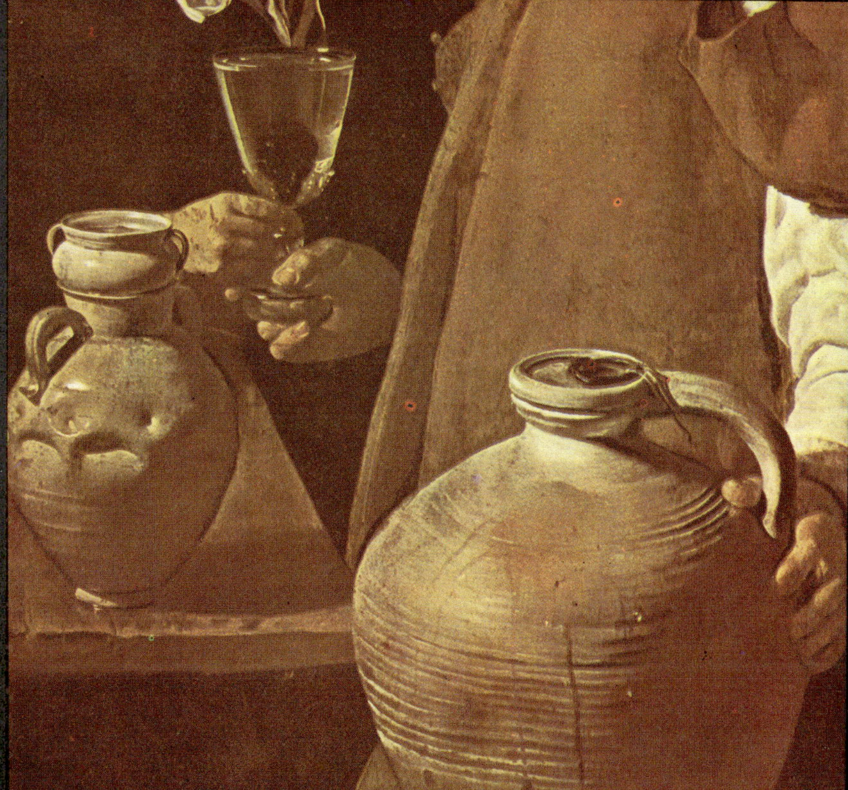

when, how, why and what?

This descriptive type of painting, portraying things about the house, flowers, fruit and goodies, etc, has existed from antiquity. It was after the Renaissance that these elements began to take their place as the main subject of a picture but, in the sixteenth century, there were many artists who painted figures into a scene of "dead nature" creating still lifes with figures. We give an example here: Vicenzo Campi's *The fruit seller,* painted about 1560.

Painted earlier still than these, there are three pictures which fit into the category of still life: there is a 1470 Madonna painted a century before Caravaggio by a pupil of Roger van de Weyden, a fifteenth-century Flemish painter; on its back is a still life, gracefully set in a niche, incorporating several objects which one associated with the Annunciation.

There is also a better-known picture, *Vase of flowers in an alcove,* painted in 1490 by Hans Memling, a German artist. Strangely, this is also painted on the back of a portrait.

Finally we come to the *Dead bird,* painted in about 1504 by the Venetian artist Japoco de'Barbari. This is the exception which proves the rule. Just as the other two paintings cannot really be called still life in the present meaning of the word, this is the only one of these pictures which is literally "dead nature".

Fig. 15. Vicenzo Campi: *The fruit seller,* Milan, Brera Gallery. This work, painted in about 1560, belongs to the type called still life with figures.

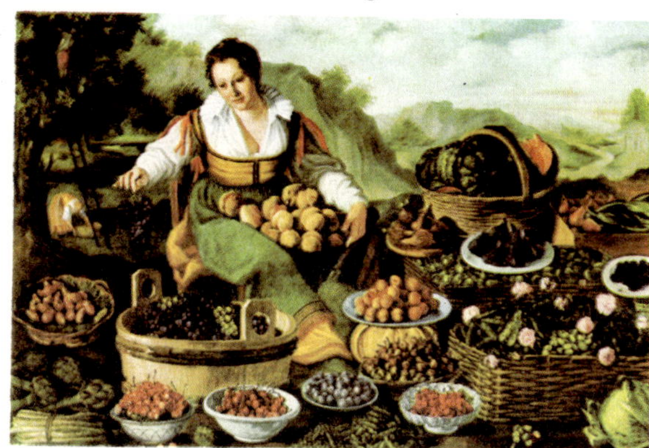

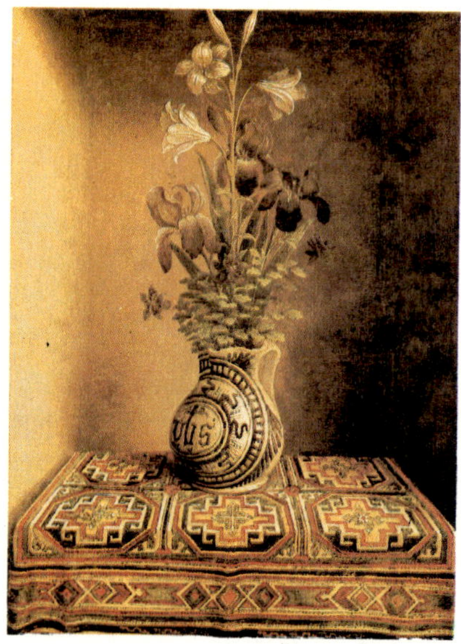

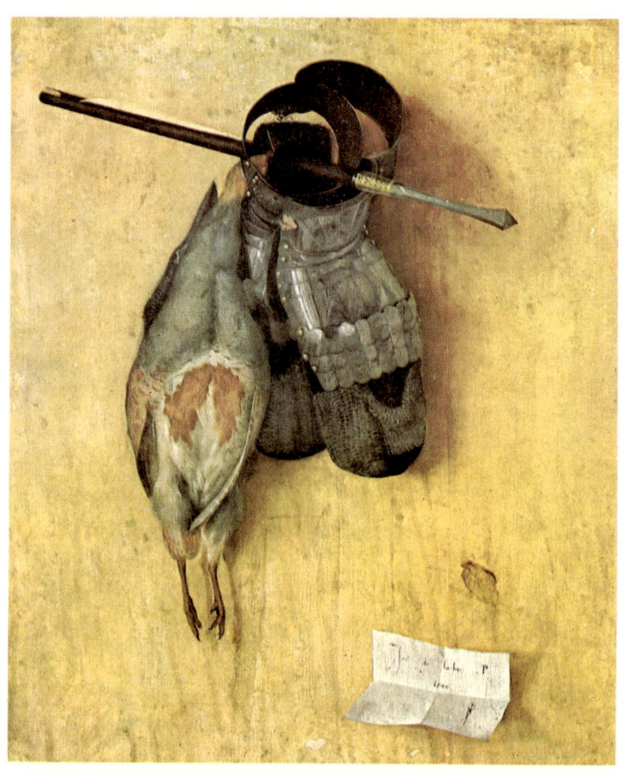

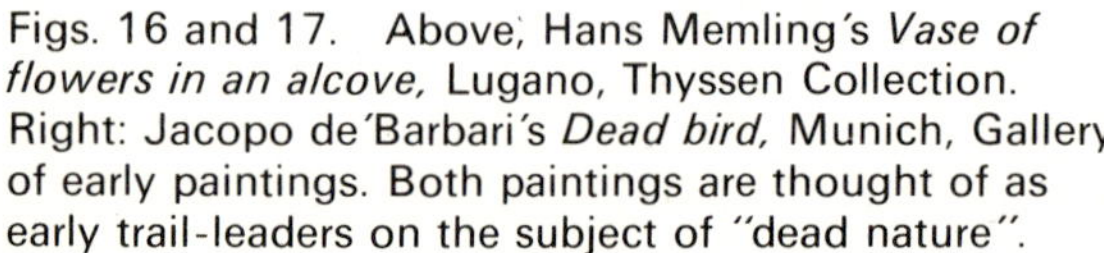

Figs. 16 and 17. Above; Hans Memling's *Vase of flowers in an alcove,* Lugano, Thyssen Collection. Right: Jacopo de'Barbari's *Dead bird,* Munich, Gallery of early paintings. Both paintings are thought of as early trail-leaders on the subject of "dead nature".

subjects of early still life

We are able to say with certainty just when still life as we know it first saw the light of day in the Low Countries and, at the same time, in Italy towards the end of the sixteenth century. In Southern Europe it grew from the talent of Caravaggio himself. In the north, perhaps, it was the logical result of the Reformation which, having downgraded religious art, must have left artists looking for something else to paint. So still life, along with other secular subjects, was eagerly taken up by artists and sculptors alike.

By the beginning of the seventeenth century three basic types of still life had been developed. Lhome's *Vanitas* shown below was one such (Fig. 18). This was intended to be a reminder of the transience and impermanence of life, with the spectre of Death just around the corner-religion at this time being represented by a human skull as a symbol of death and of the hereafter. This painting shows a candle burning down to nothingness and an hour glass, both reminding one of the brevity of life, an impermanence shared by material things —money, books, flowers and the brightly-coloured butterfly.

Soon a symbolic type of still life came into being, somehow representing the five senses: sight, hearing, touch, taste and smell. Here religion was symbolically linked with Nature —fire, wind and water. This so-called symbolic still life reappeared much later, in the eighteenth century, but this time it depicted Art with a capital A, especially in painting, sculpture and literature.

Figs. 18-21. Four paintings of subjects of early still life:

Fig. 18. Lhomés *Vanitas.* Troy Collection

Fig. 19. Linard's *The five senses and the four elements,* Algiers, Fine Art Museum.

Fig. 20. Chardin's *Paraphernalia of art,* Paris, Louvre.

Fig. 21. Louis Tessier: *Arts and science.*

18

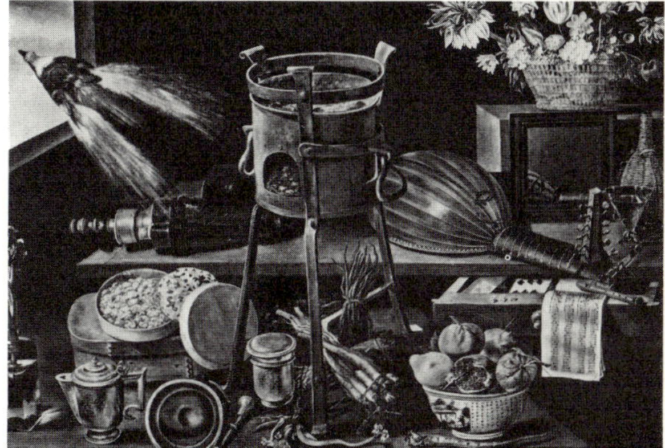

19

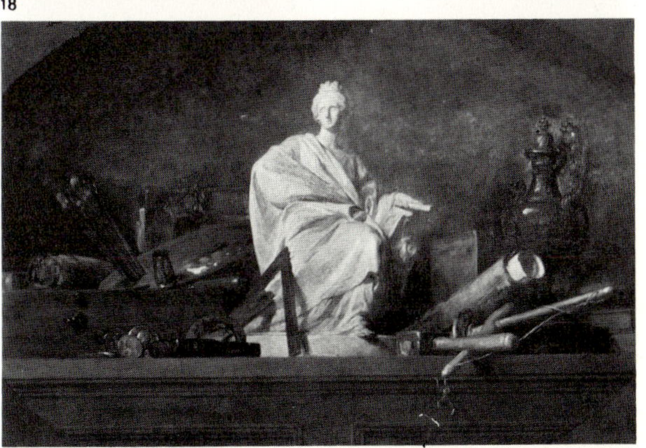

20

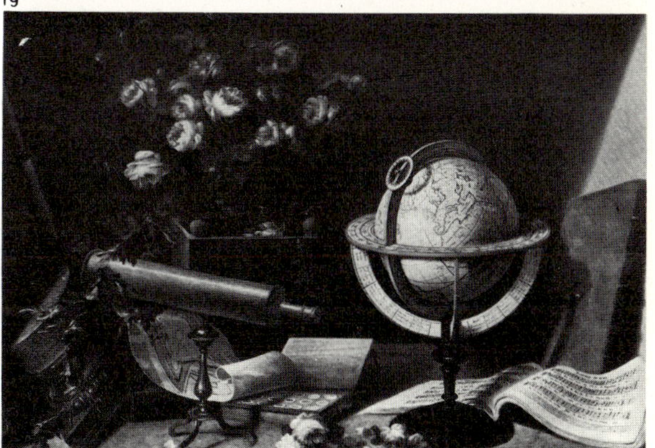

21

virtuosity and "trompe l'oeil"

Together with the theme of *Vanites* and symbolic pictures of this kind, there was a third subject for still life, using objects chosen to bring out the painter's skill. In these pictures flowers and fruit, pitchers and baskets abound, already incorporating the principles of seventeenth-century art. Artists included in their paintings little insects and tiny creatures, beetles, butterflies, snails and miniature lizards. By introducing these minute creatures, the artist tried to prove his virtuosity and to deceive the eye. The cultivation of this trick, so that an insect settled on a piece of fruit or on a table top would seem "real" to the viewer, not just painted on, led, in the middle of the seventeenth century, to a form of art called *trompe l'oeil,* a French expression meaning "deceiving the eye".

In modern art, *trompe l'oeil* reappears as Hyperrealism in still life. It's used by Ken Davies in the United States, Hockney in England, Sciltian in Italy and many, many more artists.

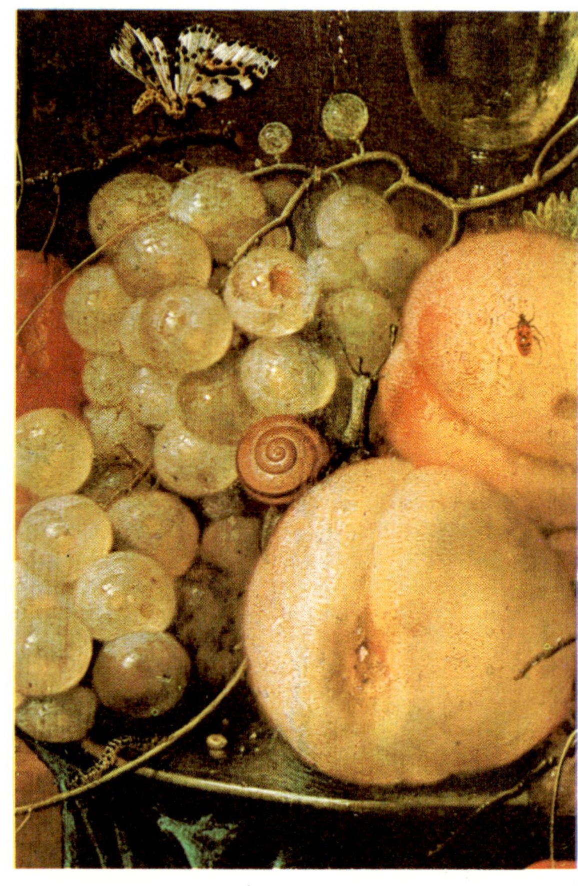

Fig. 22 (right). Detail from a still life by J. D. Coosemas, Madrid, Prado. We can see the small features of virtuosity typical of the time. He included a butterfly (top), a ladybird (right), a snail (centre) and a caterpillar (bottom left). It is from this kind of painting that the *trompe l'oeil* style later developed.

Figs. 25, 26, 27. Three examples of the early treatment of the still life theme, showing virtuosity but painted with no intention of symbolism.
Left to right: in this still life the Spaniard Sánchez Cotán adopts a primitive approach which can be found now in the contemporary works of North American artists, Ken Davies, for instance; Fig. 26, detail from a French artist, Boucle, reveals exceptional skill and minute attention to detail; lastly, another French painter, Vignon, demonstrates his mastery by including insects painted in miniature and in perspective.

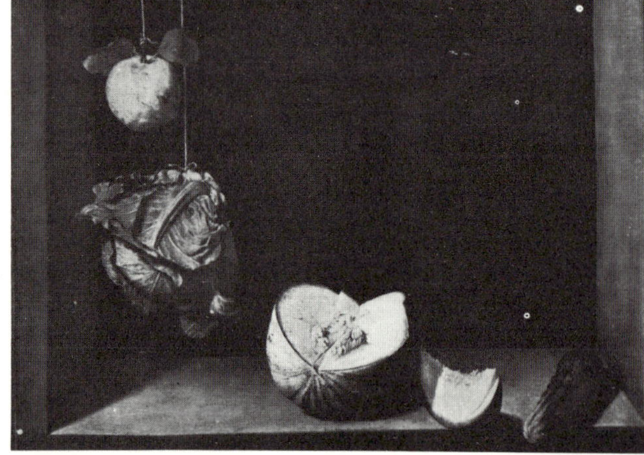

Fig. 25. Sánchez Cotán: *Still Life,* USA, California Fine Art Collection, San Diego.

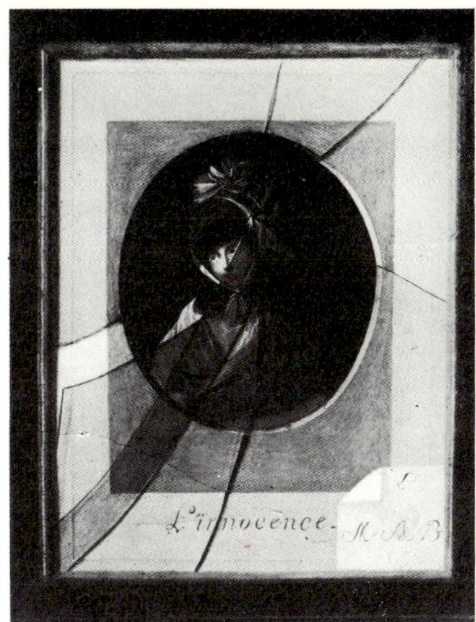

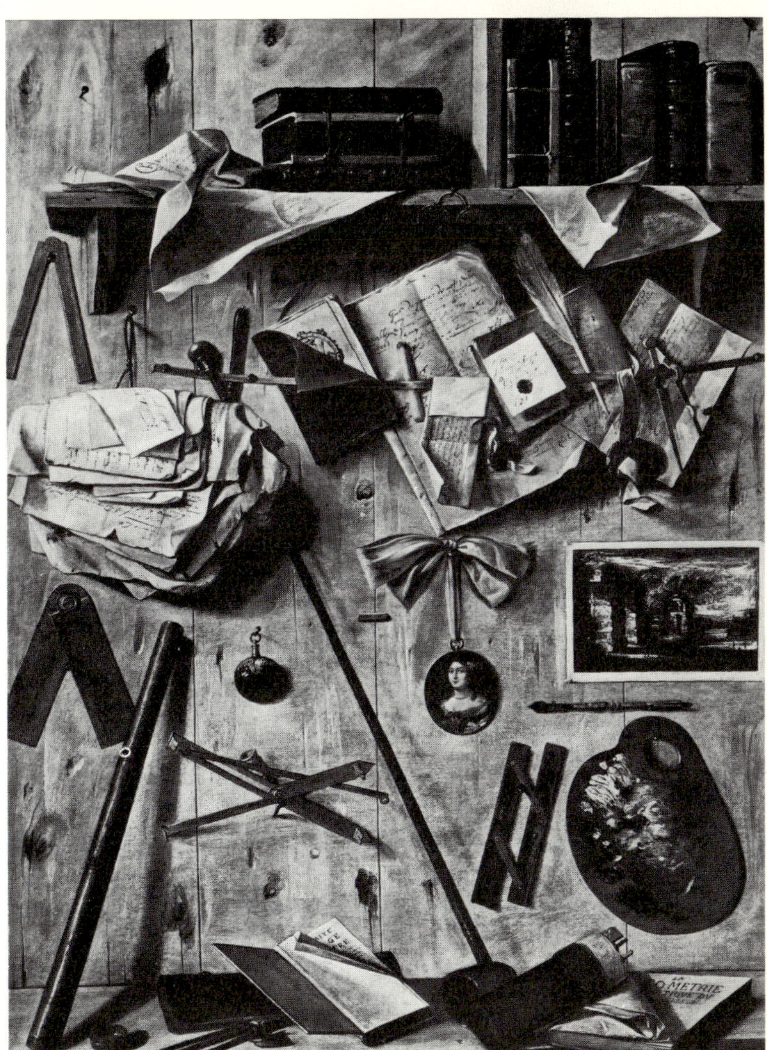

Figs. 23 and 24. Right: a typical *trompe l'oeil* by J. F. De La Motte, France, private collection; he uses effects of relief, detail and imitative technique to the maximum in the way characteristic of this subject and style. This is now fashionable again in the still lifes of some North American modern artists, as well as being echoed in certain works of contemporary Hyper-realism. Above: the ultimate in *trompe l'oeil:* painting of a framed picture with its glass broken, by Duplessis-Berteux, Paris, private collection.

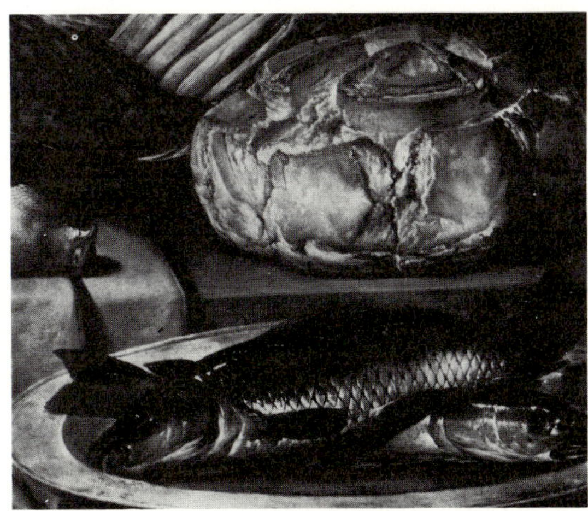

Fig. 26. Detail from P. Boucle's *Carp and pike, poultry and game,* Paris, Collection Cailleux.

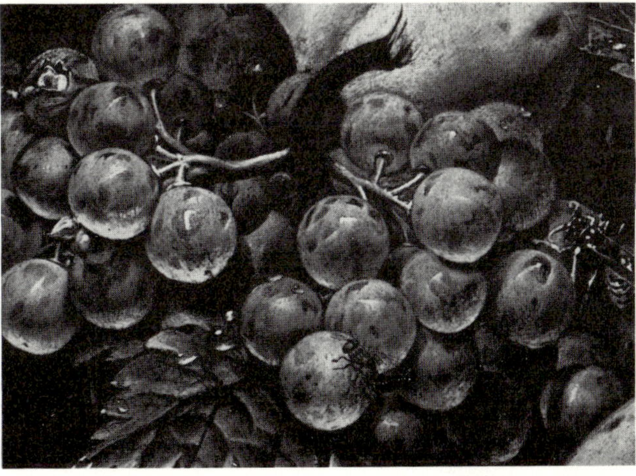

Fig. 27. Charlotte Vignon: *Peaches and grapes* (detail), Paris, J. R. Collection.

sixteenth to seventeenth centuries

The first still-life pictures as such appeared at the end of the 16th century. Outstanding among these are the works of the Dutch painters Jacobo de Ghent and Van der Ast, the Flemish master Pieter Bruegel the Elder, the Italian painter Caravaggio and the Spaniard Sánchez Cotán. Soon afterwards Jacques Linard and Louise Moillon came to the forefront in France and Van Schooten became esteemed in Holland.

The marked similarity in composition will be apparent from the illustrations in these pages. Note that Van der Ast, Van Schooten, Cotán and Moillon don't merely paint some shells or pieces of fruit but a group, or rather a heap of objects, since the merits of a simpler arrangement using fewer and more diverse elements, as already achieved by Caravaggio in his famous *Basket of fruit,* had not yet been appreciated.

In the following pages we show how this early kind of composition was superseded in the 17th century.

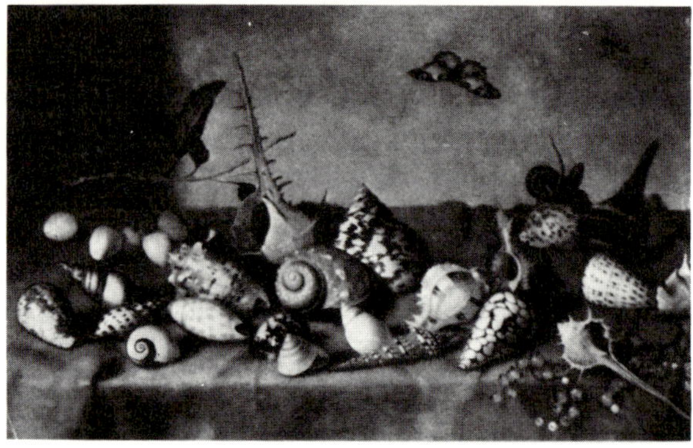

Fig. 28. Notable among the earliest Dutch still life painters is Van der Ast. The subject-matter of this picture, *Shells,* Rotterdam, Boymans Museum, was much to the taste of the townsmen interested in buying pictures and collecting treasures from the Indies.

Fig. 29. Van Schooten: *Laden table,* Sweden, Carlsson Collection. Van Schooten was another famous Dutch artist (mid-16th century). His composition is archaically symmetrical, but he stamps his own mark on his work with minute detail, like that of *trompe l'oeil.*

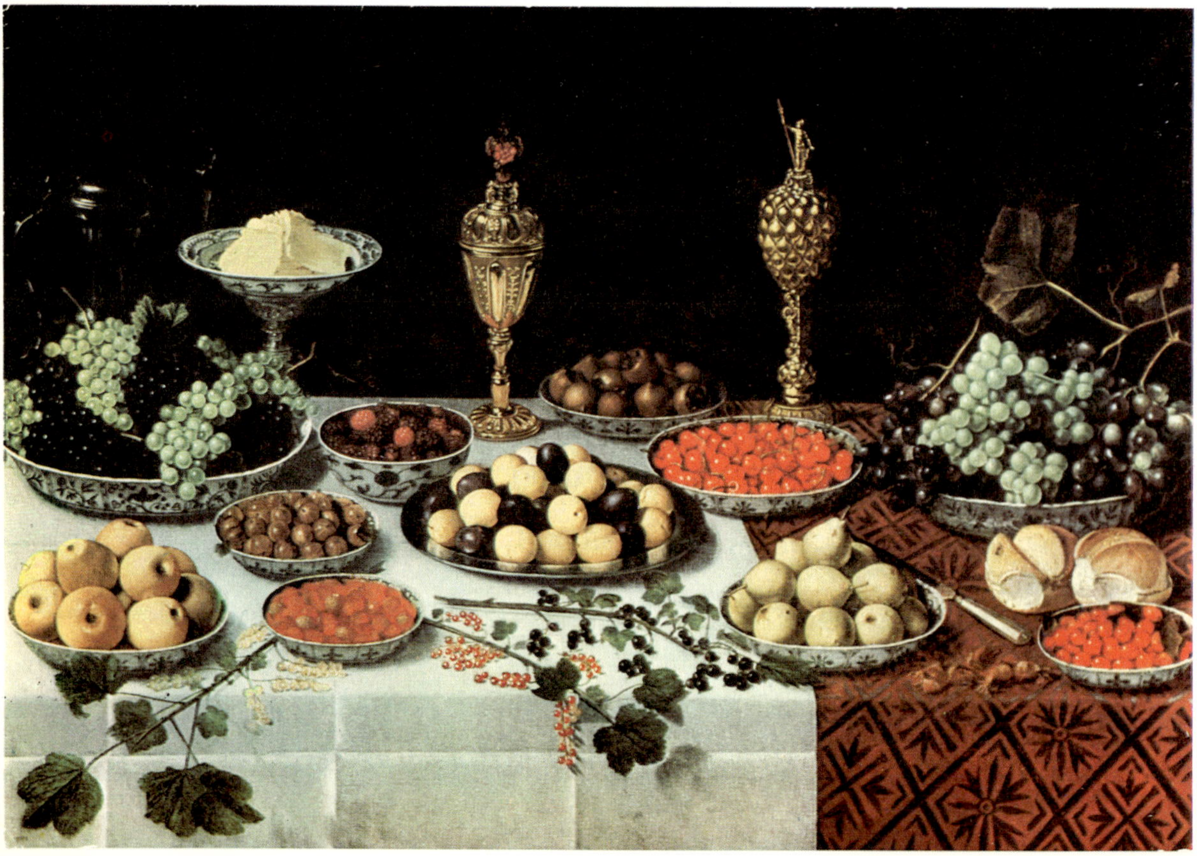

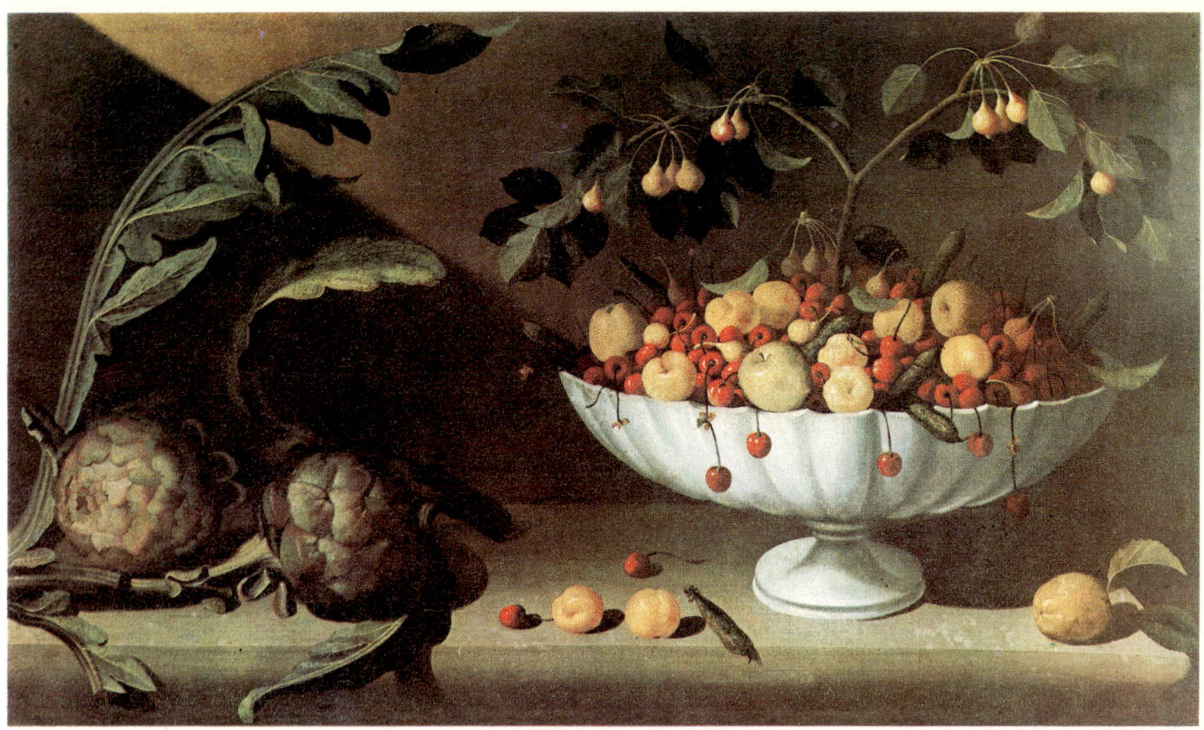

Fig. 30. Sánchez Cotán: *Still life with fruit and artichokes,* New York, Victor Spark Collection. At the end of the 16th century the works of the Carthusian monk Juan Sánchez Cotán appeared in Spain. His still lifes combine the Spanish spirit with Caravaggio's use of shadow, and with the Baroque style then emerging. Sánchez Cotán's paintings have marked personality, great simplicity and austerity. He never painted the precious metal dishes, jugs or goblets so frequently depicted by his contemporaries. His style influenced many Spanish artists of the time, and his followers included another still-life painter, Felipe Ramírez.

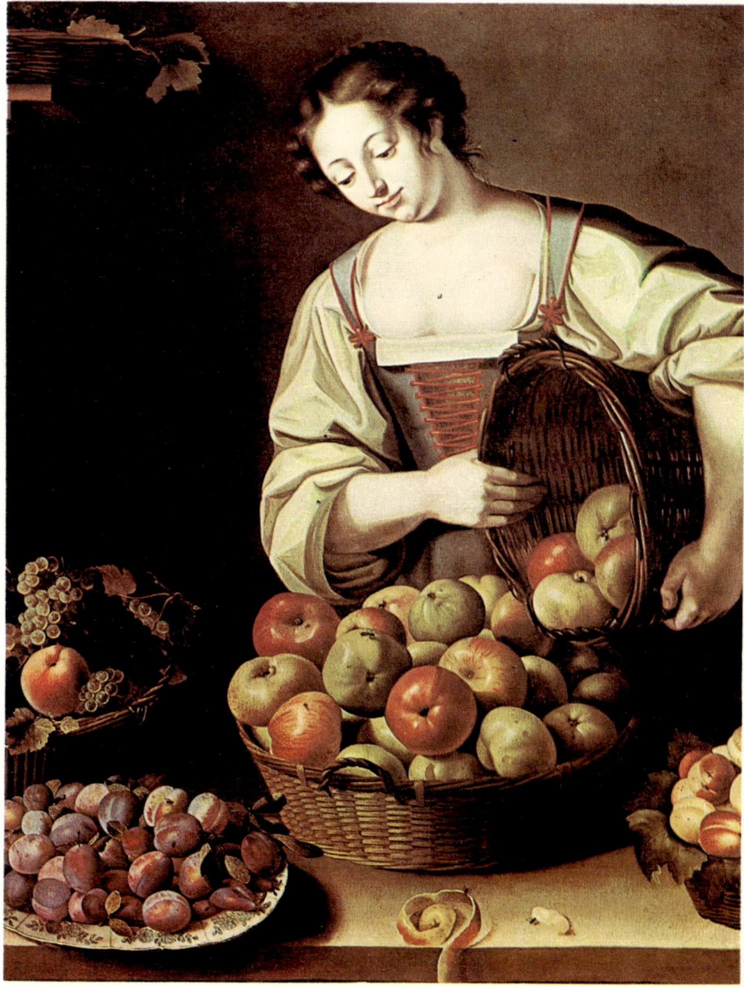

Fig. 31. Louise Moillon: *The fruit vendor,* New York, private collection. The beginning of the 17th century saw the emergence in France of an outstanding female still-life artist, the niece of François Garcier, who painted the same subject. Moillon's pictures have the mastery and personality seen in this work and it may be regarded as one of the best of its era.

the seventeenth century

In the 17th century Dutch and Flemish painters dominated this subject. In Holland, Pieter Claesz, Cooseman, Van Heem, van de Velde and others, specially Willem Heda, painted marvellous still lifes. In Flanders, Van Soon, Jan Fyt and Clara Peeters were among those who raised the level of artistic achievement.

In Spain, Zurbarán and Velazquez discovered the potential of the still life and painted wonderful pictures, such as *The water-carrier* and the famous *Vessels on a cloth,* while Juan de Valdés Leal painted his *Vanitas* and Felipe Ramírez followed the school of Sánchez Cotán.

In France, Bauguin, Stoskopff and Dupuisy were among the successful interpreters of the whole theme of Nature Morte, from a simple picture with two or three elements to the elaborate and stylized content of grandiose paintings, from the subject of "transience" to the simple still life with a few carefully-arranged pieces of fruit.

Fig. 32. Willem Heda: (top right) *Still Life,* Madrid, Prado. Heda was indubitably one of the greatest 17th century Dutch painters of still life. It has been said that Heda's pictures possess three essential factors of the art of composition: a) selection of the model based on elements with definite geometric shapes, exhibiting the principle of unity and coherence; b) use of a diagonal arrangement of composition, arrested by a tall, elegant vessel or some other element; c) careful colour harmonization.

Fig. 33. L. Bauguin: (below) *Still life with chessboard,* Paris, Louvre. This is a good example of it's kind of the "symbolic" still life. The subject seems to be a portrayal of the five senses, with the mandolin and music score representing hearing, the purse, cards and chessboard indicating touch, the mirror (background, right) for sight, the carnations for smell, and the bread and wine for taste.

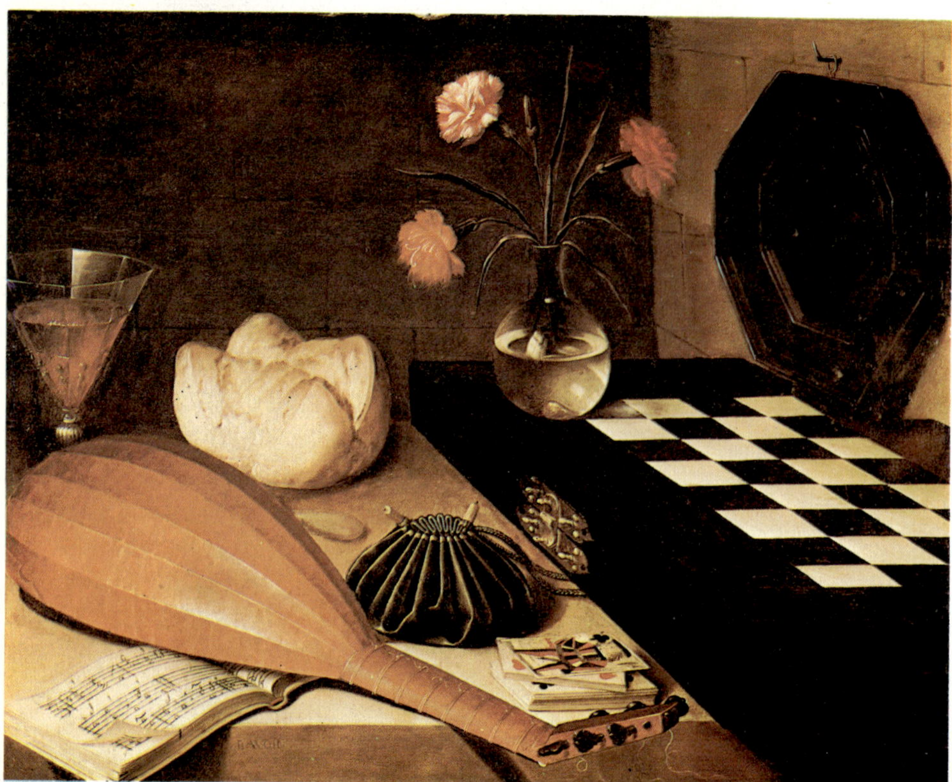

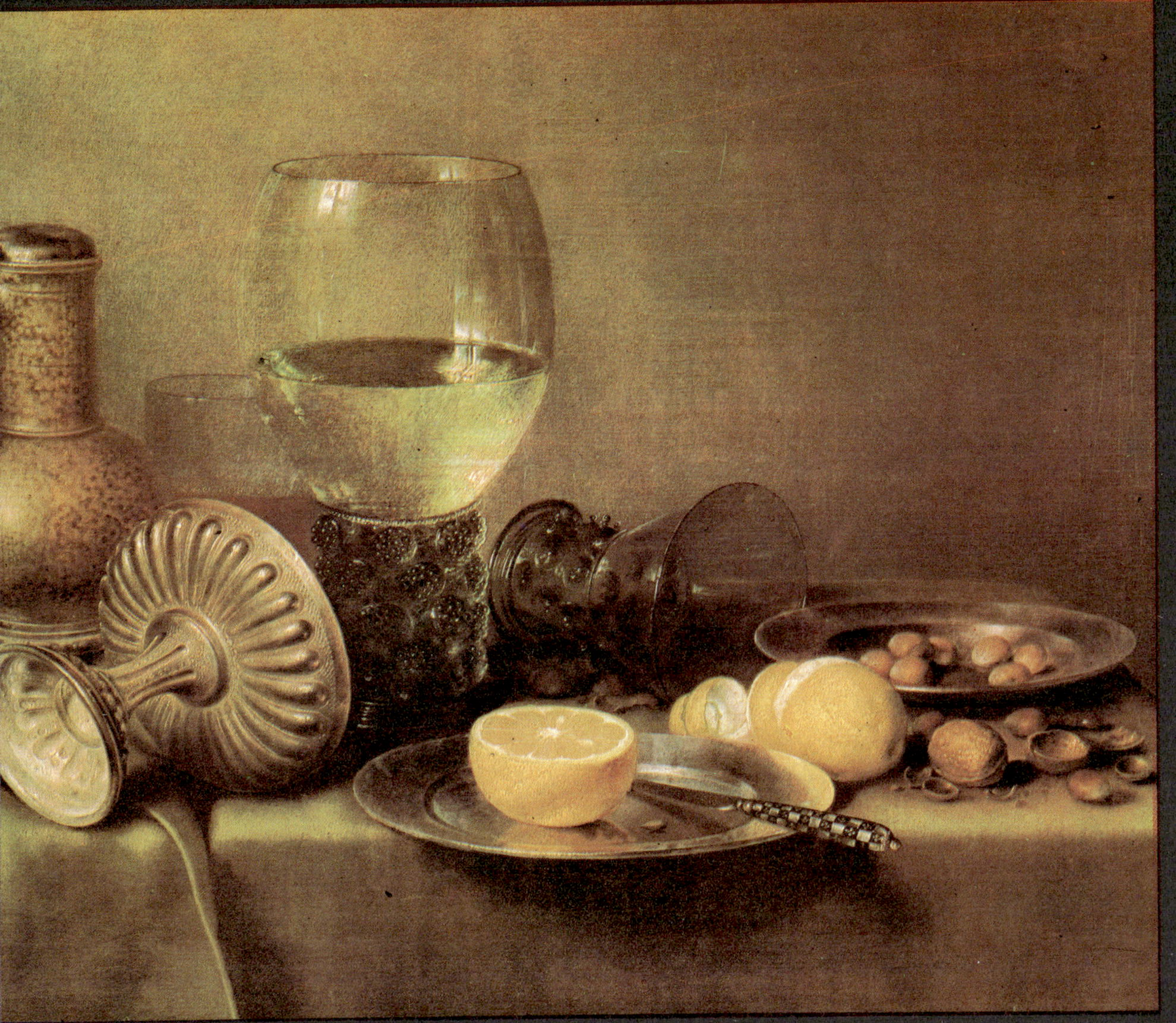

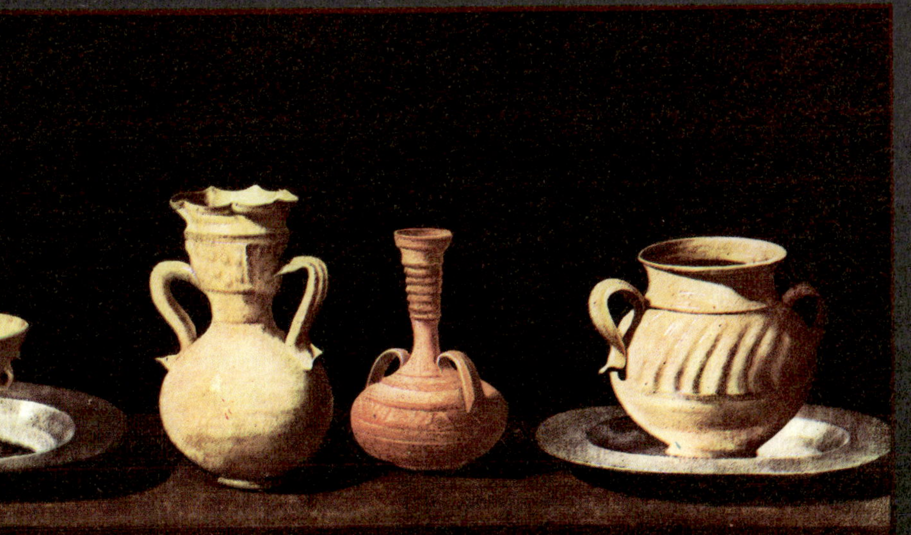

Fig. 34. Francisco Zurbarán: *Still Life,* Madrid, Prado. A contemporary and friend of Velazquez, Zurbarán was a student of Herrera the Elder in Seville, where, in his youth, he painted this famous still life with wine jugs. The picture is remarkable in its simplicity (reminiscent of Sánchez Cotán); the well-contrived impression of volume and the arrangement of the pottery defy the rule of "unity within variety" yet produce one of the most famous still lifes in Spanish classical painting.

the seventeenth century

Fig. 35. Sebastian Stoskopff: *Still life with fish*, Munich. Born in Strasbourg but living in France, Stoskopff was among the leading 17th century French painters of still life.

Fig. 36. P. Dupuis: *Plums and peaches*, France, private collection.

Fig. 37. Felipe Ramírez: *Still Life*, Madrid, Prado

35

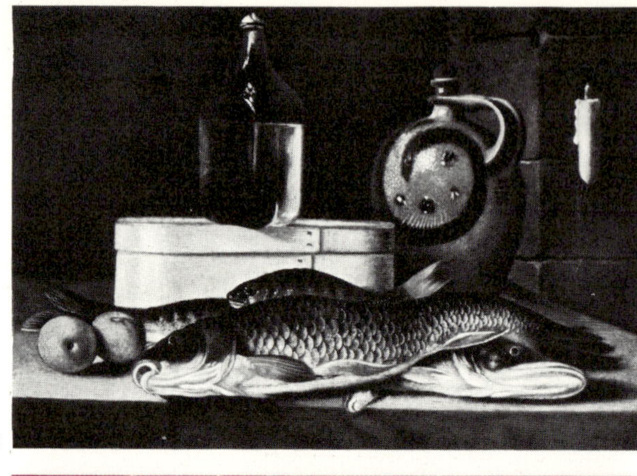

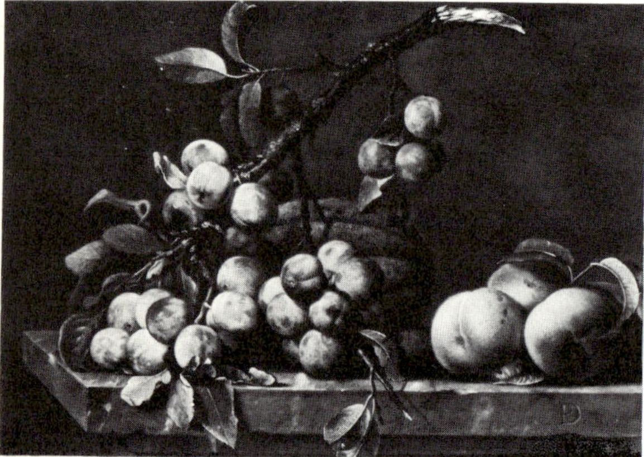

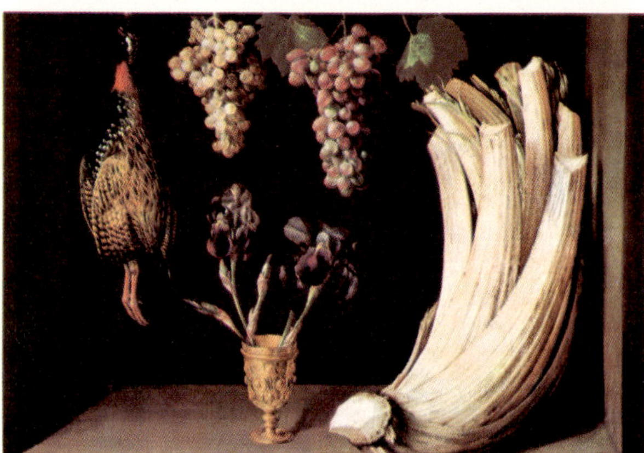

38

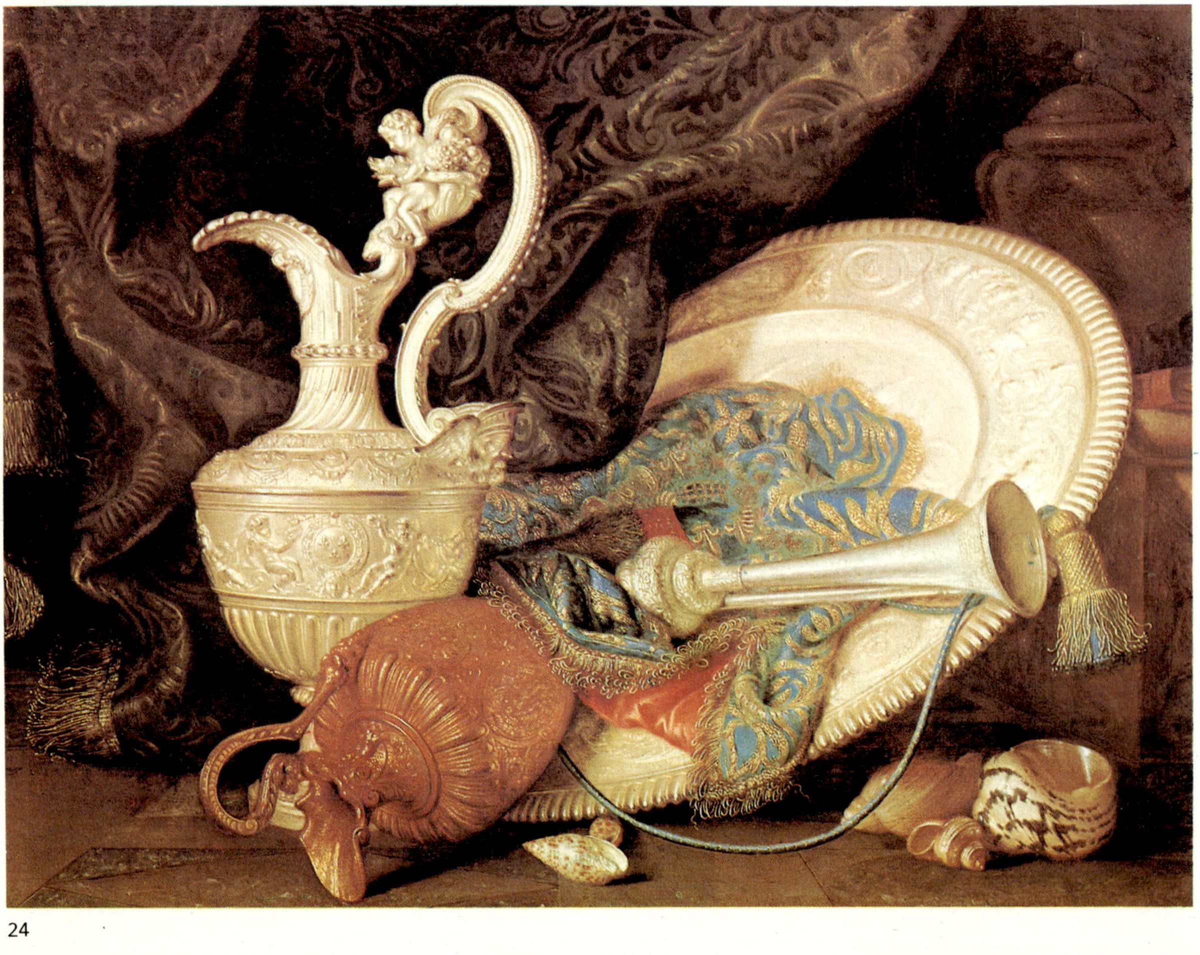

Fig. 38. (below, left) Meiffren Conté: *Pitcher, arms of France, oval dish and shells,* Brussels, Van de Brock Collection. The ostentatious courtly style of Louis XIV of France strongly influenced the decorative conception of still lifes in the second half of the 17th century.

Fig. 39. Joris Van Soon: *Still Life,* Madrid, Prado. Van Soon was a Flemish painter with a disciplined and balanced style, as portrayed below. Note how the composition reflects the beginning of the trend towards simplicity, gradually moving farther away from the Baroque. The butterfly detail is frequently found in the still lifes of the time (mid-17th century).

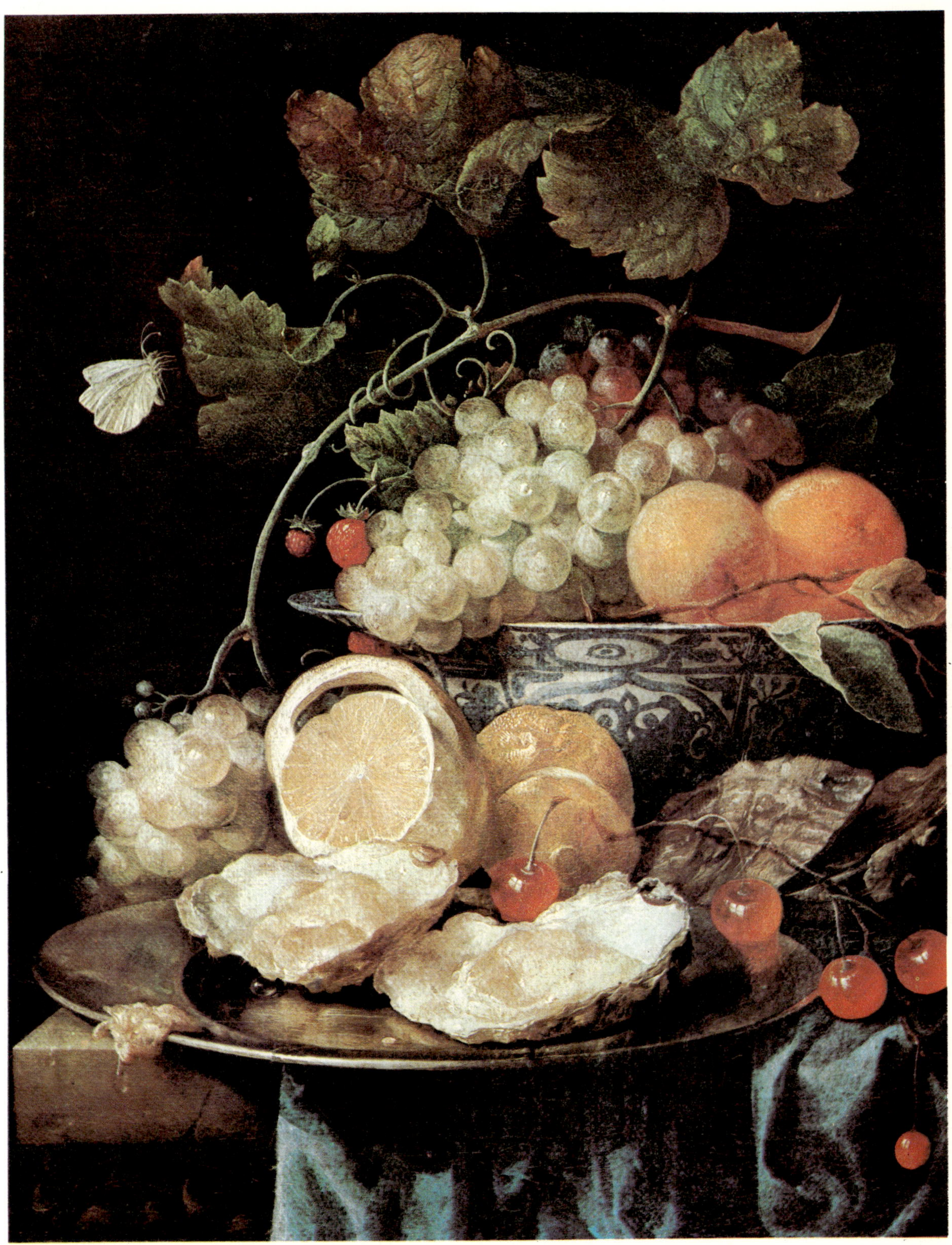

eighteenth century

France became the main centre of influence on 18th century Western art. Here this was the golden age of still life, looking to Nature as an art form, producing works of oustanding merit and following the example set by Jean Chardin, the famous French painter. Some examples of his work are shown on pages 28 and 29. Many of his contemporaries contributed towards the establishment of still life as a successful subject; two of these were Jean-Baptiste Oudry and Anne Vallayer-Coster.

One of Holland's most notable painters was Justus van Huysum, who is celebrated for his flower paintings and his innovations in the field of composition. Art in Spain had sunk into a decline, the still lifes of Luis Meléndez being an exception.

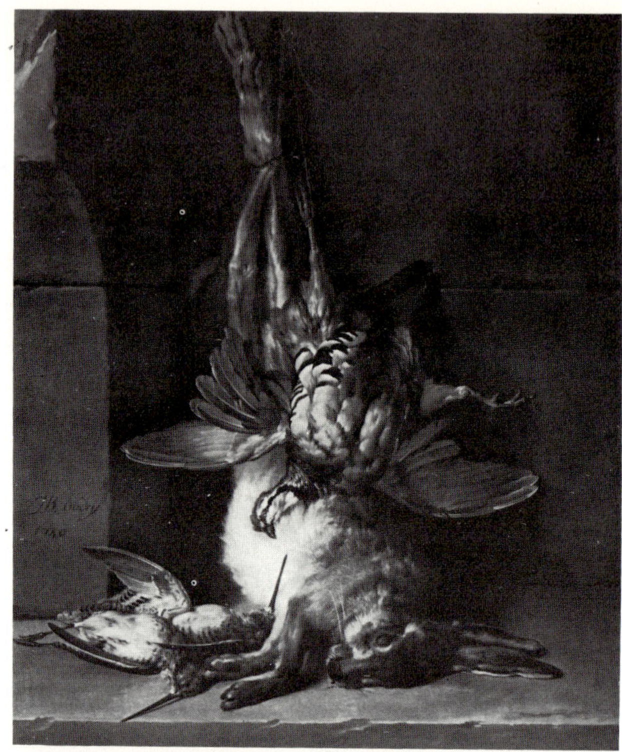

40

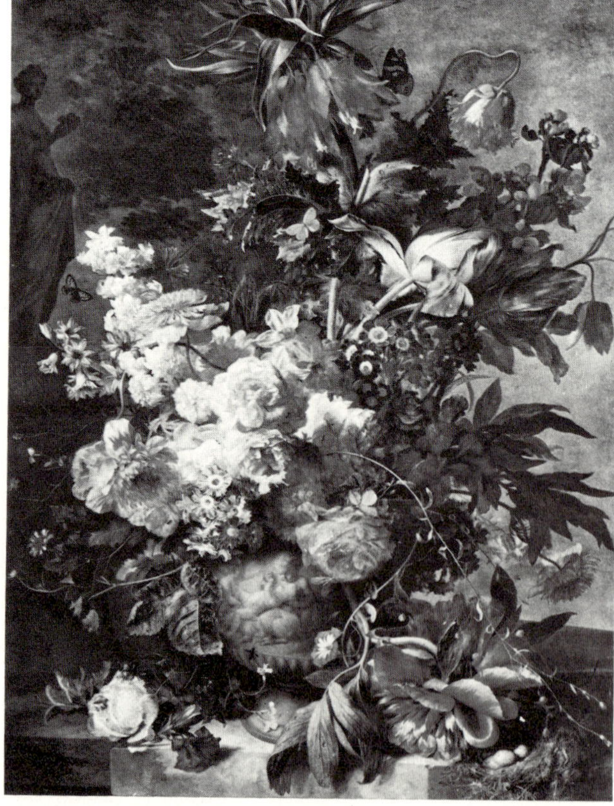

41

Fig. 40. Jean-Baptiste Oudry: *Hare, red-legged partridge and snipe,* USA, Museum ofArt, Worcester. Oudry is recognized as one of the 18th century French masters. He was appointed Court Painter to Louis XV and worked for the Beauvaus tapestry workshop, being made Director in 1734. He had an enormous capacity for work and was skilled in figure painting, portraiture and landscape, though he specialized in still lifes and, most of all, in animal pictures and hunting scenes.

Fig. 41. Jan van Huysum: *Flowers,* Amsterdam, Rijksmuseum. He was the most famous son of Justus van Huysum who also produced flower and fruit paintings. Jan brought into his still lifes the innovation of background illumination, i.e. painting the model against a light background. This had already been done by other Dutch artists, but without such deliberation.

Fig. 42. Anne Vallayer-Coster: *White tureen,* (facing page, above). Anne Vallayer-Coster might reasonably be rated the best French still-life painter of the 17th and 18th centuries. She was admitted to membership of the Royal Academy of Painting and Sculpture at the age of 26, "with particular satisfaction in recognizing her ability." She was compared with Chardin, summoned to Court to paint portraits of the Queen, and acknowledged by contemporary critics and painters as an exceptionally great artist.

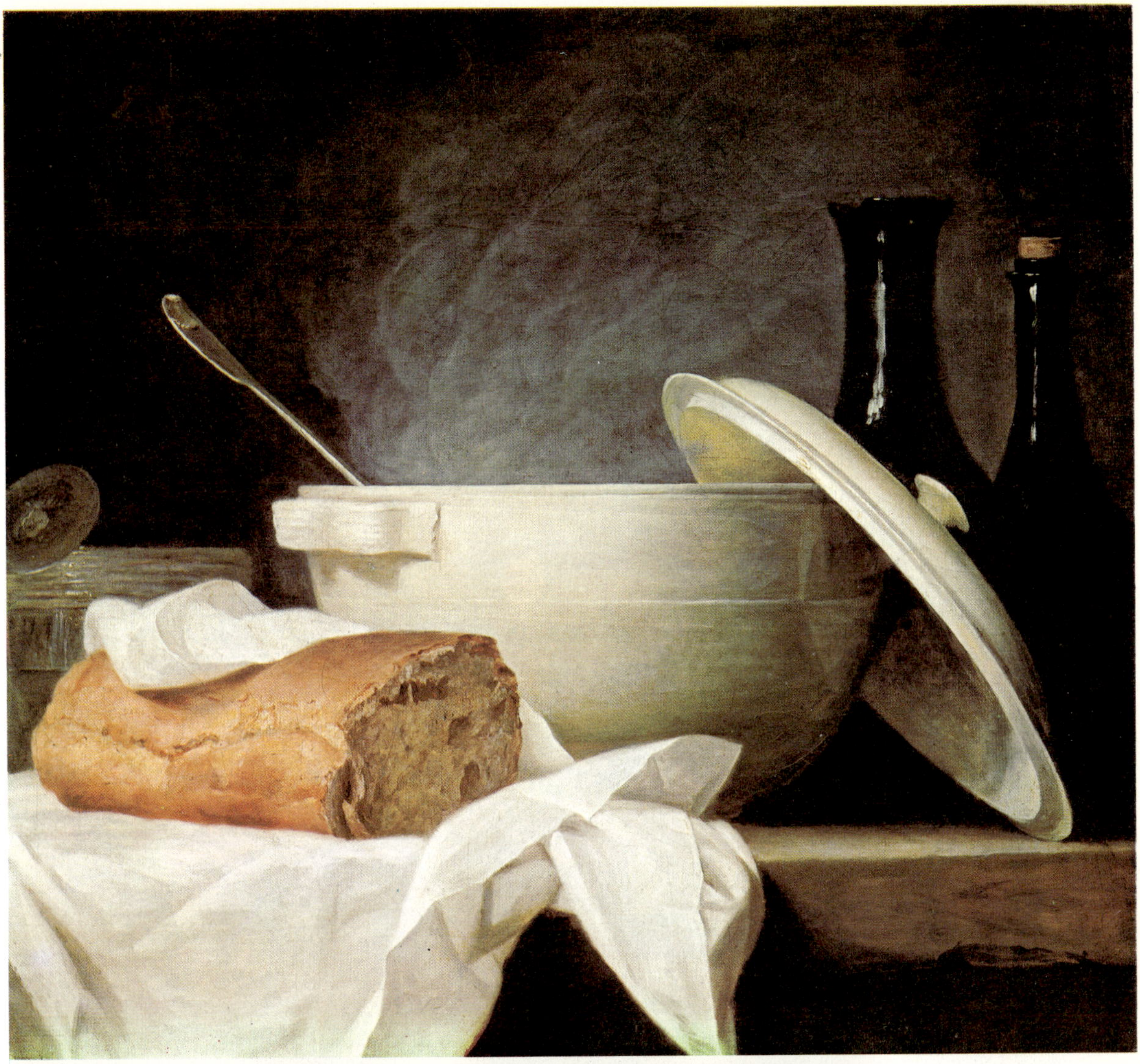

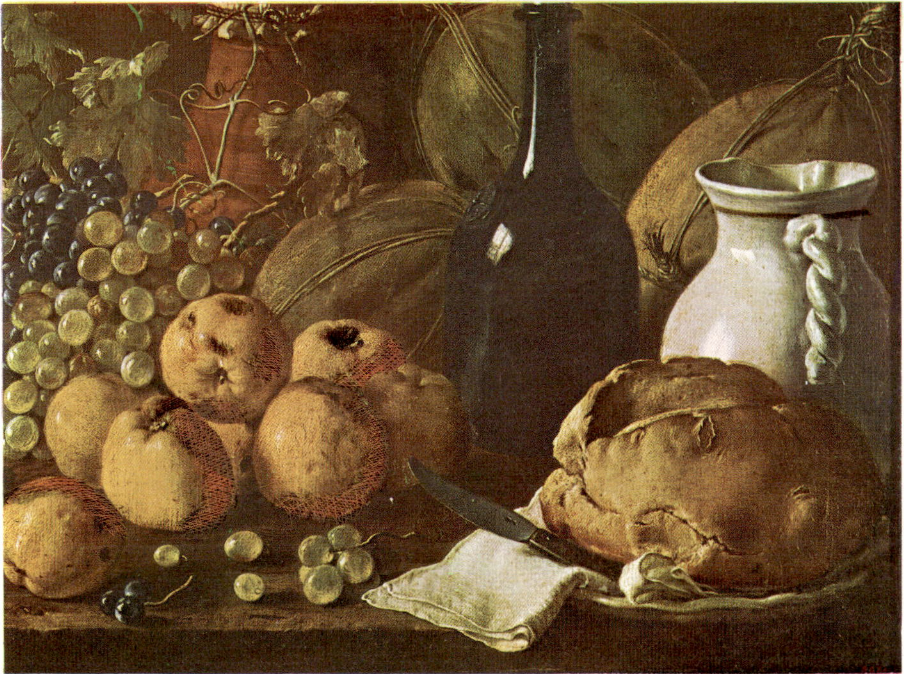

Fig. 43. Luis Meléndez: *Still Life,* Madrid, Prado. Meléndez was born in Italy of an Asturian father and Italian mother, but lived in Spain from early childhood. His style was markedly influenced by current French art, so much so that he was called "the Spanish Chardin".

eighteenth century: chardin

Pondering on the work of Jean-Baptiste Chardin, how apt it is to quote the Chinese proverb: "one picture is worth a thousand words". You have only to see Chardin's paintings reproduced here to realize immediately that you are in the presence of a consummate artist, entirely at ease when painting his still lifes. Some painters had to resort to still life because they lacked the ability to achieve the same technique and quality in figure painting. Chardin moved easily back and forth between still lifes and portraits. His most renowned paintings are: *Lady sealing a letter, Woman scrubbing, Lady drinking tea, The cook, Child with top (a brilliant portrait of the son of one of his clients, the jeweller Godefroy) and his famous self-portrait with vizor.*

Chardin, with his great skill, had the intelligence and courage to turn away from over-ornate, pretentious, opulent subjects, such as the ubiquitous silverware or the stag killed after a heroid chase and surrounded by flowers, fruit, musical instruments, etc. He rejected these clichéd, artificial scenes and created a beautiful real world from three apples, a casserole, a loaf, some pottery, with a knife placed on a tablecloth. In effect, he returned to the basic subjects of still life, as exemplified in Caravaggio's Basket of fruit or Velazquez' *The Water Seller of Seville.*

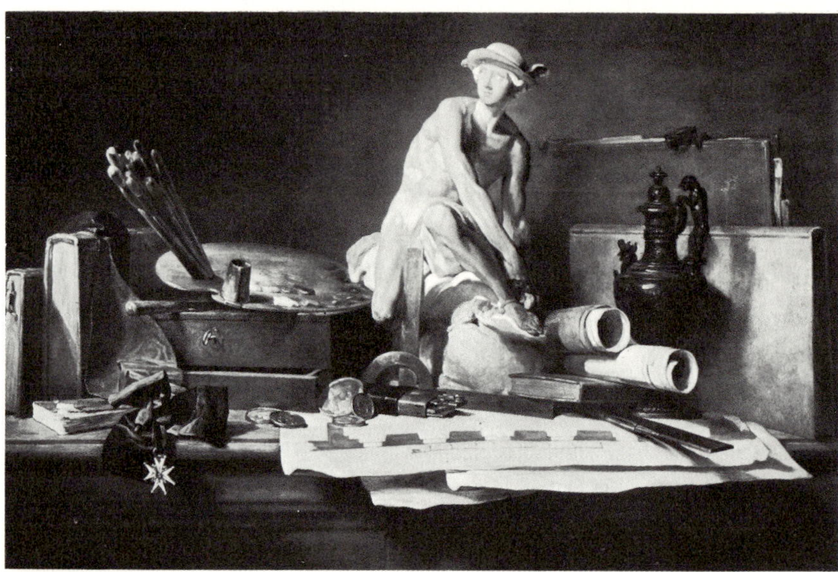

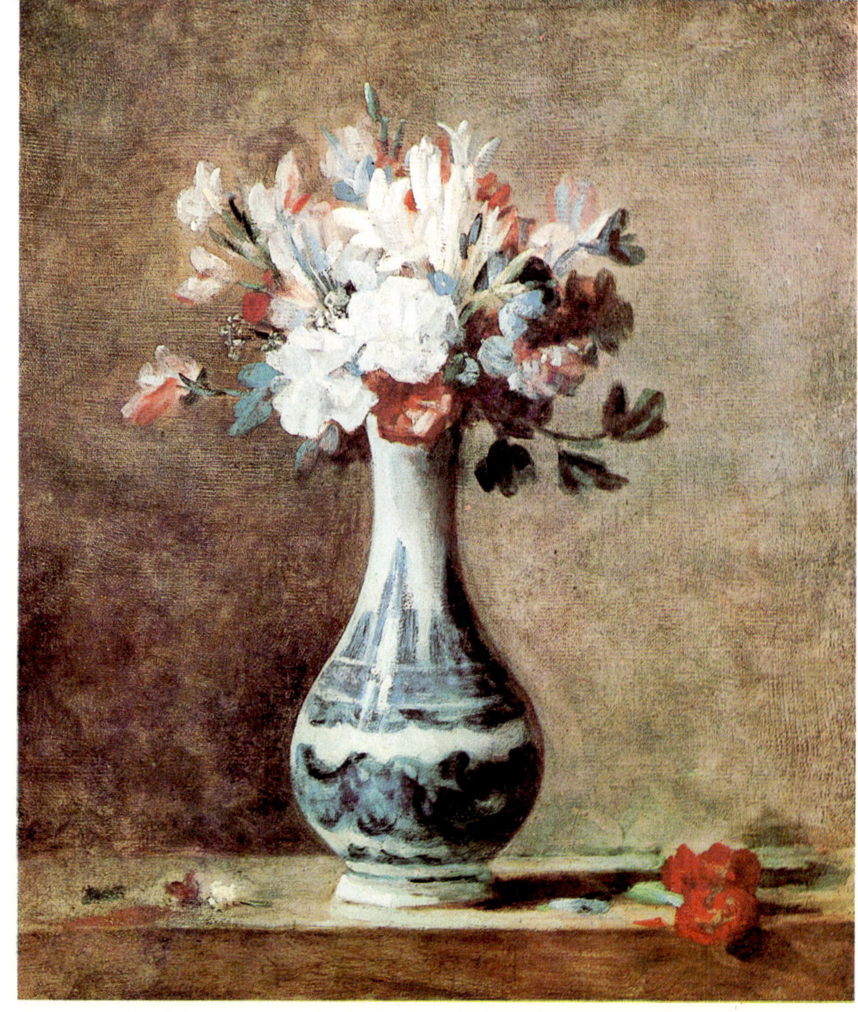

46

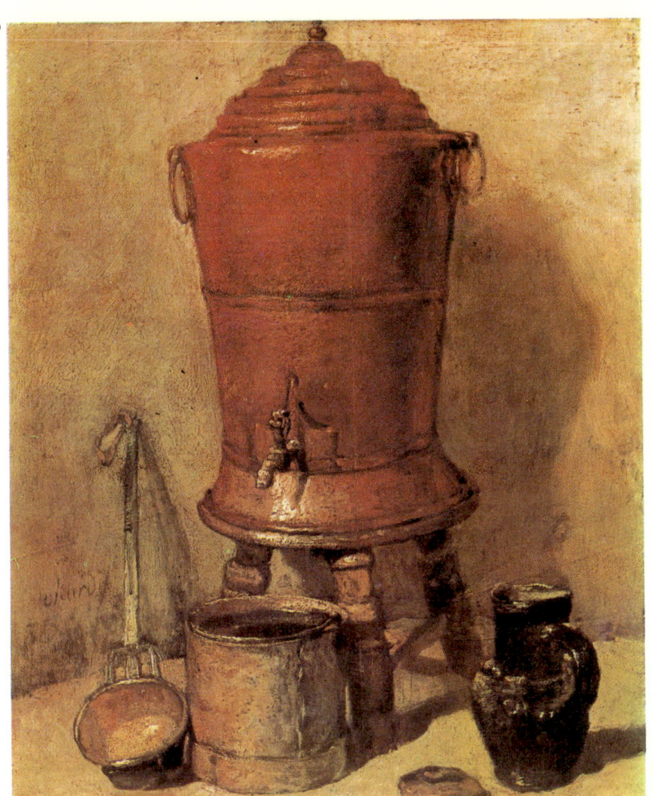

Fig. 44. (facing page, top): Chardin's The artist's tools and his rewards, USA, Minneapolis Museum.

Fig. 45. (facing page, below): *Bunch of flowers,* Edinburgh, National Gallery of Scotland.

Fig. 46. (left): *Copper urn,* Paris, Louvre.

Fig. 47. (below, top): *Copper pan,* Paris, Louvre.

Fig. 48. (below): *Opened ray fish,* Paris, Louvre.

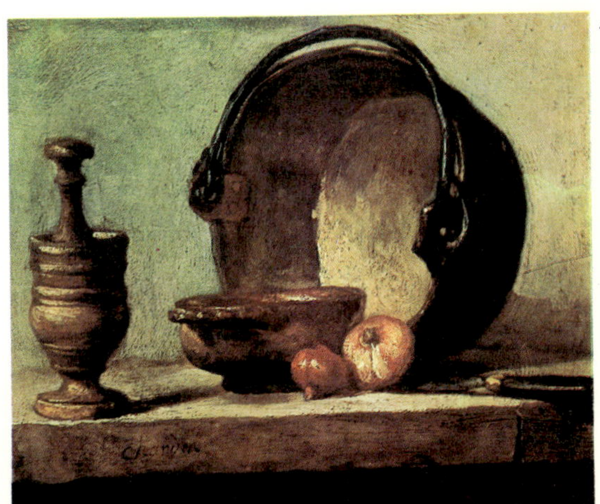

47

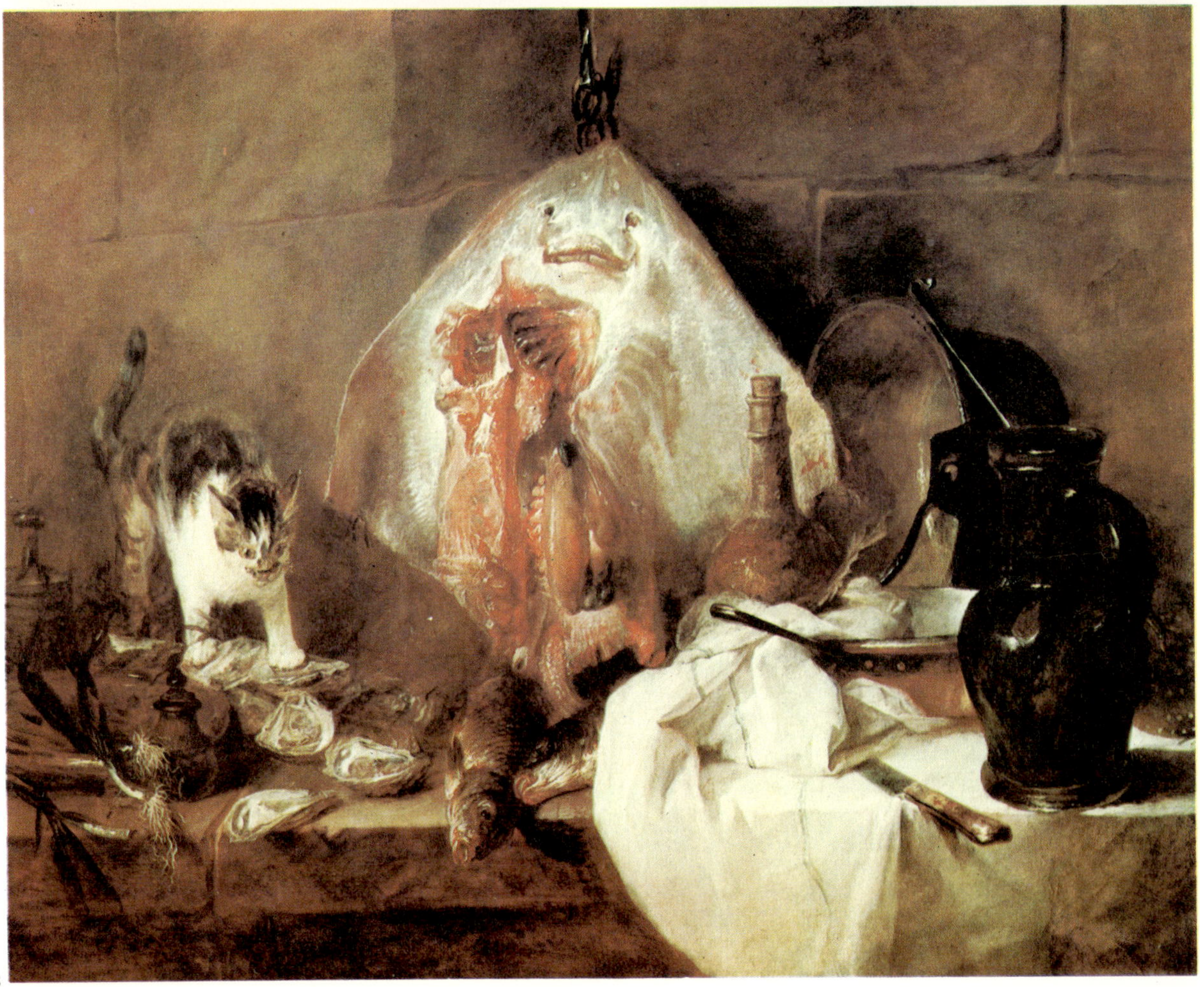

48

nineteenth and twentieth centuries

Since the 19th century, still life painting has been a much-cultivated art, practised fairly assiduously by almost all the world's leading artists: Delacroix, Courbet, Manet, Monet, Renoir, Van Gogh, then Picasso, Nonell, Matisse, Braque, Juan Gris, Dali and —last but not least, Cézanne— certainly the most important still-life painter of this time. Later, we shall be considering his sketches and pictures, and I hope you may benefit from his works and his guidance.

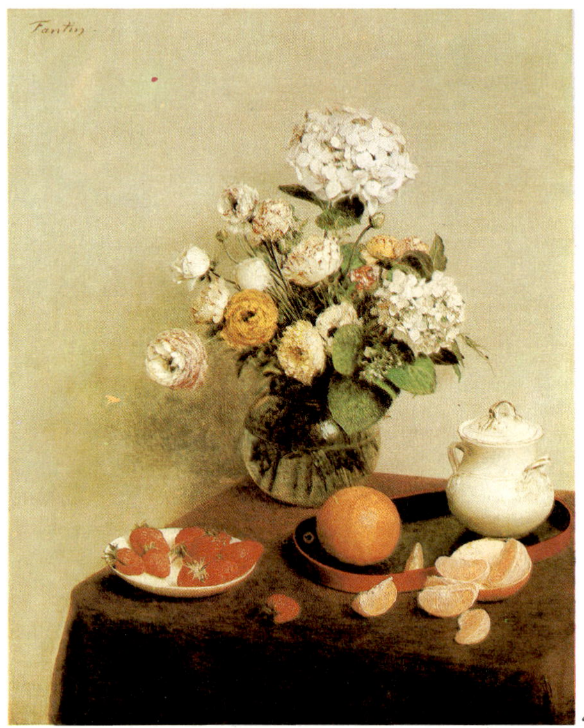

49

Fig. 49. Henri Fantin-Latour: Still life with dahlias and hydrangeas, USA, Toledo Museum of Art, Ohio In 1866 this French artist painted the exquisite picture shown above. This was four years before the first exhibition of the Impressionists, with whom he was friendly. But Fantin-Latour still continued to paint in the academic Realist style.

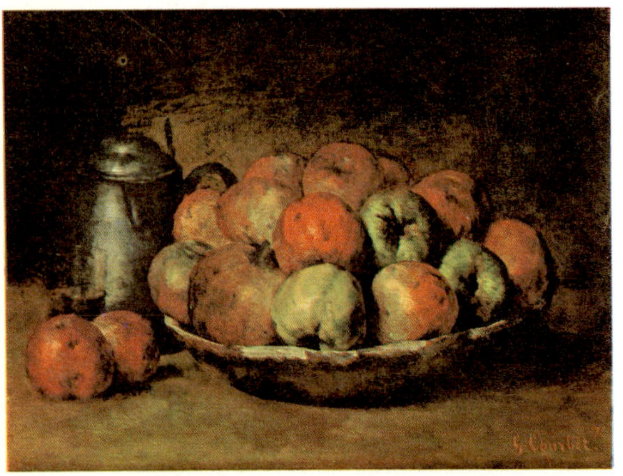

50

Fig. 50. Gustave Courbet: *Apples and pomegranates,* London, National Gallery. This quiet, unpretentious picture (left, above) was painted in 1871 while Courbet was serving a prison sentence in Paris for alleged involvement in the Vendôme Column affair when he was President of the Paris Assemblée d'Artistes.

51

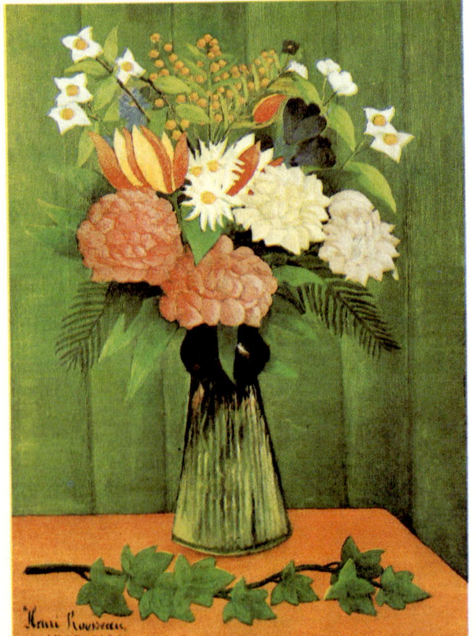

Fig. 51. Henri ("Le Douanier") Roussea: *Vase of flowers,* USA, Albright-Knox Art Gallery, Buffalo. An example of still life in a style half-way between Realism and "primitive", a style of painting defined as naive, spontaneous and childlike. Rousseau was a genuine primitive artist and, fortunately, despite his efforts to paint "well" he was unable to alter his style since judged "better than well".

nineteenth and twentieth centuries: cézanne

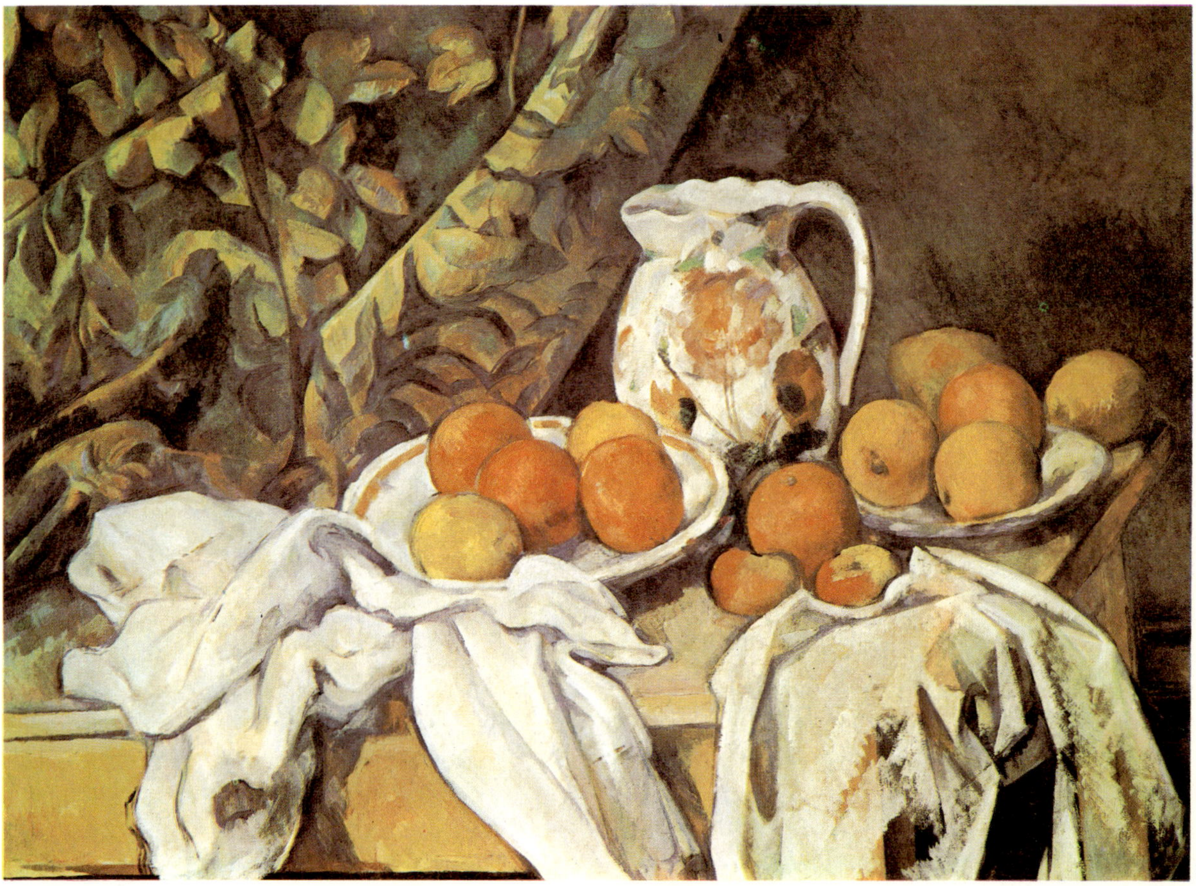

52

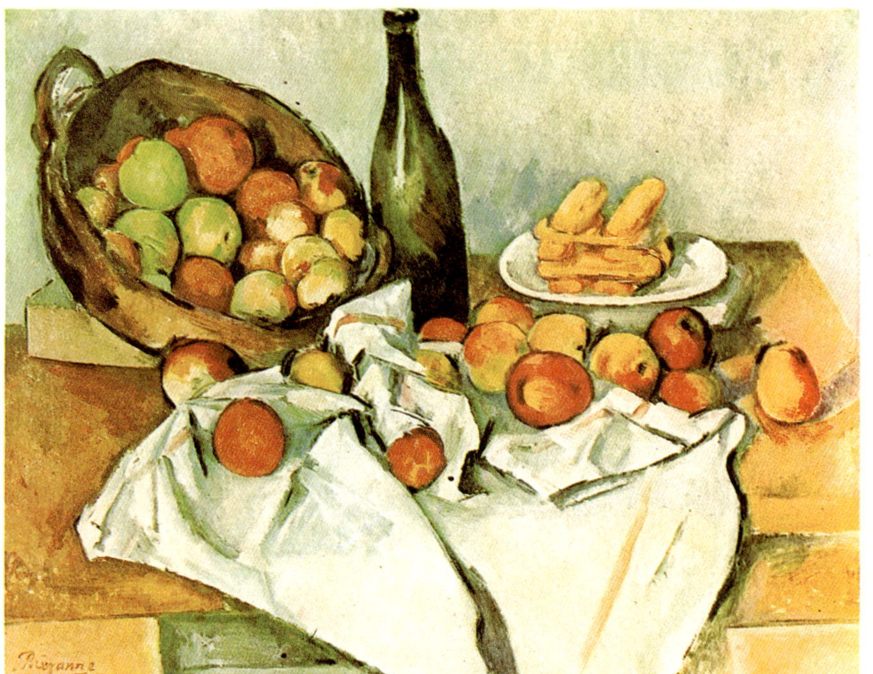

53

Fig. 52. Paul Cézanne: *Still life with drape,* Leningrad, Hermitage Museum.

Fig. 53. Paul Cézanne: *Still life with basket of apples,* USA, Institute of Art, Chicago. Cézanne is remarkable in his arrangement of the painting's components apparently haphazard— yet the result of hours of careful study.

twentieth century

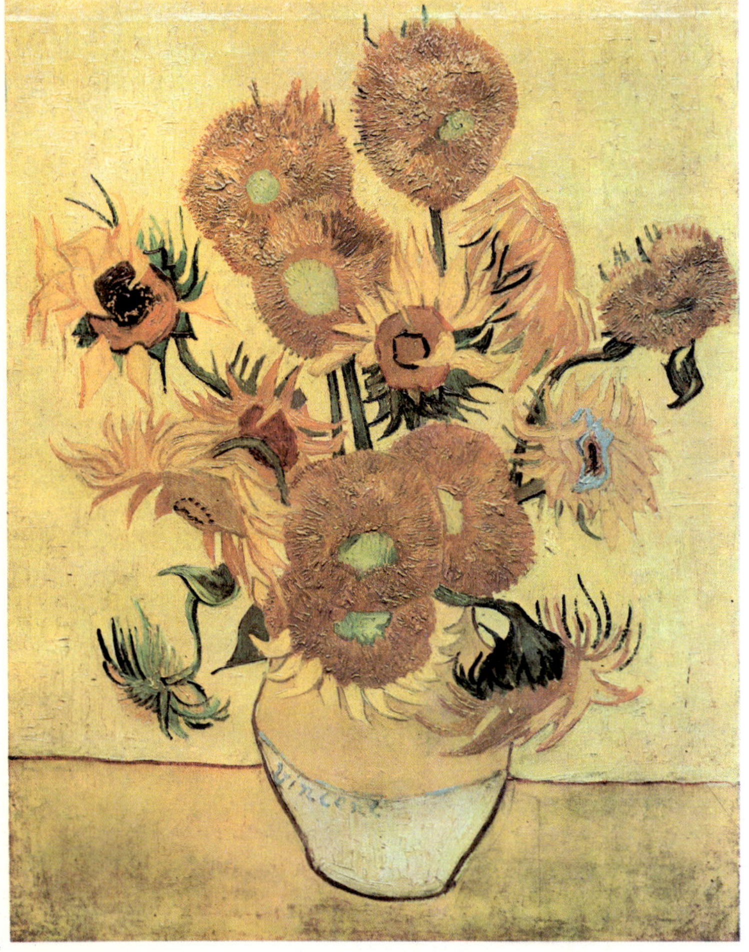

54

I have come to the end of my brief summary of the history of still life and I'll close with just two chosen pictures which may be regarded as "modern" works within the scope of Realism. These are not intended to be representative of the enormous quantity of 20th-century still-life paintings.

One picture is by van Gogh, one by Nonell. The first is strikingly Colourist, composed of flat colours giving form without volume, lacking any pattern of light and shade, yet possessing clear shapes. Here is a whole new style, an individual and masterly method of painting.

In the second, Catalan painter Isidro Nonell paints as a Valuist. Using a fluent treatment and creating outlines with brush strokes, he carefully expresses volume by means of shadows, local colours and highlights. This is a different and equally valid style of modern painting.

We'll go back later to Colourism and Valuism and examine their practical aspects and the potential they afford.

Fig. 54. Vincent van Gogh: *Vase of sunflowers,* Amsterdam, Rijksmuseum.

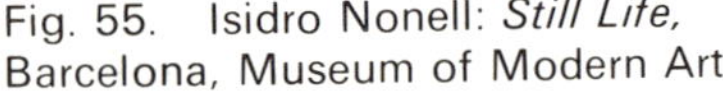

Fig. 55. Isidro Nonell: *Still Life,* Barcelona, Museum of Modern Art.

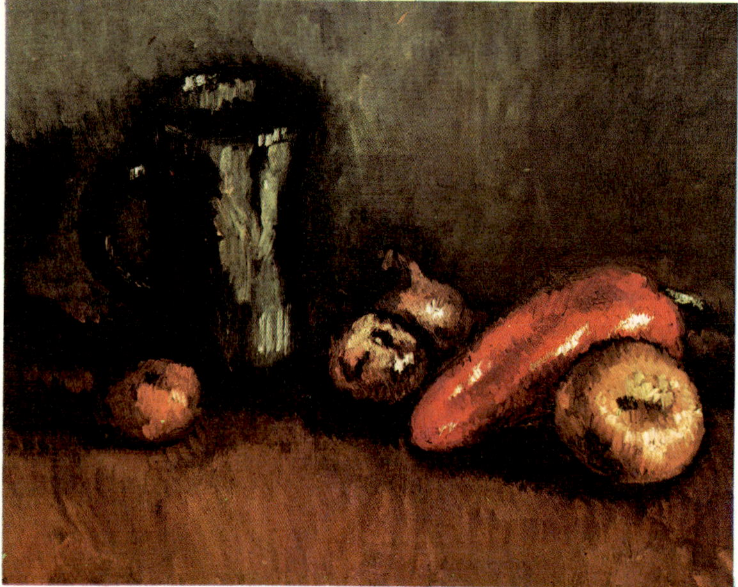

55

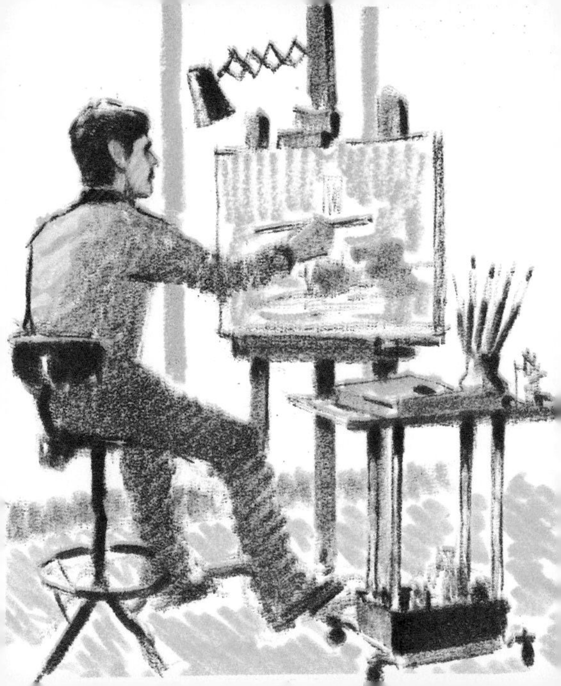

the studio

In April 1904 Pablo Ruiz Picasso came to live in Paris for the second time. A month earlier the sculptor Paco Durio had written to say that he was leaving a studio in Paris, on the slopes of Montmartre, number thirteen, rue de Ravignan (now called Place Emile Goudeau). "Plain, cheap and in a very pleasant part of the city", was the description given to Picasso by his friend.

Cheap certainly, but plain most of all, the studio was in a dilapidated old wooden tenement building inhabited by artists, writers, actors, washerwomen, stallholders and prostitutes. Picasso joked with friends that in the autumm winds and storms the dreadful building pitched and tossed like a sailing ship, so the poet Max Jacob dubbed it the "Bateau-Lavoir" ("floating laundry") which was the popular nickname for the old wooden stages moored in the Seine from which people used to do their washing. The name stuck and came into general use to describe Picasso's studio.

What was it really like, this famous "Bateau-Lavoir"? From 1905 to 1909 it became one of the frequent Paris meeting-places for artists, poets and writers —men of the calibre of Braque, Dufy, Utrillo, Rousseau, Cocteau, Apollinaire and Max Jacob.

In her book *"Extraits de Picasso et ses amis"*, Fernande Olivier, Picasso's first mistress, describes the Bateau-Lavoir:

"An ice box in winter, an oven in summer. A place redolent of work and jumble: a divan bed in one corner, a rusty little iron stove on which stood an earthenware tub used as a washbasin, beside it an unpainted wooden table, a towel and some soap. In another corner a battered black trunk served as an uncomfortable seat. A straw-bottomed chair, easels, canvases of all sizes, paint tubes scattered about the floor, brushes, jars of turpentine, no curtains..."

"To support all this, a floor of rotting planks." adds one of Picasso's biographers.

The Bateau-Lavoir studio was really quite big —up to fifteen people at a time would meet there to discuss Art with a capital A. It must have been larger than the room in Boulevard Clichy rented by Picasso during his earlier stay in Paris in 1901. Judging from the photograph below, the space could not have been more than 4 × 5 m.

Despite conditions in the small room in Boulevard Clichy and the wretched Bateau-Lavoir, Picasso produced the celebrated paintings of his "blue" period, a marvellous series now considered to be among his best works.

These details about Picasso's studios show that surroundings need not necessarily affect the speed or otherwise of creative work such as painting. All the same, certain minimum facilities —space, light and materials— are necessary. Let's consider these points, first looking at the minumum dimensions needed for a studio, though many amateurs may have to use their living rooms.

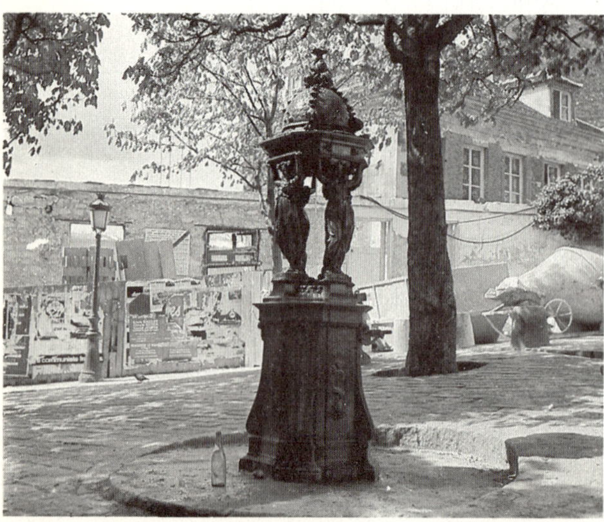

Fig. 57 A recent photograph of Place Emile Goudeau, on the slopes of Montmartre. In the background, behind the lamp-post, and half-hidden by the hoarding, is the top of the "Bateau-Lavoir", Picasso's studio in the 1900s. The Bateau-Lavoir has been in ruins since a fire a few years ago but a new building is now being erected. The square and the fountain where Picasso first met Fernande Olivier are unchanged. Picasso arrived at the Bateau-Lavoir in 1904 and moved out in 1909. During those five years his studio was a meeting-place for all the leading young artists of the day. Most of the pictures in his "blue" and "rose" periods were painted here.

A painter's studio need be only about 4 × 3.5 m; a larger room is better

From my knowledge of painters' studios, I am sure these measurements are suitable. I painted for several years in a studio with an area of 4×5 m and I now work in a room measuring 8×3.30 m, half of which is used for reading, writing, chatting with friends or listening to music.

Your workroom should have natural light. But see overleaf for more about this.

Figs. 58 A & B. Nowadays a painter's studio might look like this. The top floor of any house or flat usually has plenty of natural light. Ideally, it should be a room which can be divided into areas for painting (A) *and,* as in Fig 58 B, for reading, entertaining visitors, listening to music and so on. As these photographs show, the studio need not be very large.

A

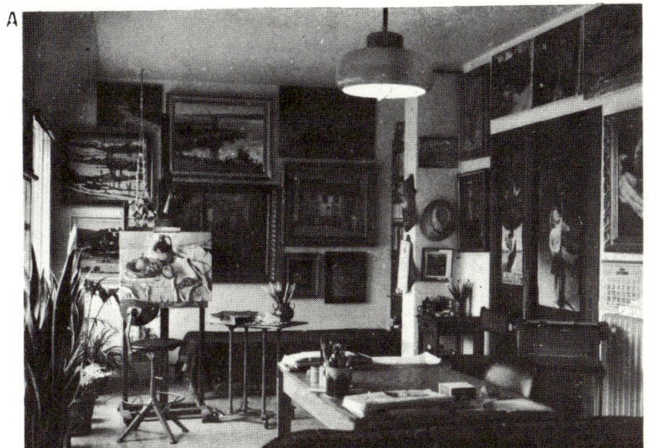

B

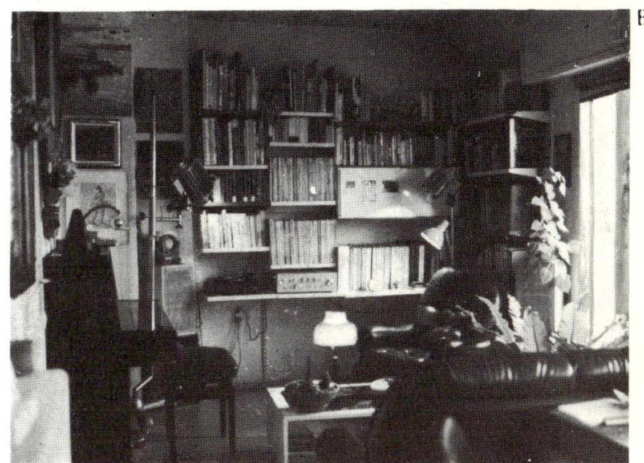

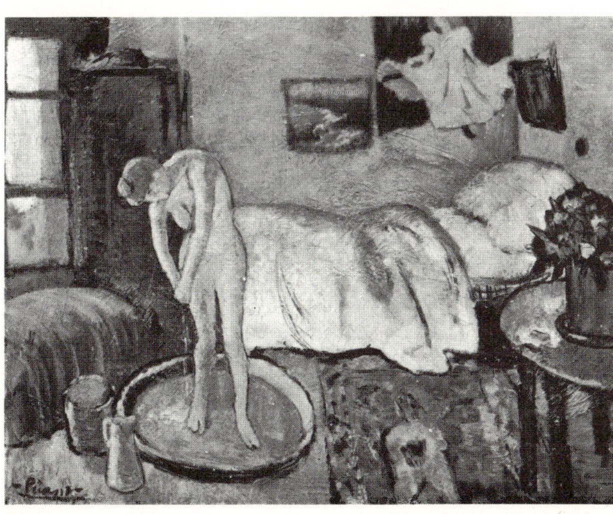

Fig. 59. *Female bather:* Picasso (1901). The room is based on his Paris lodgings in Boulevard Clichy. Its smallness did not hinder Picasso in painting this and several other pictures at the beginning of his "blue" period

the importance of light

Most painters work by daylight, but there is no reason why they should not paint by artificial light if they wish. Professionals often work on two pictures concurrently, one in the morning, by daylight and another after dark, by artificial light. This is nothing new: in 1600 Caravaggio studied and painted his models by candlelight and flambeaux (hence his strong contrasts); a little earlier, in 1586, El Greco used to arrange draperies, dummies and live models from which to work by candlelight. His marvellous paintings, including *The burial of Count Orgaz,* were painted at night. Picasso regularly painted late at the Bateau-Lavoir, using the blue gaslight for the lighting he needed. This explains the predominance of blues in his pictures and, indeed, his famous "blue" period.

A studio should have at least one big window for painting by natural light, giving the model side-frontal lighting or side lighting.

Painting by artificial light calls for two sources of light, one to illuminate the model and another to light the work. And there should be yet another lamp for lighting the whole room.

The light for the model can be a 100-watt bulb in a wide-shaded lamp, so that the painter can avoid the sharp focus and excessive contrast produced by direct lighting. For still-life painting the lamp should be about 80-100 cm away from the work; this is usually the best distance for good illumination of the model.

The painting itself needs light projected from above, preferably from a flexible or extending lamp. Again, use a 100-watt bulb. It's important to use two bulbs of the same strength, so that the lighting of the work is not too strong compared with that of the model, or vice versa. This might cause the artist to apply colours paler or darker than he wants.

LIGHTING AND STUDIO EQUIPMENT

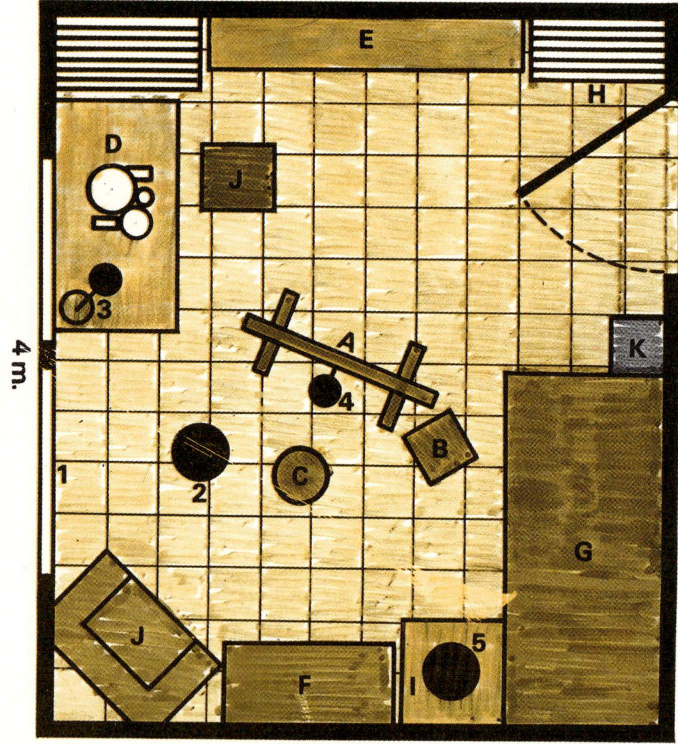

Fig. 60. Minimum dimensions for a studio showing positioning of lighting and the usual equipment:

1. Windows or light sources in the external wall
2. General lighting (artificial)
3. Table lamp, to illuminate a still life
4. Easel light, above the picture
5. Extra light for additional worktop

The studio we have in mind measures 3.5 · 4 m. We'll have a look at the equipment needed by the professional painter:

a. Studio easel
b. Small extra table
c. Painting stool
d. Rectangular table for still-life subject and for preparation of quick roughs
e. Bookcase
f. Record cabinet
g. Studio couch
h. Space for storing used and unused canvases
i. Extra working surface
j. Armchairs
k. Upright chairs

Finally, the general light should be set near the ceiling; it can be 60 or 100 watt (depending on the size of the room). Make sure that it doesn't project extra shadows to affect the lighting of the model and exaggerate highlights.

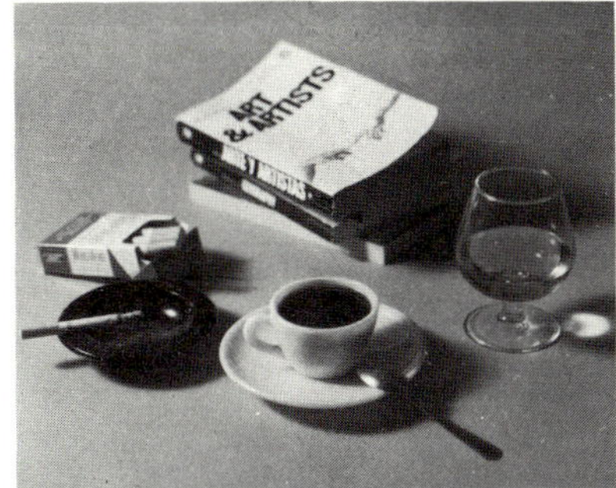

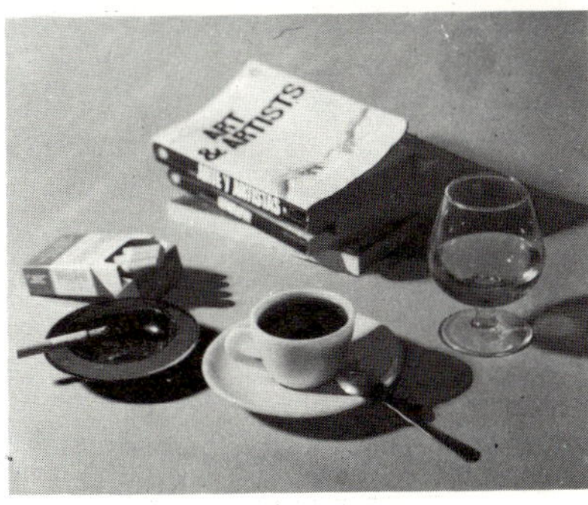

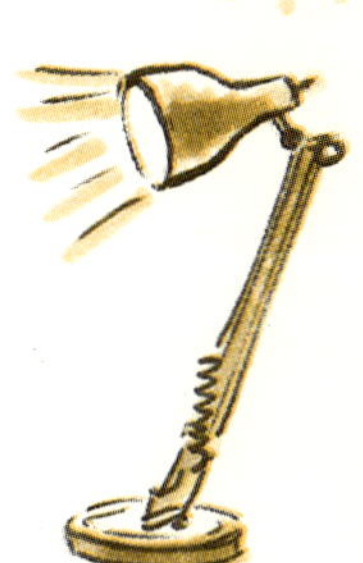

Figs. 61 and 62. Natural diffused light gives soft modelling of form; artificial light (direct light) accentuates contrast.

Fig. 63. Artificial light can over-reflect, especially when the paintbrush is horizontal, so be careful.

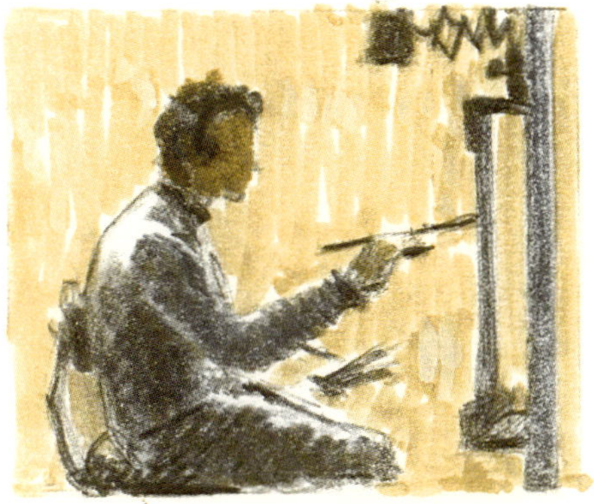

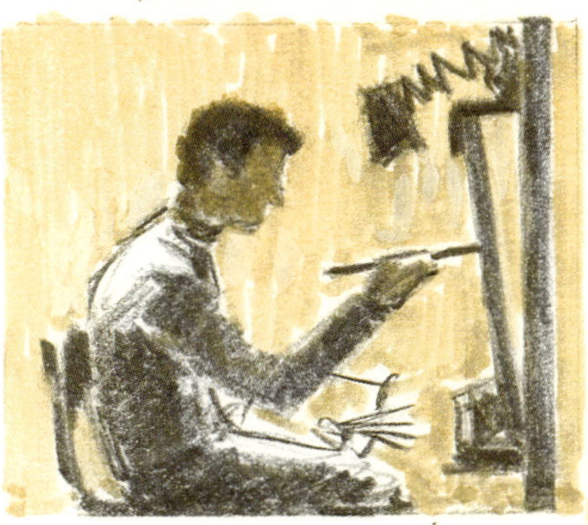

Fig. 64. Get rid of reflection by lowering the light, tilting the canvas and painting diagonally or vertically.

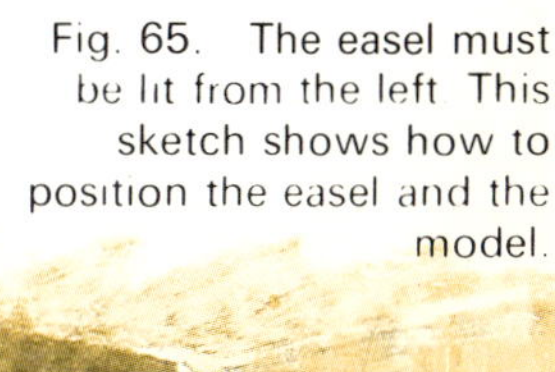

Fig. 65. The easel must be lit from the left. This sketch shows how to position the easel and the model.

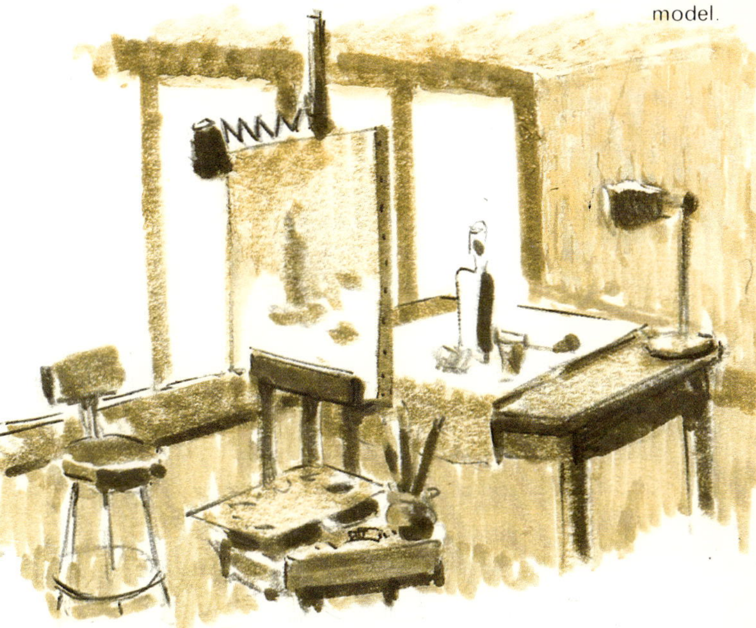

the studio easel

You'll need various items for your studio. Most are listed here in order of importance:

a. studio easel
b. artist's stool for use when painting
c. stool
d. table on which to draw, arrange the model and so on
e. chairs and a studio couch
f. bookcase
g. portfolios

The easel: there are two kinds of easel for oil painting, one for painting out of doors and one for studio work. The former is the usual three-legged folding easel, suitable for outdoor painting. If you are a complete novice you may find it better to use an outdoor easel for studio painting at home, provided that you realize that its thin legs may collapse. But a studio easel is stable enough to withstand both nervous dabbing and vigorous brush strokes.

Here we show an outdoor easel (Fig. 66) as well as some of the more usual types of studio easel.

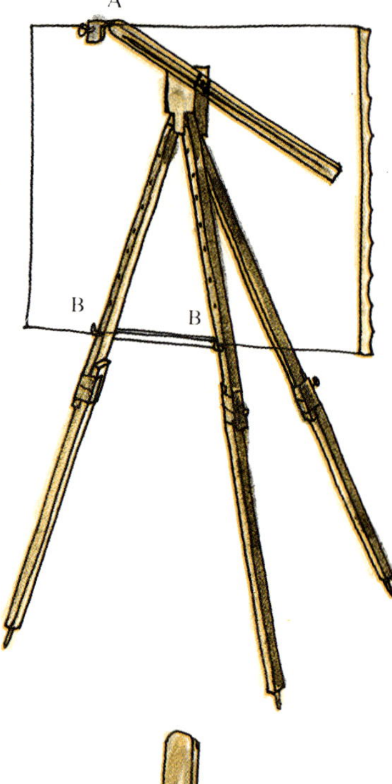

Fig. 66. Conventional outdoor easel; see how the canvas is secured by clamp (A) on the bar resting on the two pegs (B). (sometimes a bar is provided instead). It is not big enough to take large canvases. For this reason and because of its poor stability, it's not to be recommended as a studio easel.

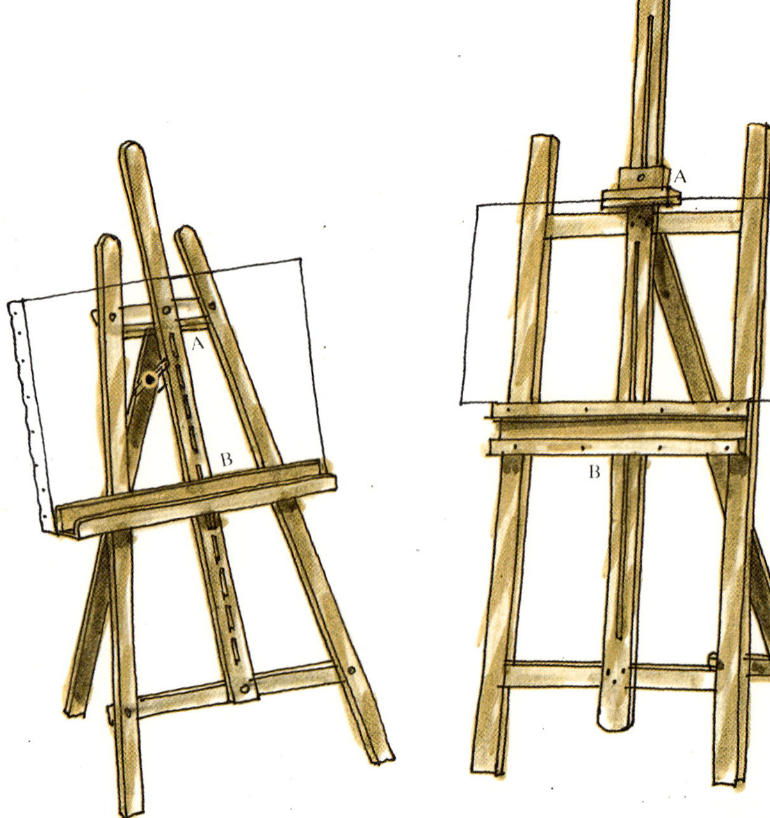

Fig. 67. (right) Tripod studio easel with toothed metal bar (A) set in the central support, allowing the ledge (B) (which takes the canvas) to be adjusted and fixed in place. It's about 1.70 m high and can be used with canvases of up to 100×81 cm. This is the type commonly used in art colleges.

Fig. 68. (far right) An up-to-date version of the previous easel, again based on the tripod design, but with greater stability. The canvas is secured by adjustable bar (A) on the central support and there is an additional ledge (B), which is useful for setting down paint tubes, brushes, rags, etc when you are working.

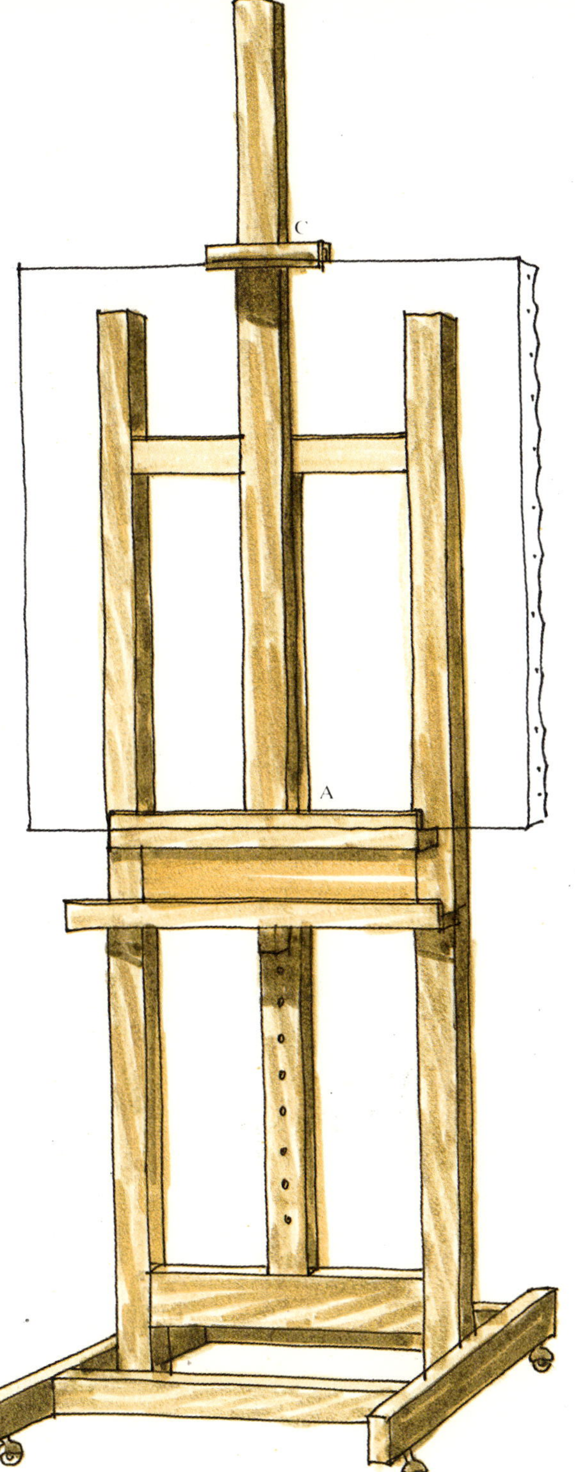

Fig. 69 A. This is the most usual studio type for the professional. It stands on a firm frame of wooden supports mounted on four castors, for easy movability or adjustment. It has two ledges (A), one to hold the canvas and the other to take paint tubes, brushes, spatulas, etc, when in use. The height of the ledges can be adjusted according to need; the central support also has an adjustable height clamp or locking bar (C) which holds the canvas in place.

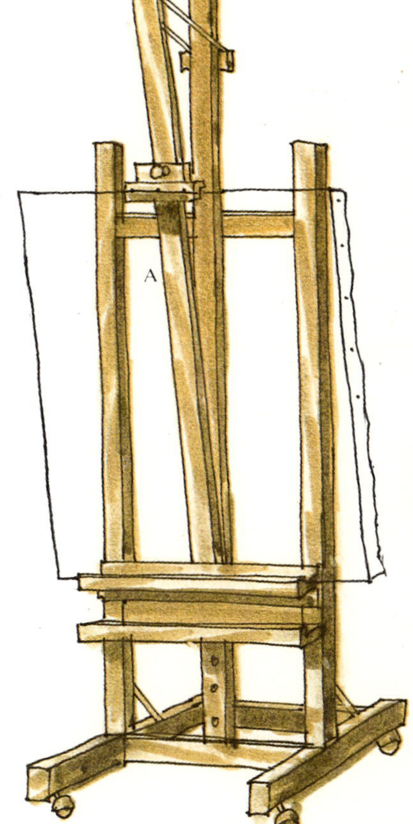

Fig. 69 B. This is almost the same as 69 A, but a little bigger, having a double-arm central support (A) which can tilt the canvas to avoid reflection. This easel is designed for larger pictures.

the studio

A painter working in his own studio really needs some kind of small workbench to put beside the easel while he works. In shops selling artists' materials you may be able to find a purpose-designed stand (Fig. 72). This is on castors, so that the painter can easily move it around the studio and can bring it right beside the easel when he is painting. It's very useful for putting more paint on the palette, picking up a rag, changing paint brushes or simply for holding the palette when the artist is not actually using it, measuring up and so on. The top of the stand is divided into compartments; there are drawers which swivel out to provide trays or additional surfaces and shelves for bottles, tins, pots, rags, etc.

You can use an ordinary small table or stand if you wish. Some time ago I converted an old typewriter trolley for this purpose, fixing a board over the top and adding drawers below, as shown in Fig. 72.

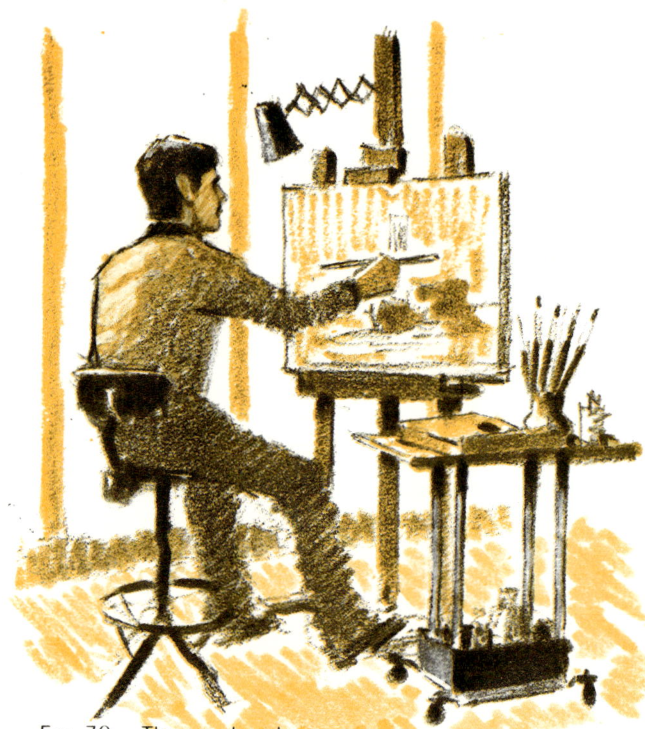

Fig. 70 The easel with extending-arm lamp, the swivel stool with backrest and the small extra workbench

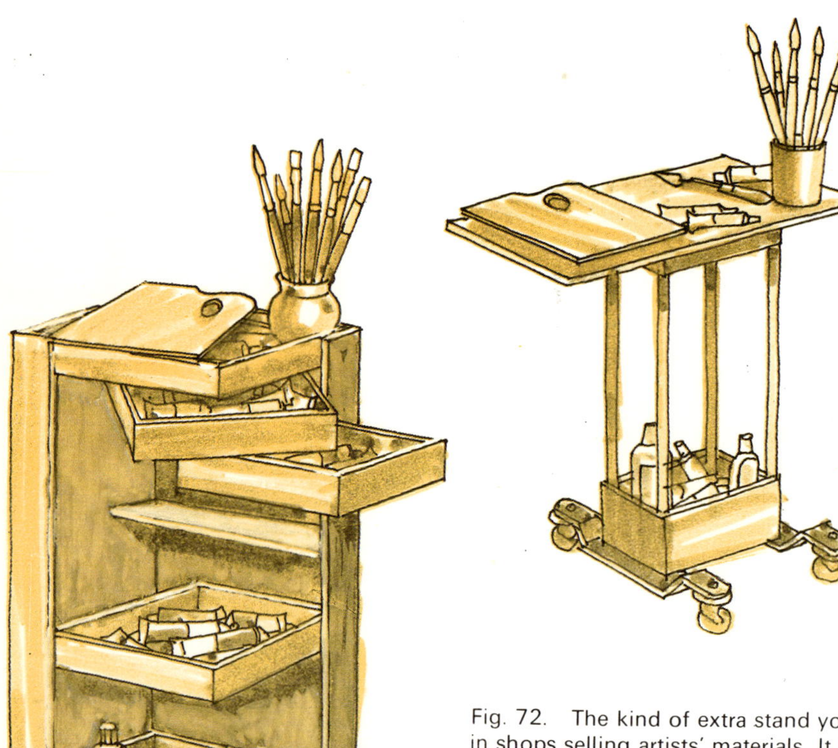

Fig. 71. For years I have used a small workbench made from an old typewriter trolley, like this.

Fig. 72. The kind of extra stand you may be able to buy in shops selling artists' materials. It has drawers and trays which swivel out and compartments or shelves for everything the painter needs tubes of paint, brushes, spatulas, bottles and rags and so on. It moves around easily on its four castors. Perhaps its only fault, apart from the high price, is the shortage of flat working surface.

The artist's stool is usually fairly high, so that he can sit down comfortably or lean forward. If you have a choice, it's a good idea to get one on castors, with an adjustable backrest, an adjustable upholstered seat and a footrest as shown in Fig. 74 (left).

Other than this very practical seat there is the conventional three-legged wooden stool with adjustable seat which can be made more comfortable with a small flat cushion.

A studio also needs an ordinary table about 140×80 cm, large enough to display a still-life subject. The artist can also use this for drawing, either by propping a drawing-board against it or by adding a simple block which changes it into a desk (Fig. 76).

A bookcase is vital —any artist needs a small library of books on drawing and painting, books on art and art techniques to broaden his knowledge and refresh his memory.

Of course, there must be space for large portfolios, a studio couch and chairs. You'll need at least two portfolios, one for storing drawing paper and one for finished work.

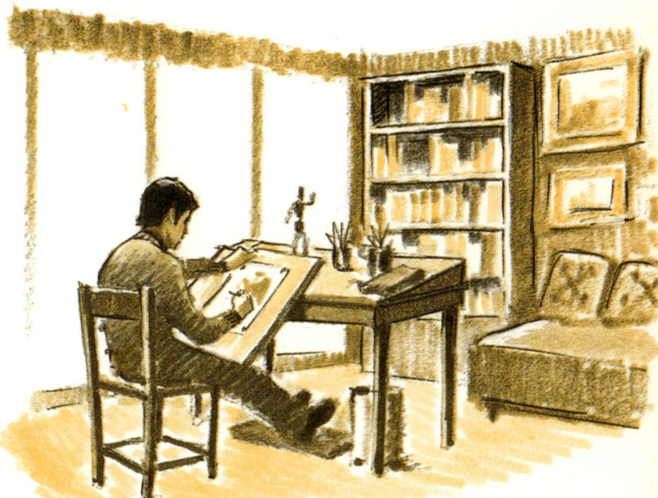

Fig. 73. Sketch of a studio corner, showing the bookcase and the studio couch, with the artist working at a drawing-board resting against the table.

Fig. 74. Left: stool with adjustable backrest, seat and footrest (A). Right: conventional wooden stool with adjustable seat.

Fig. 75. You'll need at least two portfolios in the studio, for storing paper and finished work. A portfolio rack like this is very useful. You can get them from art shops.

Fig. 76. A wooden block like this will convert a table into a desk; it makes drawing and sketching less tiring.

canvases and boards for oil-painting

The usual surfaces for oil-painting are linen or hemp canvases prepared by the application of a coat of paint called *primer,* and mounted on a wooden stretcher. Canvas can be *primed* merely by applying a coat of acrylic white, but it's not a good idea to do this oneself —it's a job for the specialist.

Art shops sell excellent prepared canvases in a range from rough to smooth work surfaces to suit the style of painting. Don't use rough-grain canvas for small pictures. Prepared canvases are sold mounted on wooden stretchers, the tautness depending on four small wedges tapped into the four corners of the stretcher. Prepared canvas is also sold in widths of from 0.7 to 2 metres.

For small pictures, canvas board (cloth-covered cardboard) or a prepared laminated wooden panel can be used. In an emergency, an ordinary piece of good quality, thick cardboard can be *primed* by thoroughly sizing the surface or by applying a coat of oil paint thinned with turps. You can paint on unprimed cardboard, canvas or wood, but the oil colours will be absorbed, spoiling the quality and slowing down the work. Good quality, thick drawing paper will take oil painting quite well.

Canvases, board and wooden panels are sold in a range of sizes. There is an international table of sizes, classified by subject —figure, landscape or marine— so that an artist can choose between various sizes in three different proportions, "figure" canvas being squarer than the "landscape", with "marine" being the widest in relation to its height.

Table of international sizes, in centimetres, of oil-painting stretchers

No.	Figure	Landscape	Marine	REMARKS
1	22×16	22×14	22×12	• With this table it's easy in the shop to buy whatever canvas you need; one only needs to ask for the required proportion (Figure, Landscape or Marine) and the number or size of canvas, for example, "a number 12 Landscape canvas".. • Board and panels are manufactured in Table sizes 1 to 8 only. • An artist can, of course, change the proportion and paint a portrait on a Landscape canvas. And he need not keep to the measurements in this international table he can always use a square canvas that is wider than any in the range for, say, Marine.
2	24×19	24×16	24×14	
3	27×22	27×19	27= 16	
4	33×24	33×22	33×19	
5	35×27	35×24	35×22	
6	41×33	41×27	41×24	
8	46×38	46×33	46×27	
10	55×46	55×38	55×33	
12	61×50	61×46	61×38	
15	65×54	65×50	65×46	
20	73×60	73×54	73×50	
25	81×65	81×60	81×54	
30	92×73	92×65	92×60	
40	100×81	100×73	100×65	
50	116×89	116×81	116×73	
60	130×97	130×89	130×81	
80	146×114	146×97	146×90	
100	162×130	162×114	162×97	
120	195×130	195×114	195×97	

HOW TO MAKE AN OIL-PAINTING STRETCHER

Making the stretcher: it's more convenient to buy a ready-made stretcher than to make it yourself. But if you live a long way from the shops or if you would rather make your own, this is how to do it:

Fig. 77. A stretcher consists of four pieces of wood jointed together so that, when mounted, the canvas can be tautened, using four small wedges pushed into slots in the stretcher's inside corners. If the stretcher is very large, it can be reinforced by a central bar.

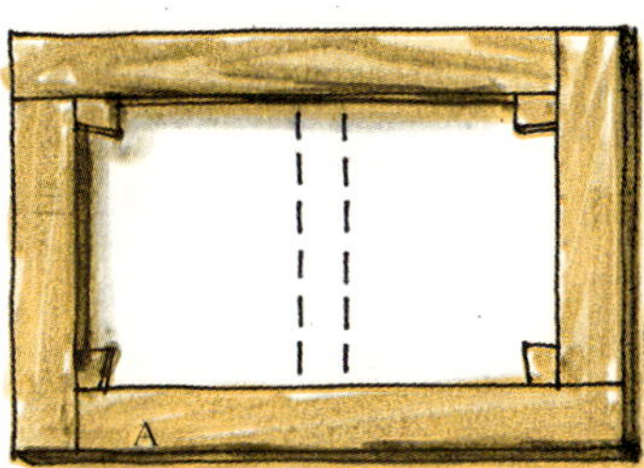

Fig. 78. To understand the jointing of the stretcher see A, the shape of a piece of the stretcher; B and C, the two ends seen in cross-section; D, a perspective drawing of a corner of the assembled frame; E and F, drawings showing the end of each of the pieces unassembled; G, a further drawing to show that the innèr tongue, F, of the piece tapers diagonally inwards to allow the wedge to be inserted. The shape and method of insertion is shown in sketch H.

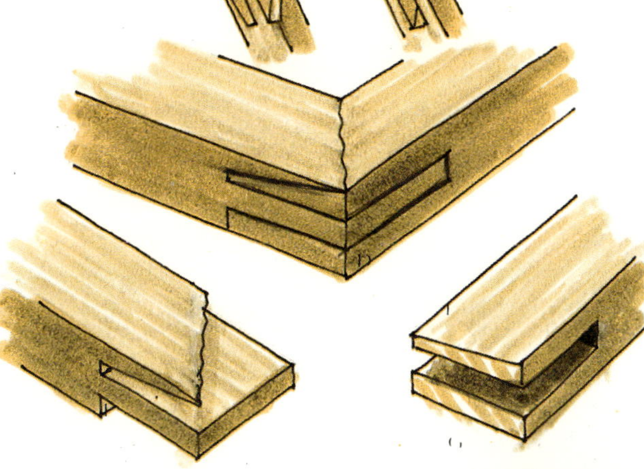

If you look carefully at this set of sketches and detail drawings, from A to H, you will see that the four pieces are bevelled inwards, i.e. they narrow towards the inside edge of the frame.

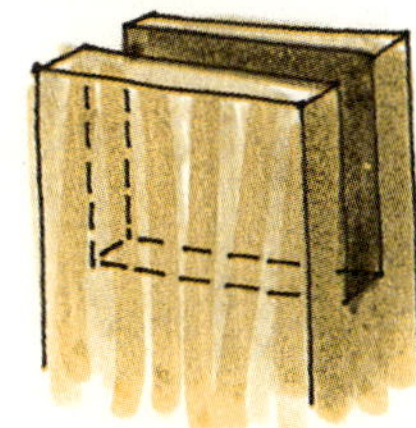

The bevelled shape of the pieces prevents the inner edge from touching the canvas and so producing a mark or extra line around the picture, since after a while this would become indelible. Note at H in the figure below how the stretcher is assembled and the wedge inserted.

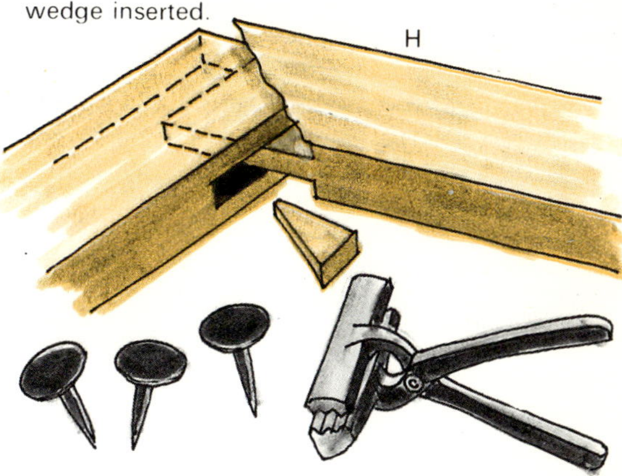

Mounting the canvas

Cut the canvas about 3 cm oversize, lay it on a table or on the floor and place the frame over it *without wedges,* taking care that the threads of the cloth, warp and weft, are parallel with the pieces of the stretcher. To mount the canvas you need special pliers with wide, flat jaws to hold the canvas taut when it is being secured; You'll also need a hammer and some short large-headed, fine-pointed tacks. The special pliers are not absolutely essential.

To tack down the canvas, begin by "making a diamond", as the initiated say, i.e. first hammer in four tacks, one in the middle of each side, in the order shown in Fig. 79 (1, 2, 3, 4). Then put in another two tacks —one on either side of No. 1— two more —one on each side of No. 2— and so on, adding pairs until there are enough along each piece of the stretcher. Obviously, from tack No. 2 onwards the canvas must be gripped and pulled taut while each tack is hammered in, and you should try to judge the degree of tautness needed to mount the canvas evenly. For the fold at each corner, see Fig. 80. When the canvas has been tacked down, pulled taut and mounted, knock in the wedges.

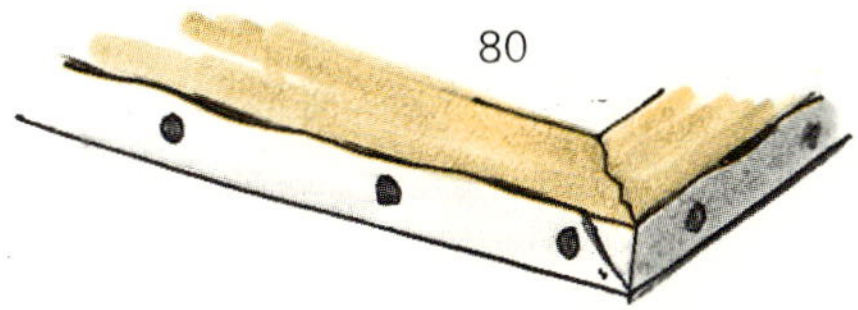

brushes for oil-painting

The brushes most commonly used for oil-painting are made of hog bristle. You can use sable brushes to paint in small details, draw lines, form outlines, etc. These bristle brushes are made in three different shapes, called in specialist shops "round", "flat" and "filbert". In some countries you can still find a type of brush with a fan-shaped tip, made especially for overpainting with transparent paint, merging shape or colour in problem parts of the picture. Sable brushes come round or flat. Brushes for oil-painting are long, 28 to 30 cm. The thickness of the tip of bristle varies according to the number on the handle. These numbers run from 1 to 24 using the even numbers (1, 2, 4, 6, 8, 10, etc). For oil-painting you need an assortment of about fifteen brushes. The most important are listed below:

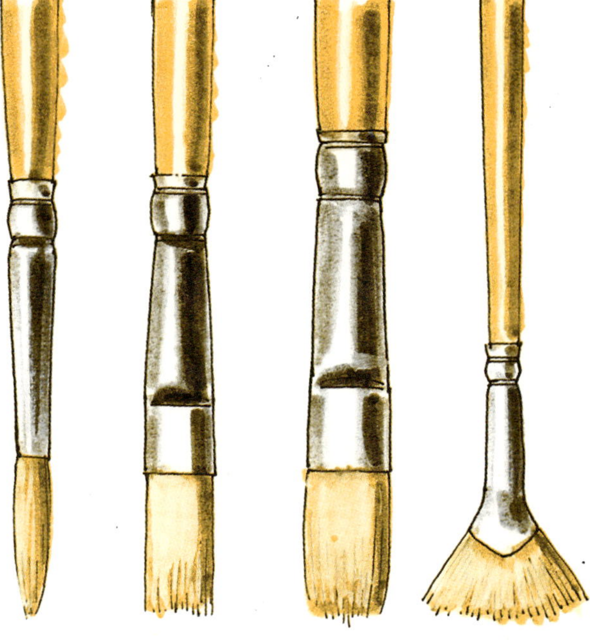

Fig. 81. Round hog, No. 6

Fig. 82. Flat hog, N. 8

Fig. 83. "Bright" hog, No. 12

Fig. 84. "Fan" hog, No. 4

Assortment of brushes for oil-painting

1 round hog, No. 4
1 flat hog, No. 4
1 round sable, No. 4
1 round hog, No. 6
2 flat hog, No. 6
1 round sable, No. 6
2 flat hog, No. 8
1 "filbert" hog, No. 8
2 flat hog, No. 12
1 "filbert" hog, No. 12
1 "filbert" hog, No. 18
1 "filbert" hog, No. 24

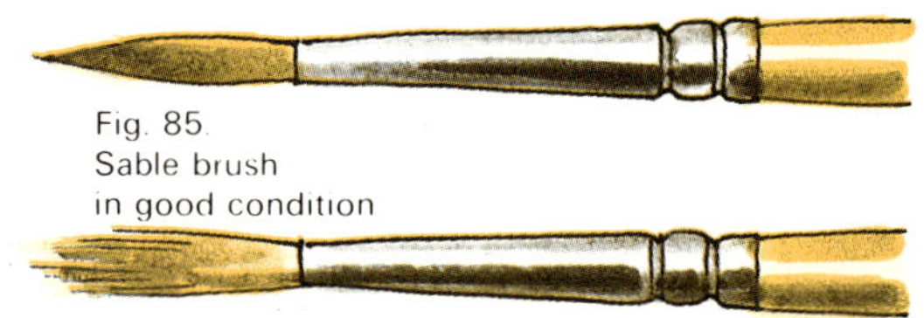

Fig. 85. Sable brush in good condition

Fig. 86. Sable brush in poor condition

A sable brush should always have a good tip. It should be cleaned carefully after use, so that the bristles don't drop out when the brush dries, making it useless.

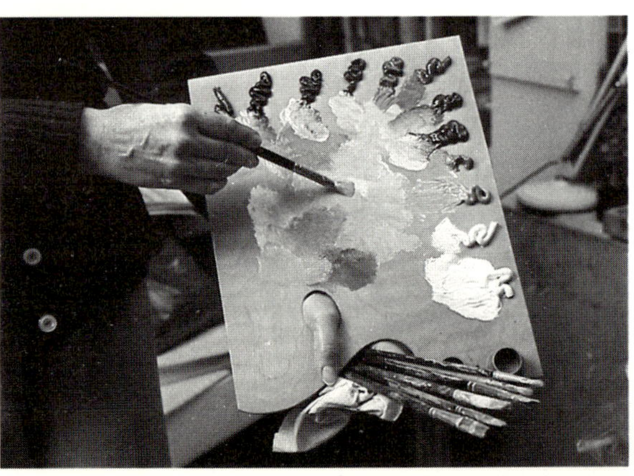

Fig. 87. This illustration shows how the palette should be held, in the left hand, with the four or five brushes you are using. The left hand also holds a rag for wiping the brushes. Hold the palette more or less flat while you hold the current brush with your right hand, mixing the colours and taking up the paint you need.

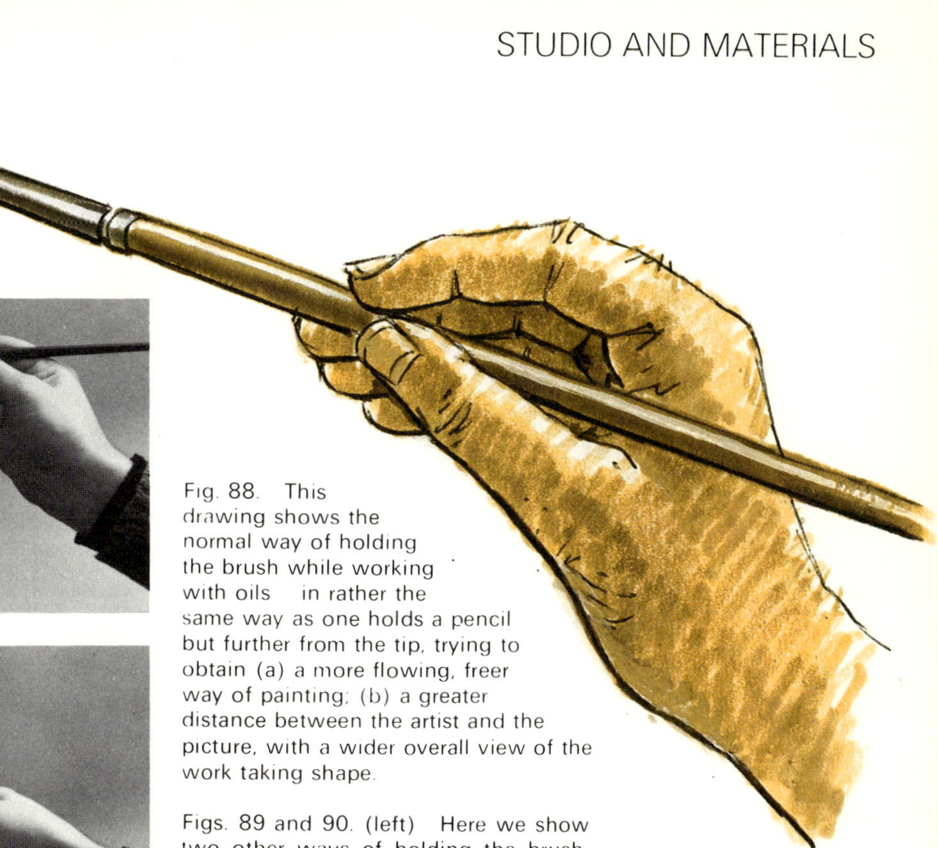

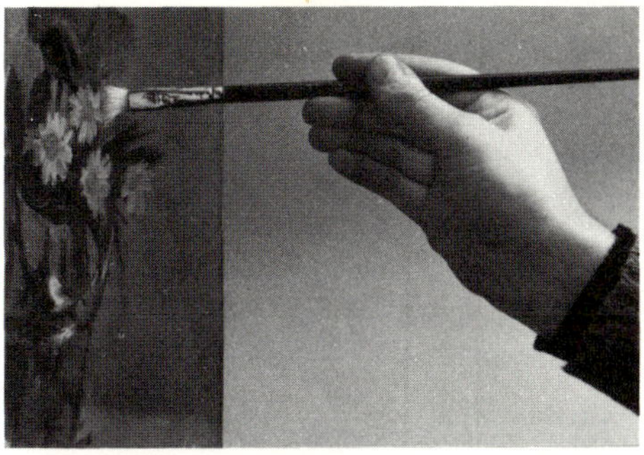

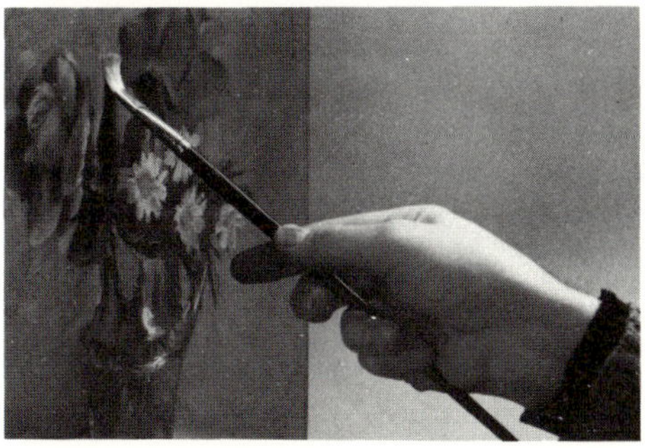

Fig. 88. This drawing shows the normal way of holding the brush while working with oils in rather the same way as one holds a pencil but further from the tip, trying to obtain (a) a more flowing, freer way of painting; (b) a greater distance between the artist and the picture, with a wider overall view of the work taking shape.

Figs. 89 and 90. (left) Here we show two other ways of holding the brush. Above: holding it straight and painting horizontally; below: painting vertically, with the handle of the brush along your palm.

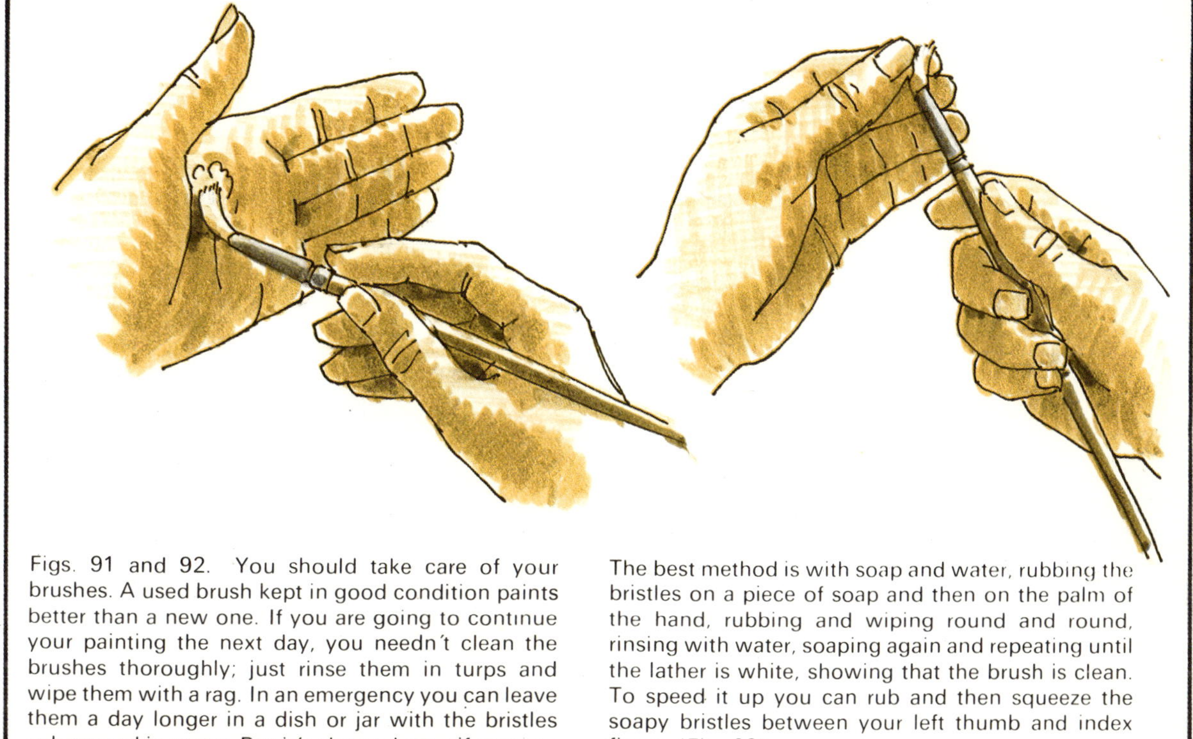

Figs. 91 and 92. You should take care of your brushes. A used brush kept in good condition paints better than a new one. If you are going to continue your painting the next day, you needn't clean the brushes thoroughly; just rinse them in turps and wipe them with a rag. In an emergency you can leave them a day longer in a dish or jar with the bristles submerged in water. But it's always better if you can wash the brushes thoroughly immediately after use. The best method is with soap and water, rubbing the bristles on a piece of soap and then on the palm of the hand, rubbing and wiping round and round, rinsing with water, soaping again and repeating until the lather is white, showing that the brush is clean. To speed it up you can rub and then squeeze the soapy bristles between your left thumb and index finger (Fig. 92).

palette knives

A palette knife is a sort of wooden-handled knife with a rounded-off and flexible steel blade but with no cutting edge. Palette knives are usually trowel-shaped. They are used for scraping paint off a painted area, cleaning the palette or painting. Painting with a palette knife requires special dexterity in using two or three spatulas instead of brushes.

A mahlstick is a light stick of wood about a metre long, with a ball-shaped tip. You use it to steady the hand when fine detail or when a very precise finish has to be applied and you can't rest the hand directly on the picture or on still wet adjacent areas. Mahlsticks are rarely used these days.

The solvents most often used in oil painting are essence of turpentine and linseed oil. Some artists use a mixture of the two, others (myself included) use essence of turpentine alone.

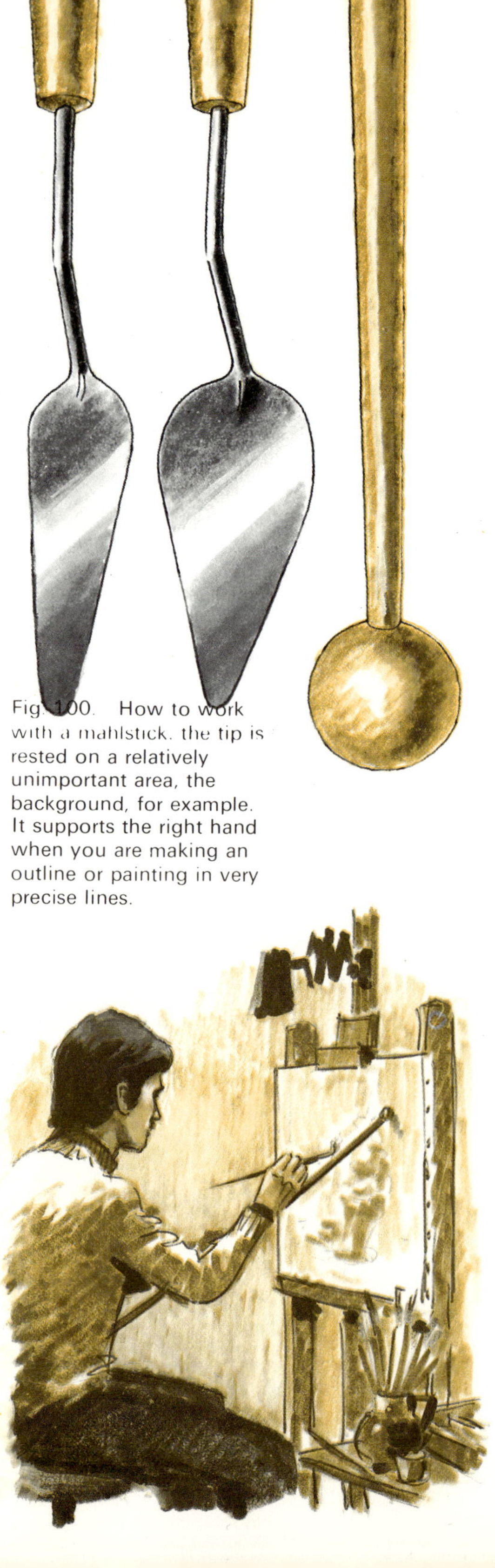

Fig. 100. How to work with a mahlstick, the tip is rested on a relatively unimportant area, the background, for example. It supports the right hand when you are making an outline or painting in very precise lines.

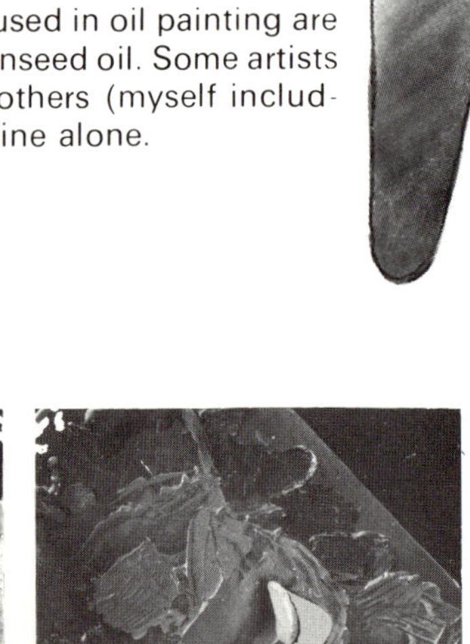

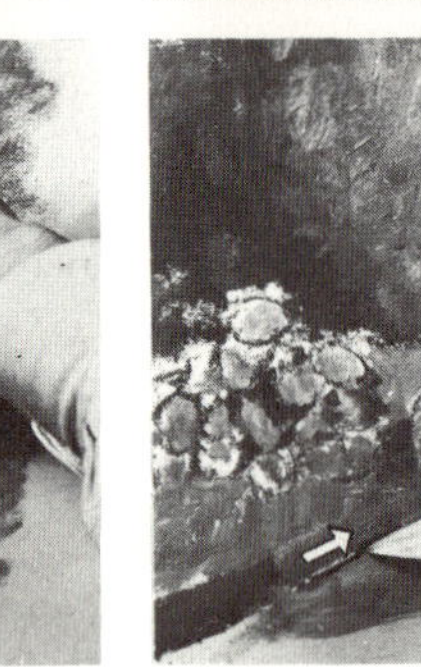

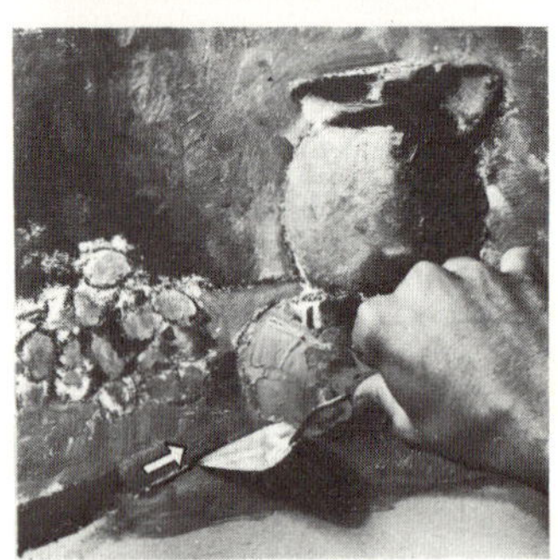

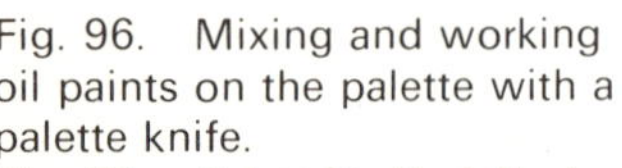

Fig. 96. Mixing and working oil paints on the palette with a palette knife.
Fig. 97. Palette knife full of oil colour, ready for use.

Fig. 98. Using a palette knife to get circular, curved shapes.
Fig. 99. Using the palette knife to get outlines on an already-painted area.

solvents and oil

The more linseed oil you use, the longer your painting takes to dry, but the shinier it will be. By contrast, essence of turpentine dries quickly, leaving a matt finish. Here is a case for remembering the basic rule of "thick on thin", warning us that we should paint the first layer or two with practically no oil, using distilled turpentine only, so that the paint applied to this surface will not crack as it would on a slightly damp surface.

You can buy special dippers (Fig. 102) to hold the solvents while you are painting. These are usually metal with a clip-on base which can be attached to the palette. Double or single dippers are obtainable, but when you are painting in the studio you may find a larger pot more useful.

Charcoal and an aerosol fixative may be necessary for the first stage or composition of the picture.

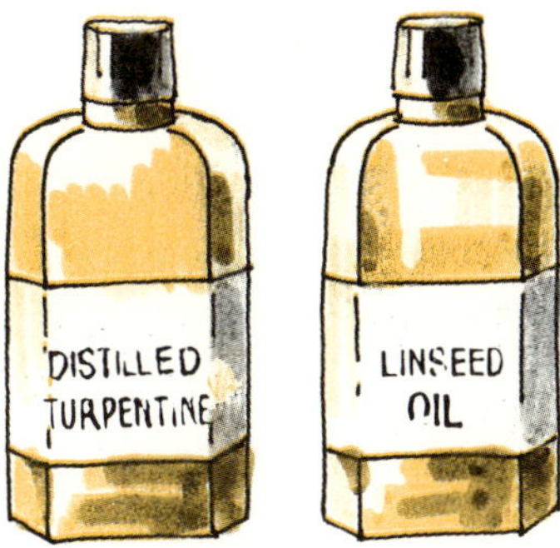

Fig. 101. Use good quality, distilled turpentine and linseed oil. But buy a larger bottle of ordinary white spirit for rinsing your hands, cleaning brushes, palette and so on.

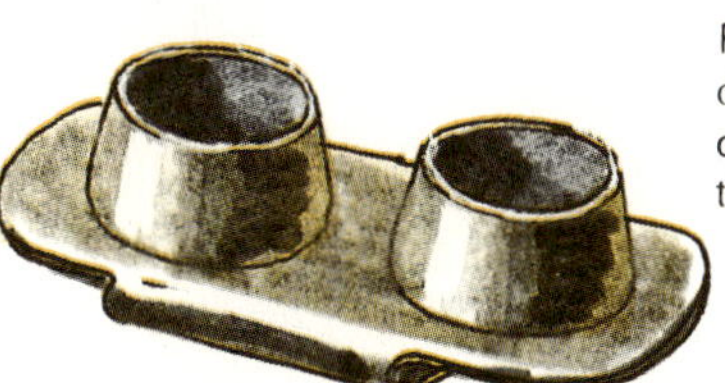

Fig. 102. Double dipper and single dipper (attached to the palette).

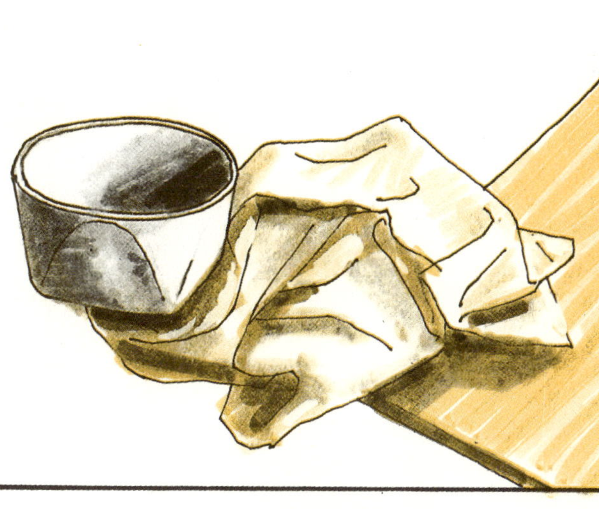

Fig. 103. Rags: old cotton or linen rags are always very useful. Try them for wiping brushes, drying or cleaning your hands, cleaning the palette, or even rubbing out a section of your painting.

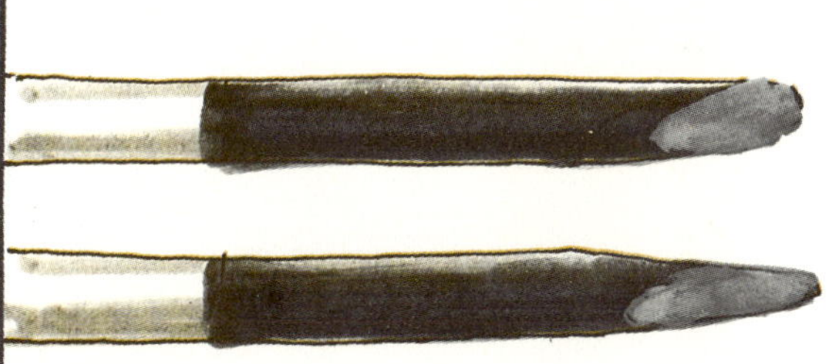

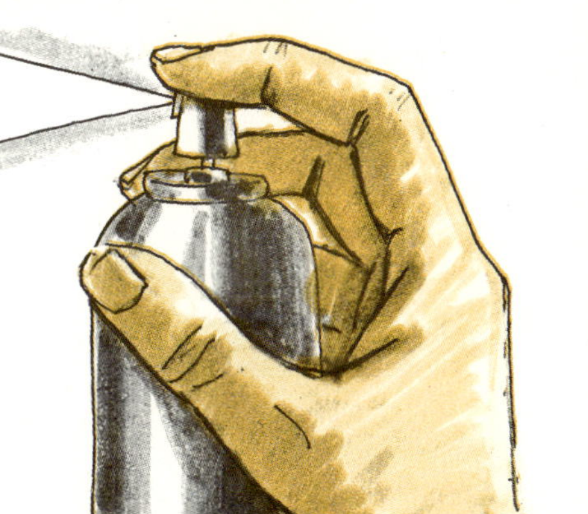

Figs. 104 and 105. You may use a charcoal drawing on which to base an oil painting. If so, you'll need an aerosol fixative for the charcoal.

oil colours

At this stage it's a good idea to establish what oil colours you're going to use, how much you'll need and which brands are thought best.

Manufacturers of oil colours offer a very extensive colour chart with more than 75 different colours. Most professionals consider that just 14 colours are enough. These 14 colours are listed below and are shown on the palette (facing page). As to the amount of each colour needed, there are usually three or more sizes of container and the medium size, or No. 6 tube, should be enough for all colours except titanium white. For this, a large, or No. 10, tube is advisable, since white is the colour most used. Finally, as to high-quality oil colours, I think that the following brands deserve mention: Talens, Rembrandt and Academie, Le Franc, Reeves and Windsor and Newton.

Fig. 106. *The palette:* there are wooden, plastic and metal palettes. Most professional artists use a wooden palette, either oval or oblong. This illustration shows how and in what order the colours are placed on the palette. note the position of the hands, especially the left and, which holds palette and brushes as well as a rag for wiping brushes, hands, etc.

Fig. 107. Actual sizes of tubes, Nos. 3, 6 and 10, approximately 10 cc, 20 cc and 60 cc.

Range of oil colours commonly used by professional artists

1. Titanium white*
2. Lemon cadmium yellow
3. Cadmium yellow*
4. Yellow ochre
5. Raw sienna*
6. Burnt sienna
7. Burnt umber*
8. Cadmium red*
9. Rose madder deep*
10. Permanent green*
11. Viridian*
12. Cobalt blue
13. Ultramarine deep*
14. Prussian blue*

Ivory black should be added to this list. The colours marked with an asterisk are indispensable; the others are useful but not vital.

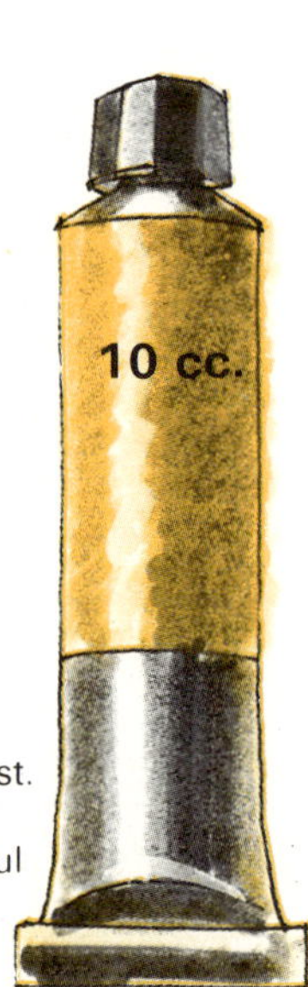

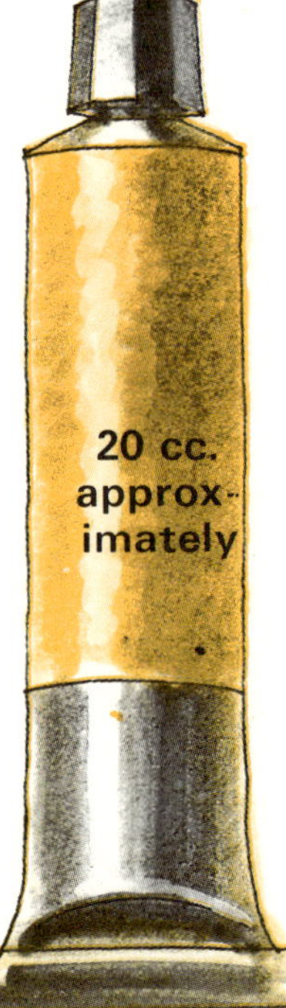

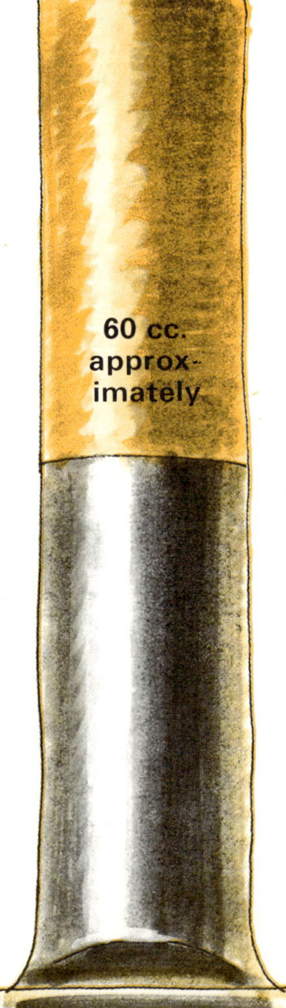

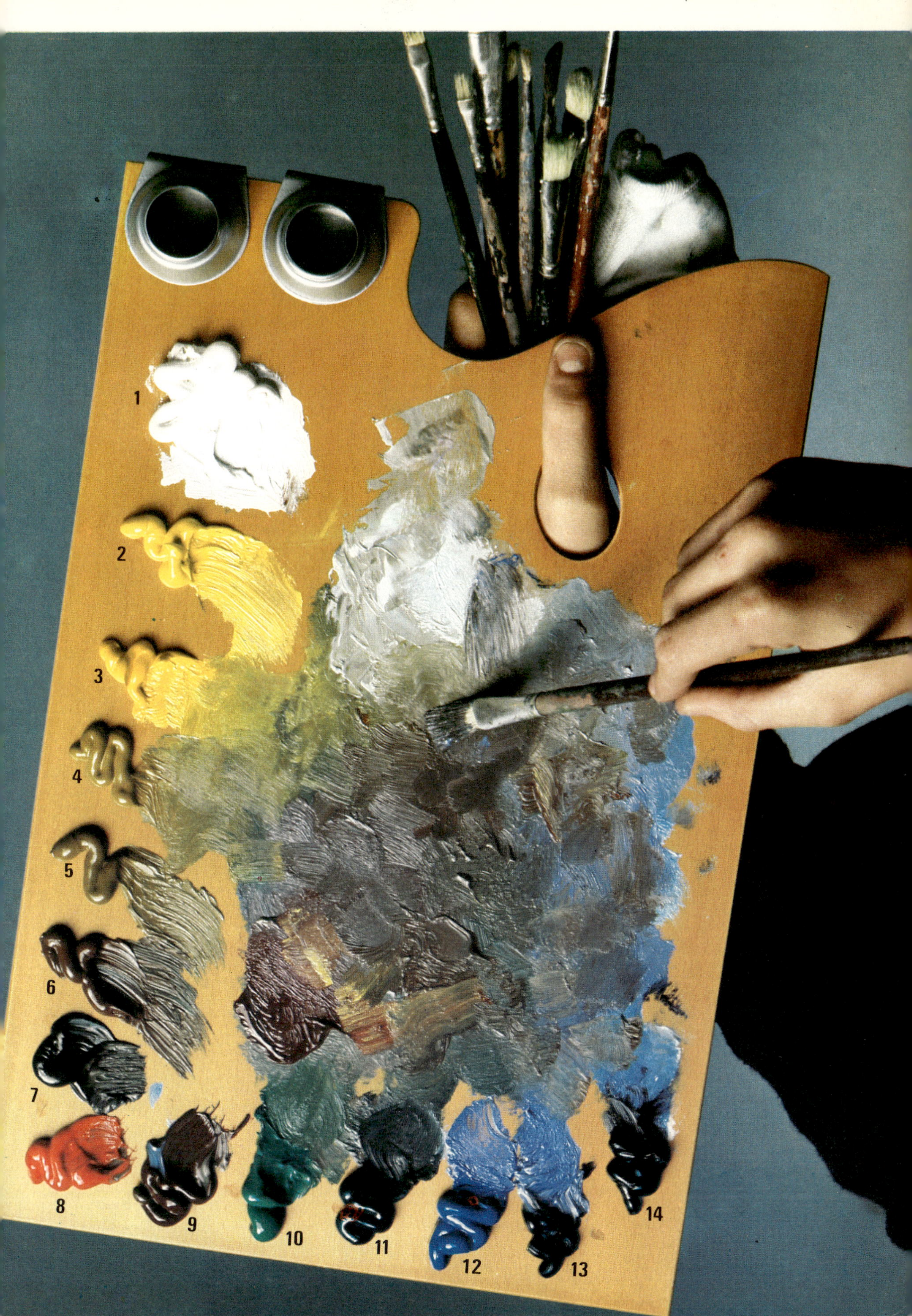

1
2
3
4
5
6
7
8
9
10
11
12
13
14

how to keep your equipment

A special box for your oil-paints, etc, is not needed when you are working on still lifes. But it is part of an artist's equipment for outdoor painting: for country landscapes, urban scenes or marine pictures. A portable oil-painting kit can be used in the studio too, as a useful unit which the artist can use for picking up and putting down brushes, tubes and paint rags. The easel box shown in Fig. 109 could well replace the working surface mentioned on page 40. (1)

Fig. 108. One of the usual types of box for outdoor oil painting. A sheet of cardboard for your picture is carried inside the box and the lid is used as a holder.

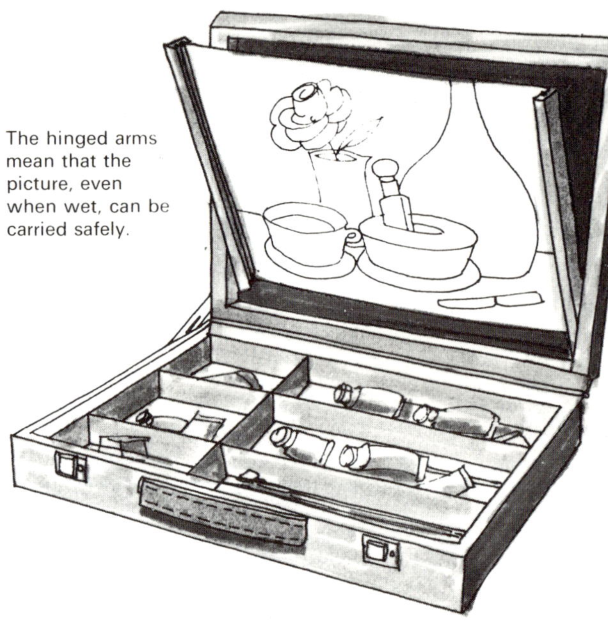

The hinged arms mean that the picture, even when wet, can be carried safely.

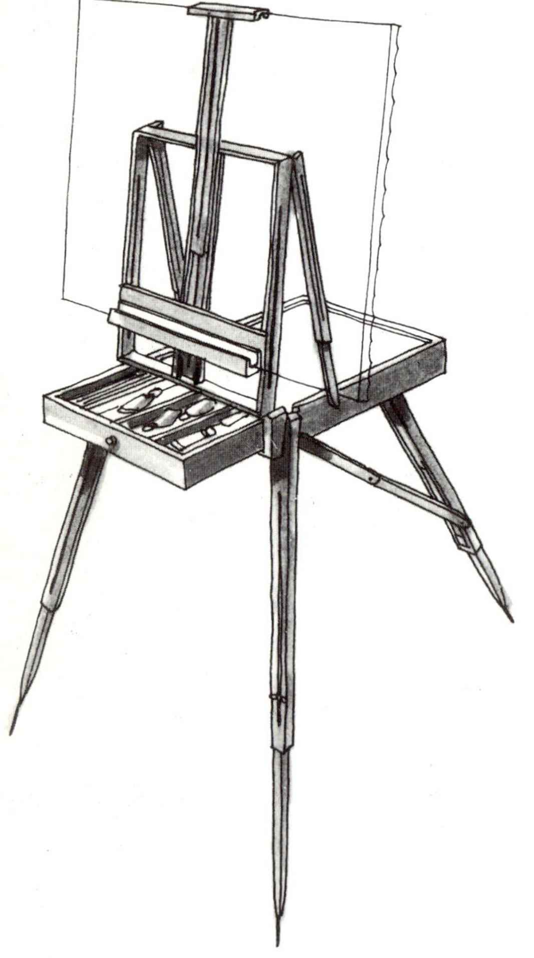

Fig. 109. The easel box is often used for carrying easel, box of painting materials, and canvas, all packed into a single unit. With legs extended and the top part folded it forms a satisfactory workbench for studio painting. Figure 109B shows the easel folded, with the canvas kept in place.

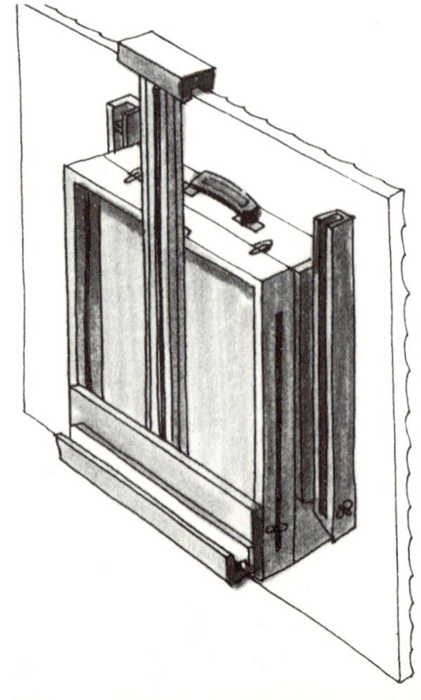

(1) See the book *Oils* in this series, in which the materials necessary for oil painting are discussed at length.

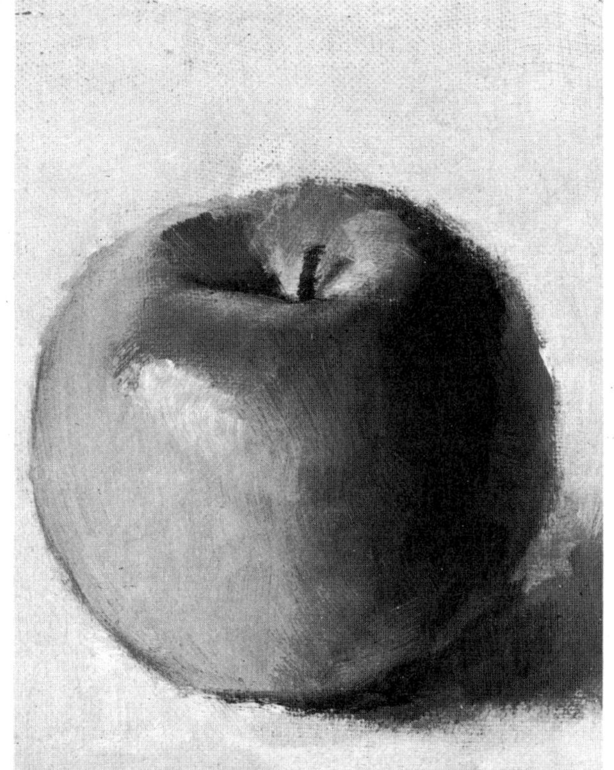

study of shapes

Even as a young man, Paul Cézanne was attracted to still life and the study of shapes and volume. In about 1860 he copied a detail from a still life by a Dutch painter which was exhibited in the museum of Aix-en-Provence. Cézanne selected from the picture the part from which he could best study spherical volume: a dish of peaches (Fig. 111). In April 1904, two years before his death, Cézanne wrote to his friend Bernard: "All forms in Nature fall into the cylinder, the sphere or the cube, everything in proper perspective." This approach, expressed earlier in other letters, at artists' gatherings and in conversation with his friends, was applied by Cézanne in his late works and was taken up by many artists at the beginning of this century. From the geometric theory Picasso developed Cubism and this became a basic principle in drawing and painting.

Cézanne's theory is especially valid when it comes to examining the shape of the objects making up a still life. We need little analysis of these objects to see that a table, a pile of books and a tablecloth with a rectangular design are essentially cube-shaped; an apple, a grape, an onion and a cooking-pot are basically spherical; a glass, a cup and a bottle are cylindrical.

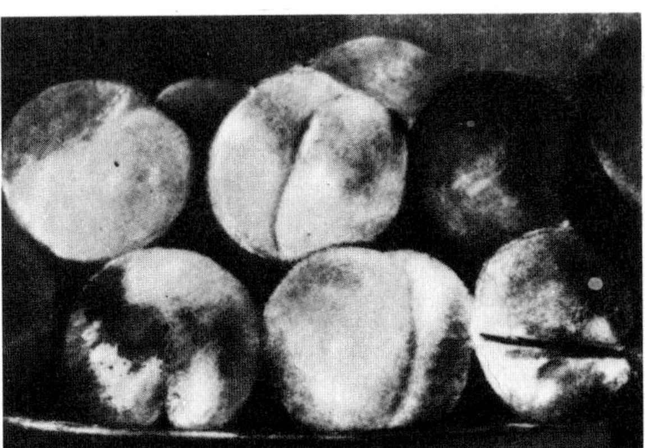

The cube, the sphere and the cylinder

Here is a list of objects classified by shape; you'll see that their structure falls into one of the above categories.

Square or cube	Sphere	Circle and cylinder
table	various fruits	wine glass or tumbler
book or books	apple	cup
box or case	peach	bottle
tablecloth	plum	casserole
objects with no precise shape but which fit into the shape of a square or a cube, for example a flower, a banana, a bunch of grapes.	melon	saucer
	orange, etc.	ashtray
	tomato	other pottery or china objects
	onion	jugs and vases
	potato	pots and bottles
	head of garlic	other containers
	pitcher	
	earthenware jar	
	pottery or glass	

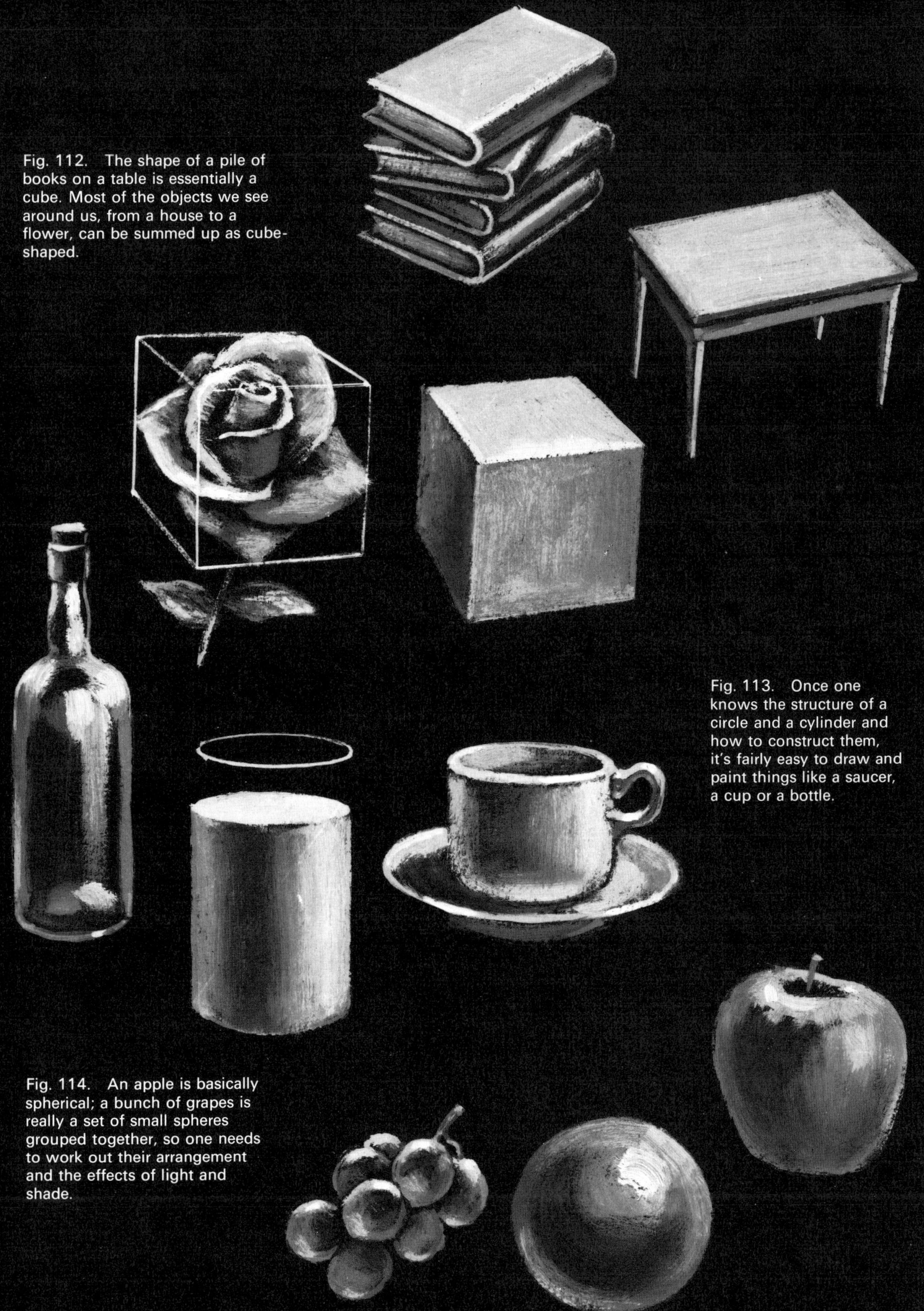

Fig. 112. The shape of a pile of books on a table is essentially a cube. Most of the objects we see around us, from a house to a flower, can be summed up as cube-shaped.

Fig. 113. Once one knows the structure of a circle and a cylinder and how to construct them, it's fairly easy to draw and paint things like a saucer, a cup or a bottle.

Fig. 114. An apple is basically spherical; a bunch of grapes is really a set of small spheres grouped together, so one needs to work out their arrangement and the effects of light and shade.

construction and perspective

The cube, the square and the rectangle always present a problem of perspective. By solving this problem the artist can represent the third dimension: depth. As you know, there are basically two kinds of perspective depending on whether the object is viewed from the front (parallel perspective) or in three-quarters position (oblique perspective). Parallel perspective and oblique perspective can be mastered using three essentials:

The horizon line
The centre of vision
The vanishing points

The *horizon line* is always at eye level; you'll find it by looking straight ahead. The *centre of vision* lies on the horizon line, in the very middle of the observer's angle of vision. The *vanishing points* are determined by the oblique lines of the object and run into the distance, meeting at the horizon line. With parallel perspective there is only one vanishing point: the centre of vision. With oblique perspective there are two vanishing points whatever the centre of vision.

As you will see in Fig. 120, the shape of the cylinder derives from the shape of a cube or a parallelepiped.

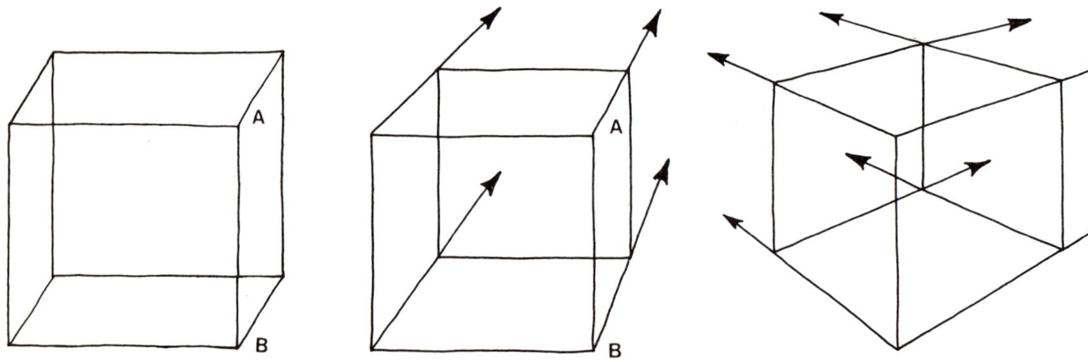

Fig. 115. If the outlines of a cube are drawn in parallel, including the lines inclined towards greater distance (lines A and B), the cube lacks perspective and therefore lacks depth.

Fig. 116. If all the lines in this cube except for lines A and B are kept parallel, the cube is drawn in *parallel perspective.*

Fig. 117. If the lines of a cube form two sets, each converging towards the horizon but not parallel to each other, the cube is drawn in *oblique perspective.*

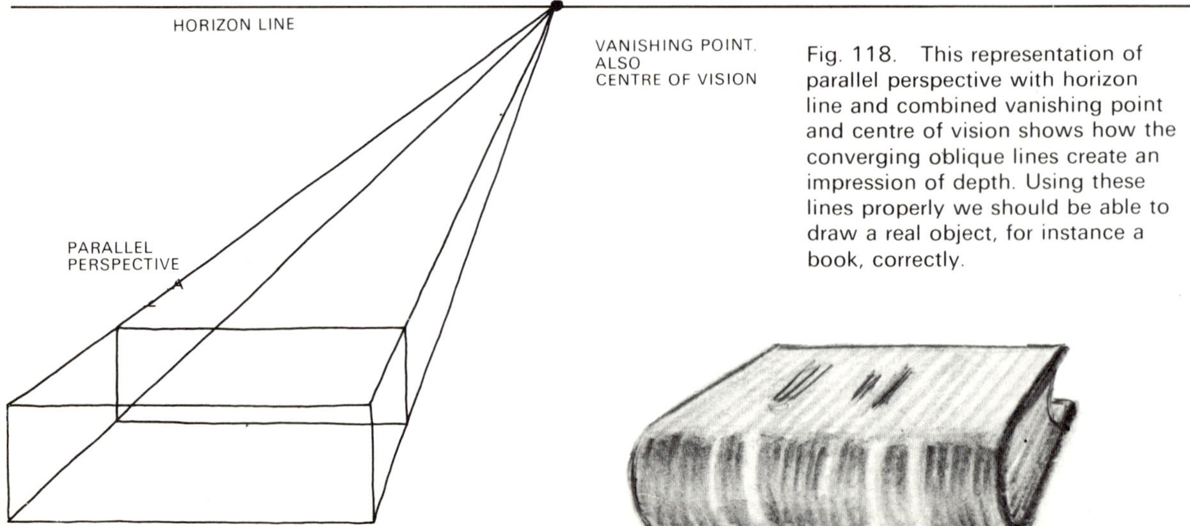

Fig. 118. This representation of parallel perspective with horizon line and combined vanishing point and centre of vision shows how the converging oblique lines create an impression of depth. Using these lines properly we should be able to draw a real object, for instance a book, correctly.

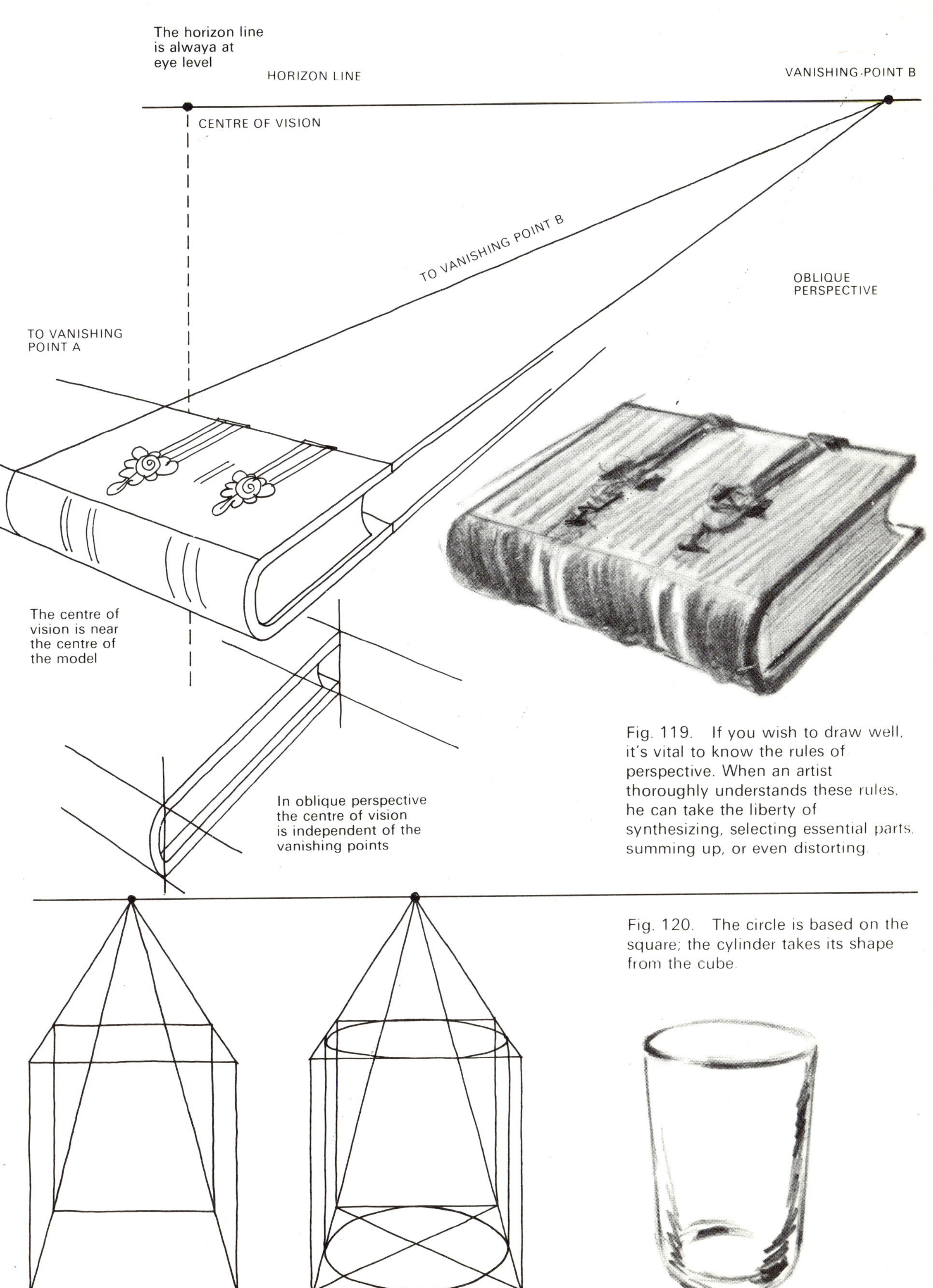

Fig. 119. If you wish to draw well, it's vital to know the rules of perspective. When an artist thoroughly understands these rules, he can take the liberty of synthesizing, selecting essential parts, summing up, or even distorting.

Fig. 120. The circle is based on the square; the cylinder takes its shape from the cube.

structure

In modern painting it is generally accepted that many artists alter and distort perspective, deliberately dispensing with horizon lines, centres of vision and vanishing points, for example, portraying the base of a bottle as a rectangle or constructing a cube without representing depth. There is nothing wrong with this; in fact it might even be good if you reach this stage through the need to create an individual style and personal form of expression. But I honestly believe that, to arrive at what Van Gogh called "inaccuracies that are more real than the truth", you must first know how to draw a cube, cylinder and circle correctly from memory —as easily as signing your name. We'll now see that it's not as easy as it sounds.

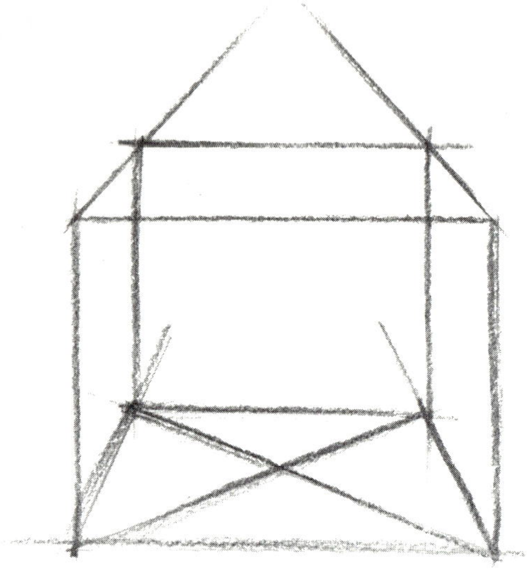

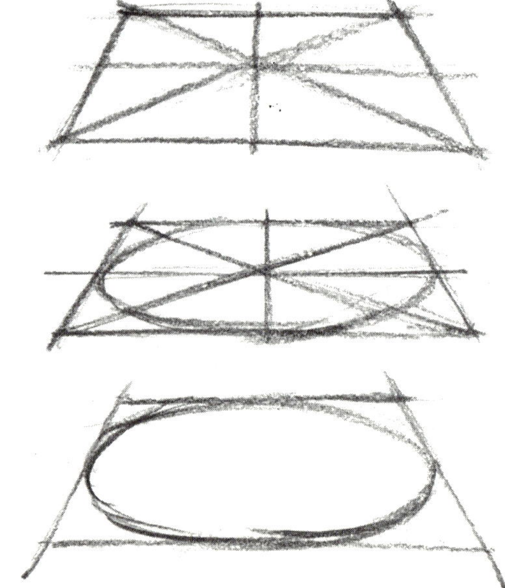

Fig. 121. Drawing from memory without using ruler or set-square,try to get sketches like these: a cube, a square and a circle. Can you do it?

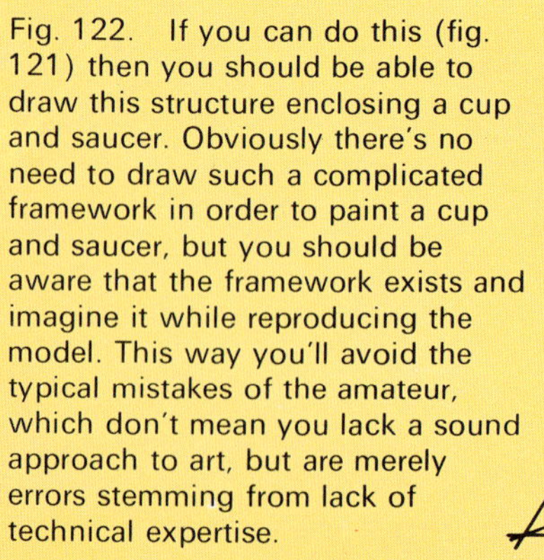

Fig. 122. If you can do this (fig. 121) then you should be able to draw this structure enclosing a cup and saucer. Obviously there's no need to draw such a complicated framework in order to paint a cup and saucer, but you should be aware that the framework exists and imagine it while reproducing the model. This way you'll avoid the typical mistakes of the amateur, which don't mean you lack a sound approach to art, but are merely errors stemming from lack of technical expertise.

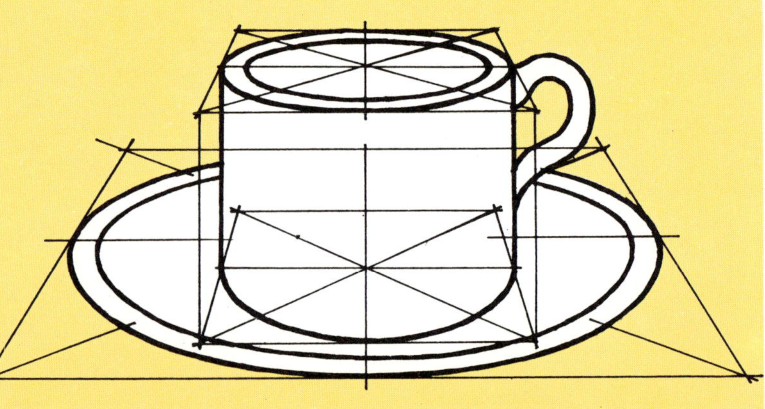

common mistakes

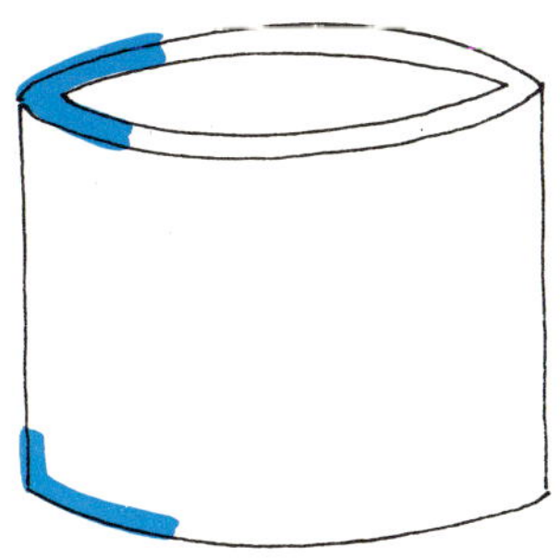

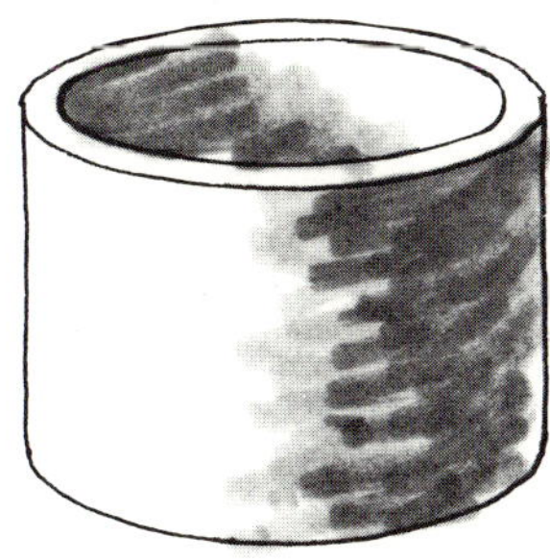

Fig. 123. In the base of this cylinder you can see the common error of drawing a circle incorrectly. In the vertices of that base there's an angular shape which is false.

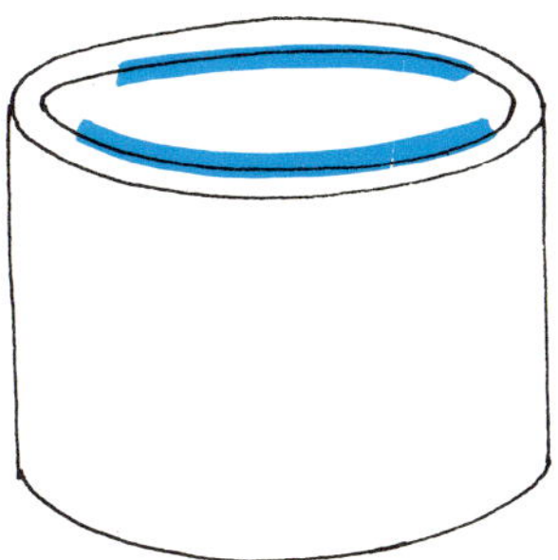

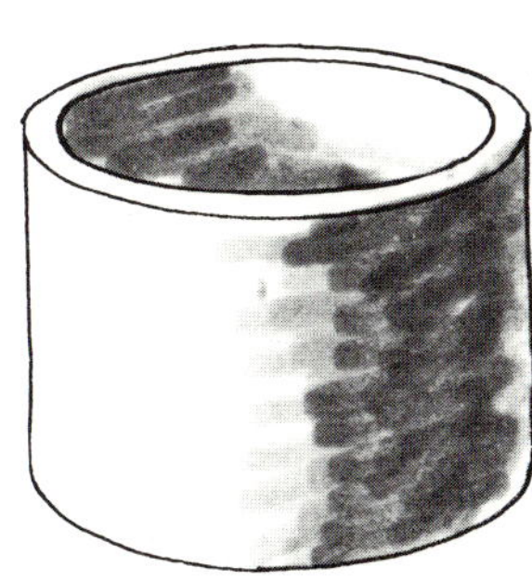

Fig. 124. Another common mistake: trying to depict the thickness of the cylinder (far left) by drawing two circles, one inside the other, without perspective.

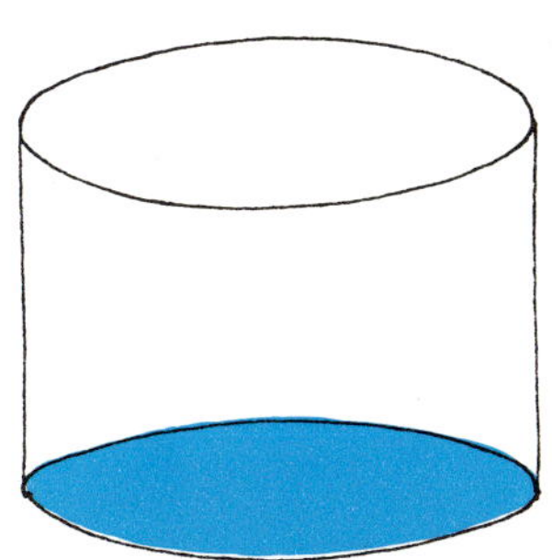

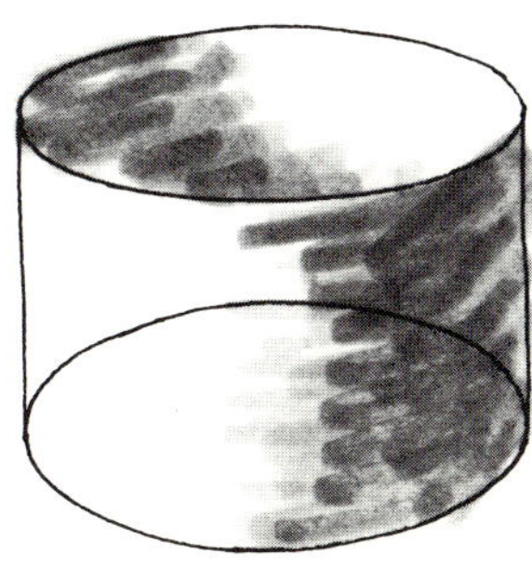

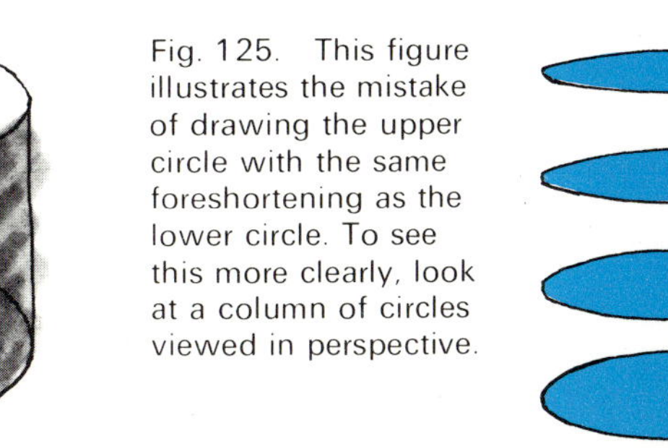

Fig. 125. This figure illustrates the mistake of drawing the upper circle with the same foreshortening as the lower circle. To see this more clearly, look at a column of circles viewed in perspective.

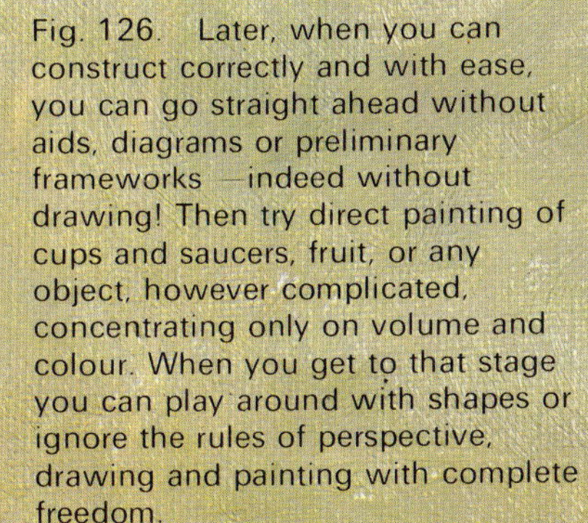

Fig. 126. Later, when you can construct correctly and with ease, you can go straight ahead without aids, diagrams or preliminary frameworks —indeed without drawing! Then try direct painting of cups and saucers, fruit, or any object, however complicated, concentrating only on volume and colour. When you get to that stage you can play around with shapes or ignore the rules of perspective, drawing and painting with complete freedom.

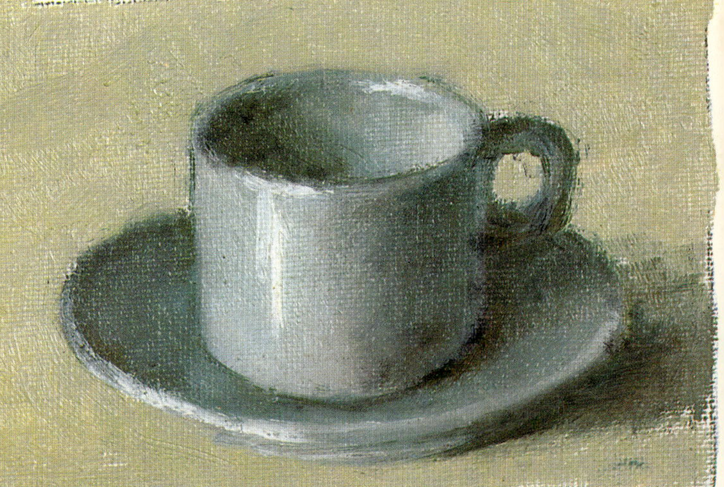

dimensions and proportions

Imagine that you have the model in front of you and that you are going to start a picture on a blank canvas. Assuming that the choice and arrangement of the different parts of your still life have already been worked out, now the problems of the picture itself begin. What size should you paint the model? Where should the model be positioned in the picture —towards the right or left, towards the top or bottom? In a still life, the size of your painted object should never be bigger than its actual size; yet you shouldn't make the elements in the model so tiny that, when painted, they look too small and the surrounding space too big. (This often happens when you've chosen too large a canvas.) Don't "blow up" the model too much, leaving scarcely any space around it. All these problems are solved by the old trick of using a cardboard frame in order to see the model within a frame and then to decide its size and position in the picture.

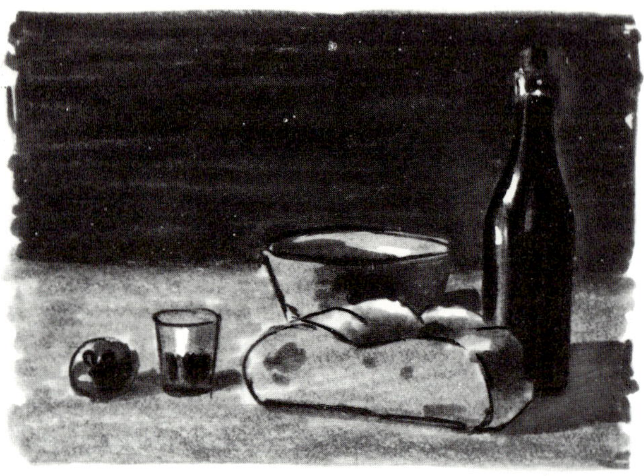

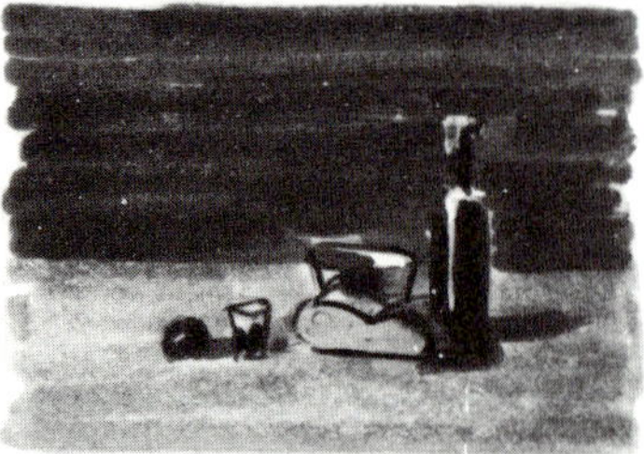

Fig. 127. Scaling down the model so that it looks lost in a vast area of canvas is the amateur's common mistake. A good way to avoid this is to paint the objects actual size and work on a canvas at the lower end of the range of sizes (No. 12 downwards).

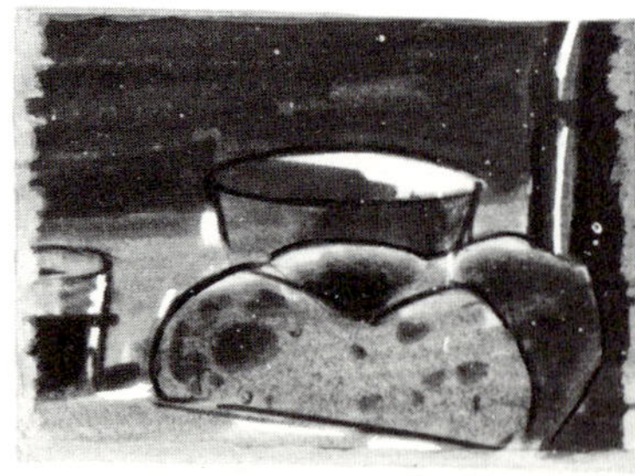

Fig. 128. "Blowing up" the model too much (or working with too small a canvas) is also a pitfall.

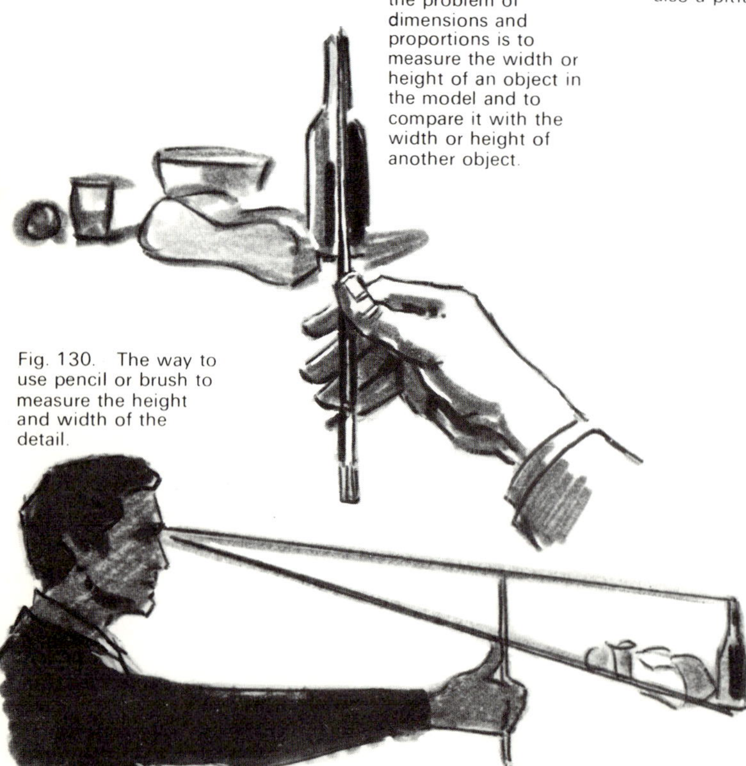

Fig. 129. One of the classic solutions to the problem of dimensions and proportions is to measure the width or height of an object in the model and to compare it with the width or height of another object.

Fig. 130. The way to use pencil or brush to measure the height and width of the detail.

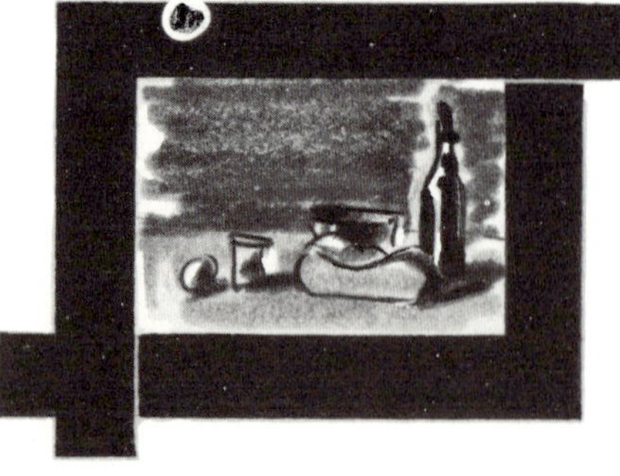

Fig. 131. Use two right-angled pieces of black cardboard placed one over the other; this way you can judge what the model will look like when framed. This will help you to fix the right position and proportion for the subject within your picture.

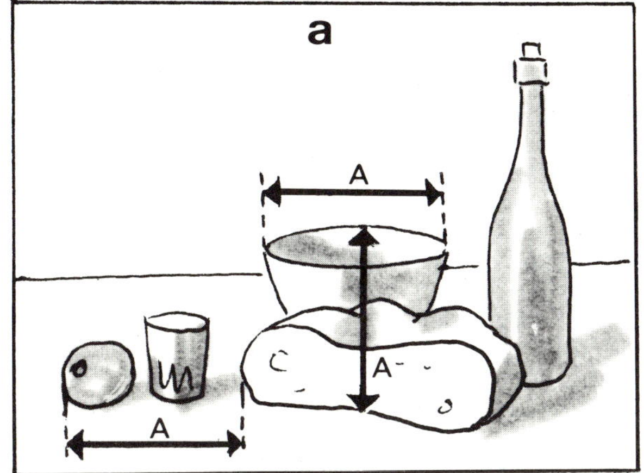

All problems of good construction or *good drawing,* which is the same thing —can be solved by means of three "magic formulae":

To work out dimensions

a) compare various distances;
b) look for reference points from which to project basic lines;
c) imagine some lines which determine the position of some things in relation to others.

The rest is a matter of speed, of mental calculations and of your own ability to see the work as a whole, so that you are really "in charge" of the picture. Remember the advice that Ingres gave his students: "Draw from a distance, as if you were all-powerful and all-seeing giants".

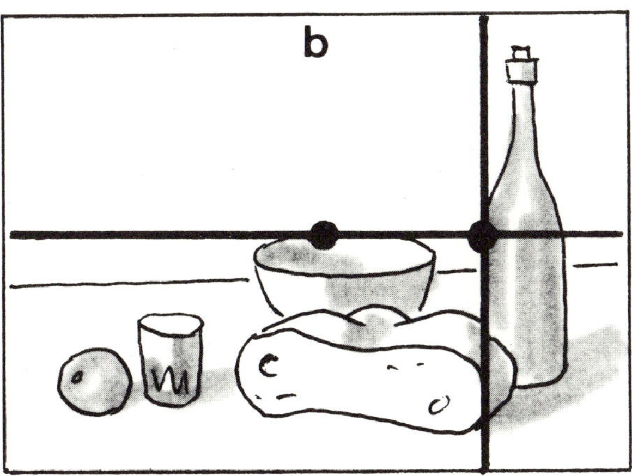

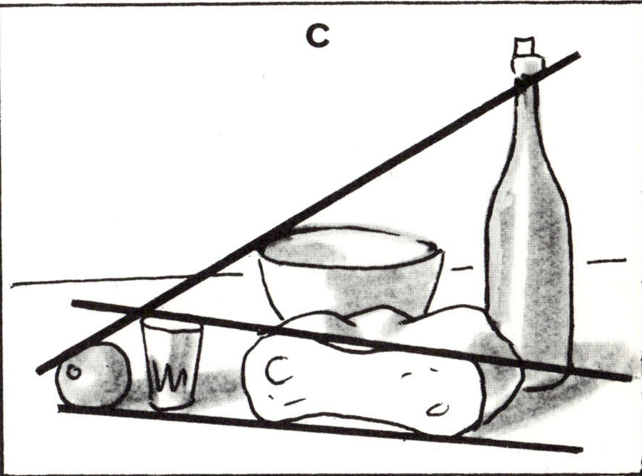

Fig. 132. Every subject provides imaginary horizontal and vertical lines for comparing distances.

Fig. 133. Look for reference points and sum up the relative position of outlines.

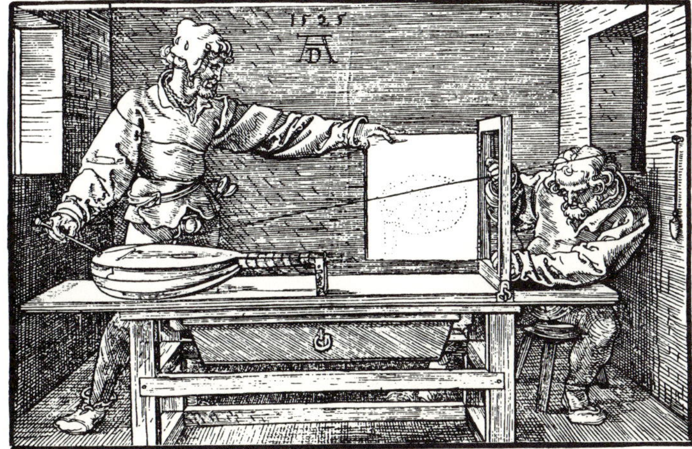

Fig. 134. Albrecht Dürer, the great 16th century artist, devised various kinds of apparatus for mechanical "drawing" which can nowadays be done with a pantograph. An invention of his which was intended to copy plans on any scale —like a pantograph— was one of those that never went beyond the drawing board.

chiaroscuro and tonal values

Light outlines and colours objects. Shade defines the form and brings out the volume. To portray volume we draw or paint tones of different intensity, or "values", comparing and evaluating certain tones and looking at the tonal value: this tone is lighter than that; the tone here is darker than the one there. Relative values therefore constitute a basic aspect of both drawing and painting. Later in this book I'll explain that it may sometimes be possible to disregard effects of light and shade, tonal values, atmosphere and even volume. But obviously you must learn the basics before you can depart from them.

This oil painting of an apple illustrates the factors determining the volume of objects. In order to depict volume you must know how to

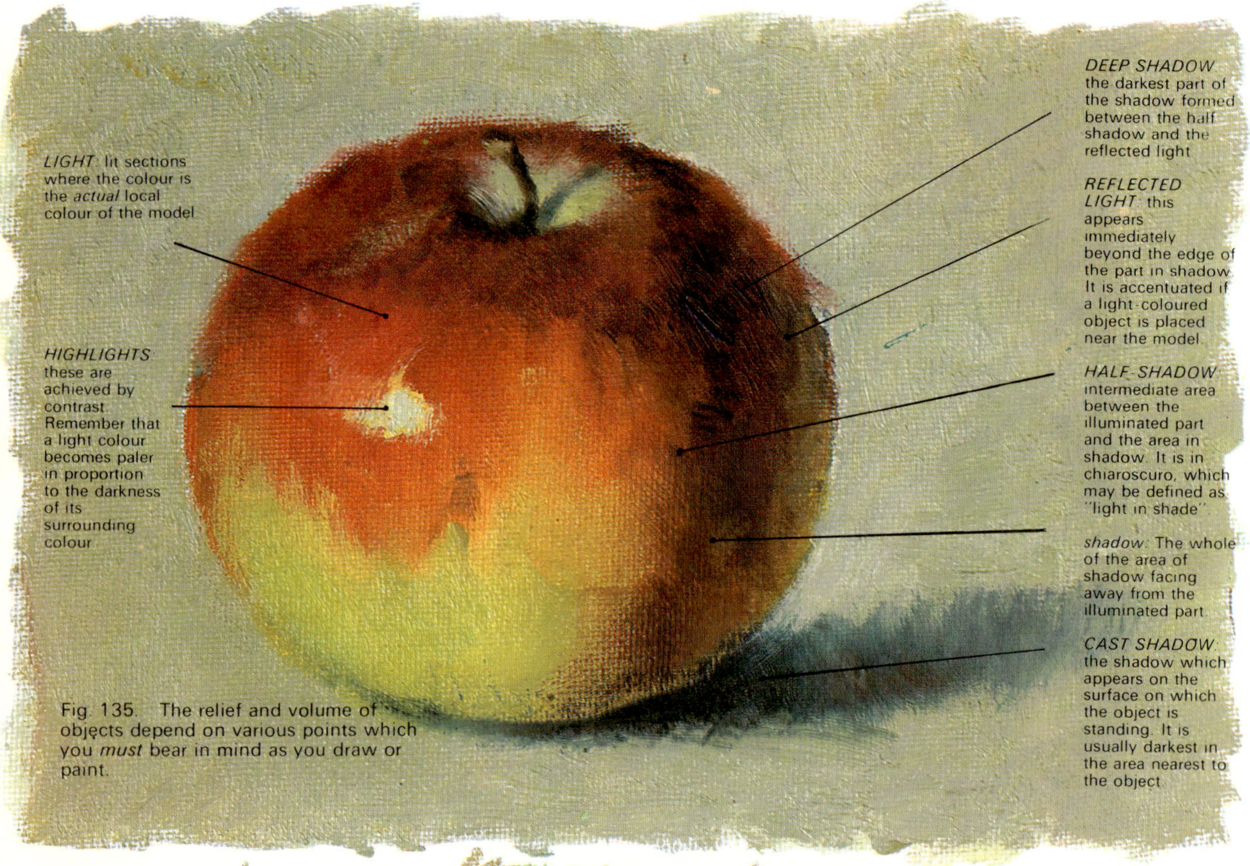

LIGHT: lit sections where the colour is the *actual* local colour of the model.

HIGHLIGHTS: these are achieved by contrast. Remember that a light colour becomes paler in proportion to the darkness of its surrounding colour.

DEEP SHADOW: the darkest part of the shadow formed between the half shadow and the reflected light.

REFLECTED LIGHT: this appears immediately beyond the edge of the part in shadow. It is accentuated if a light-coloured object is placed near the model.

HALF-SHADOW: intermediate area between the illuminated part and the area in shadow. It is in chiaroscuro, which may be defined as "light in shade".

shadow: The whole of the area of shadow facing away from the illuminated part.

CAST SHADOW: the shadow which appears on the surface on which the object is standing. It is usually darkest in the area nearest to the object.

Fig. 135. The relief and volume of objects depend on various points which you *must* bear in mind as you draw or paint.

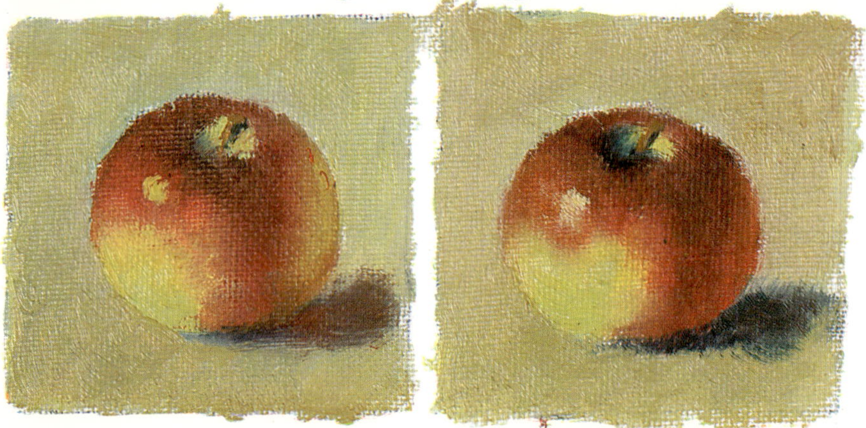

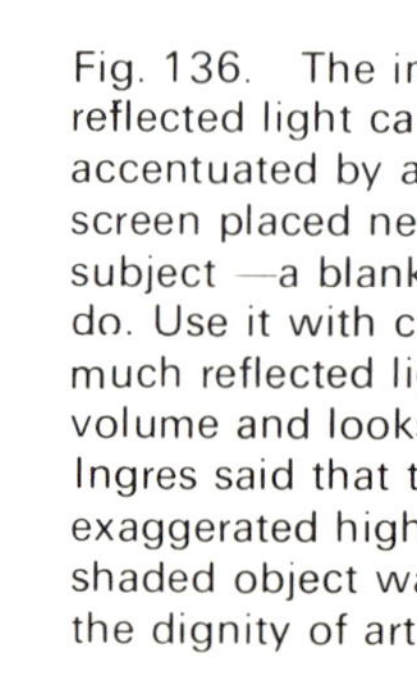

Fig. 136. The intensity of reflected light can be accentuated by a reflector screen placed near the subject —a blank canvas will do. Use it with caution! Too much reflected light destroys volume and looks artificial. Ingres said that to introduce exaggerated highlights in a shaded object was to debase the dignity of art.

work with light and shade, together with *tonal values.* The latter involves seeing and understanding, observing and comparing the different gradations of tone which make the shape. There's no need for hundreds of colour variations; it's possible to represent the whole range of the model's tones simply using white, black and five shades of grey.

Fig. 137. Here's an interesting exercise using an apple; paint in oils, using white and black only as I have done. You'll find that you don't need a huge number of tones —just the few which can convey the volume.

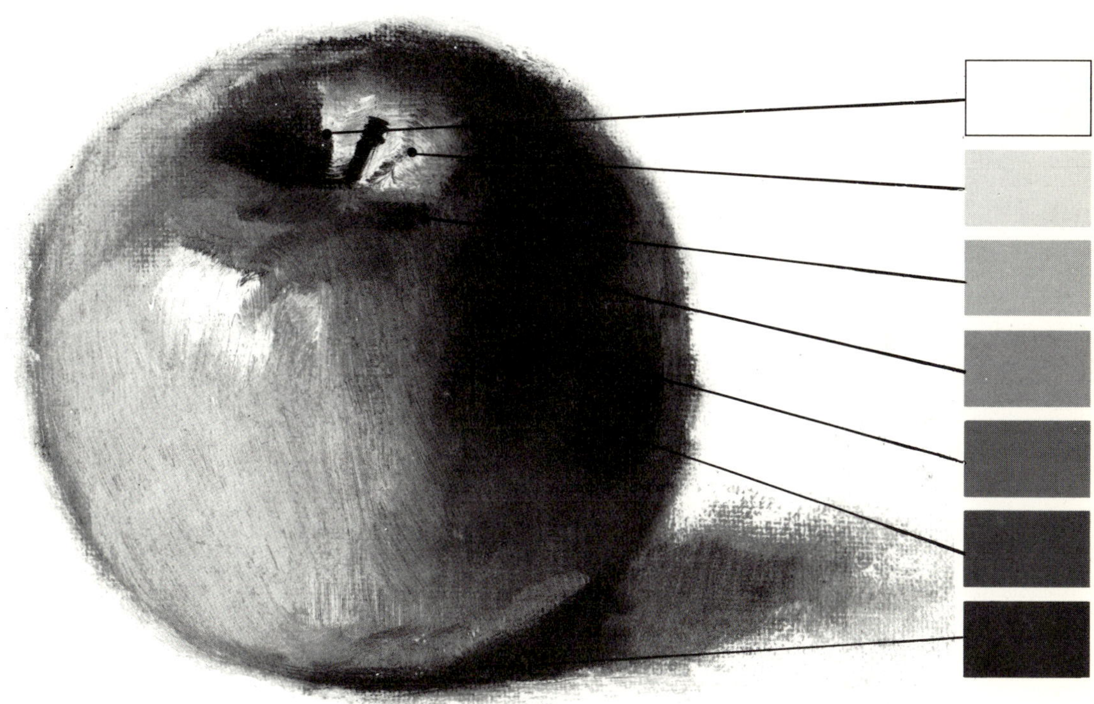

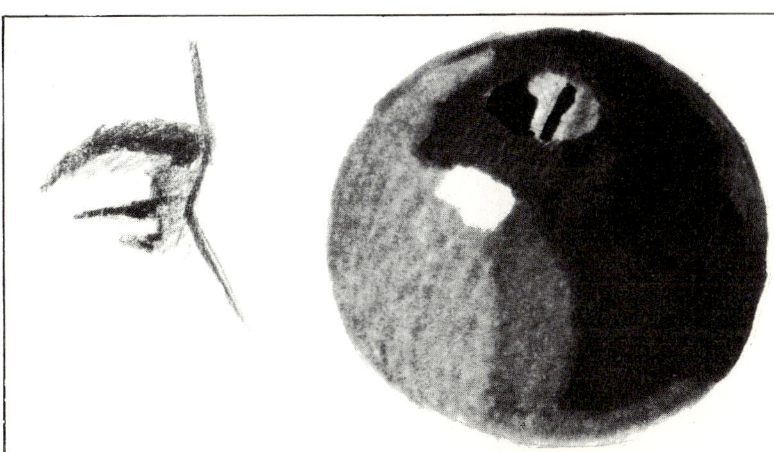

Fig. 138. A very common way of picking out tones is to look at the model with narrowed eyes. Then it seems blurred, the small details disappear and the differing tonal values which express volume show up clearly.

contrast

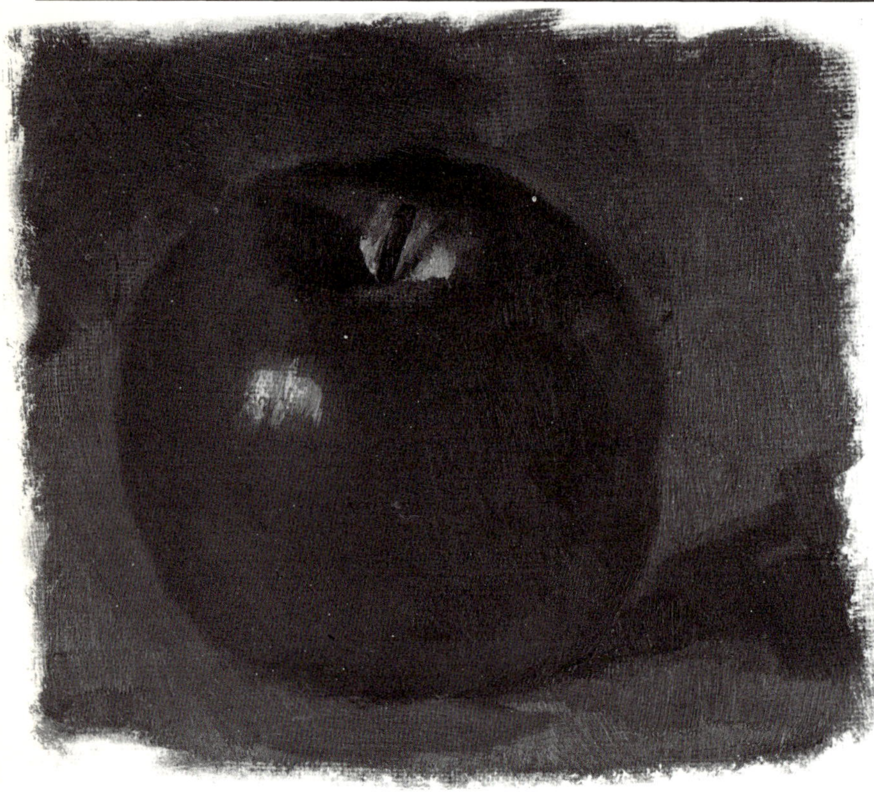

Tonal values affect contrast; contrast decisively influences the impression of volume.

Fig. 139. BAD: complete lack of contrast resulting from over-emphasized tonal values. This presents a range of tones that is too dark and includes no light of medium greys. It's a very common fault of the inexperienced painter who misuses black or dark colours.

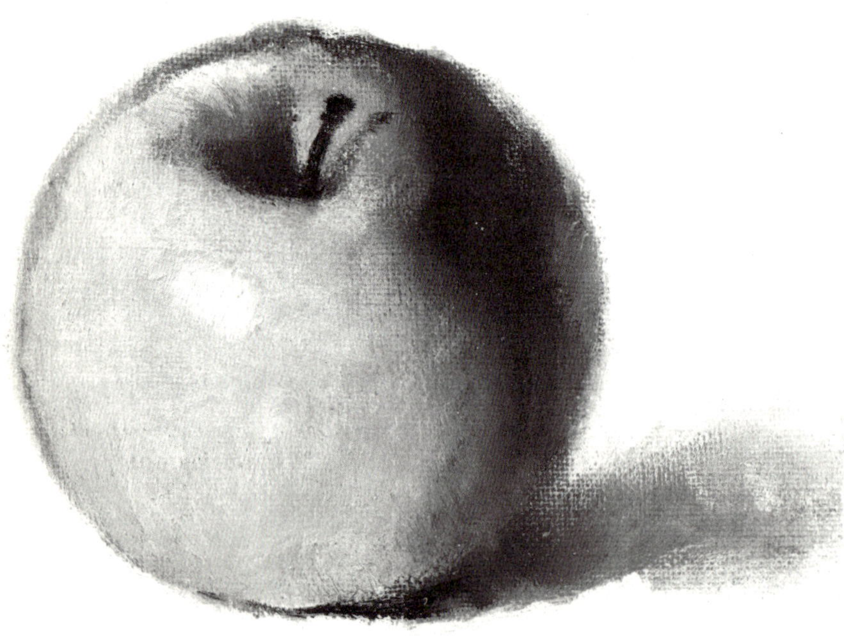

Fig. 140. BAD: too much contrast with tonal values too light. The half-tones and light greys are almost colourless; white is misused and this light, pastel appearance is produced. What's more, it's accompanied by "deep shadow" which, though very dark, conveys scarcely any volume.

atmosphere

You can convey the feeling of space and depth between foreground and background by accentuating contrast in the nearest objects while, at the same time, lessening colour or making greyer tones in the more distant areas. We'll discuss this below, using practical examples to illustrate this basic rule of contrast and atmosphere. Just remember that an illusion of space can also come from blurred outlines, especially in the farther planes.

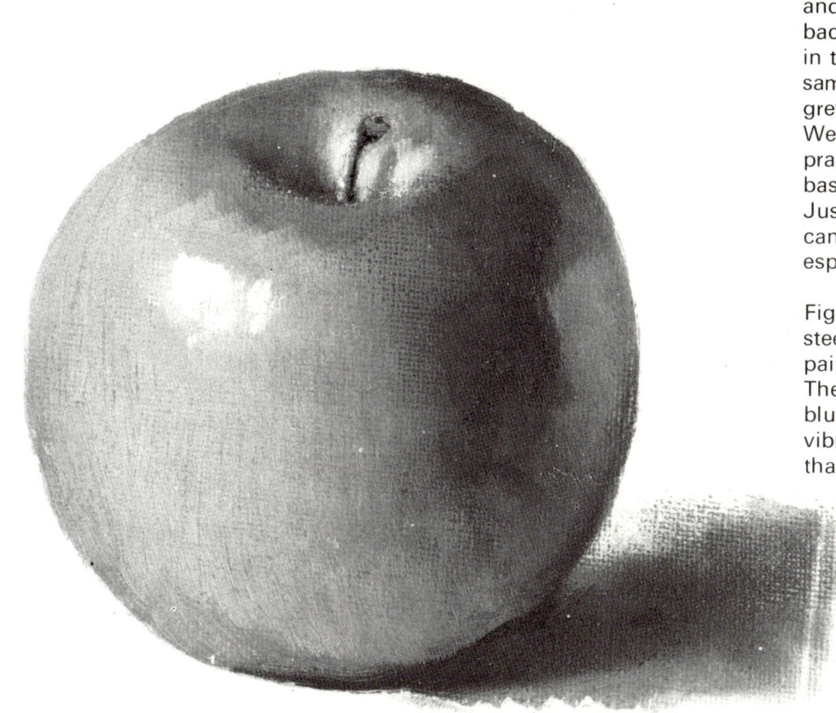

Fig. 141. BAD: this rigidity, hard as a steel mould, is not the style of a good painter. Here there is no atmosphere. The outline should be broken or blurred; this would represent the vibration of light and make one believe that the contours continue to the back.

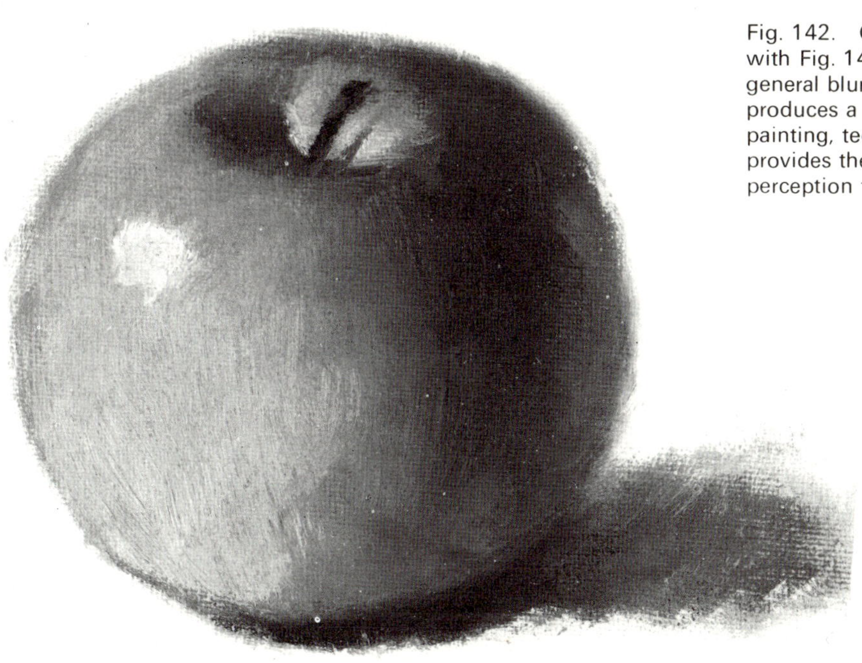

Fig. 142. GOOD: compare this apple with Fig. 141. You'll see that the general blurring of outline and form produces a more realistic picture. This painting, technically good, also provides the spontaneity and perception found in modern art.

how to provide contrasts

Let's put the apple on a surface such as it might appear in a still life. If the colours and tones of that surface are like those of the apple, the apple won't show up clearly and may look glued to the background,as if there were no space around the fruit (see Fig. 143).

So we may have to produce contrasts even if there are none! This is a trick of the trade. In Fig. 144 you can see that the surface near the lit part of the apple (A) has been made slightly darker, while near the part in shadow (B) it has been made slightly paler, showing up the shape of the apple and bringing it "off" the surface. The same effects can be seen in the parts marked C and D.

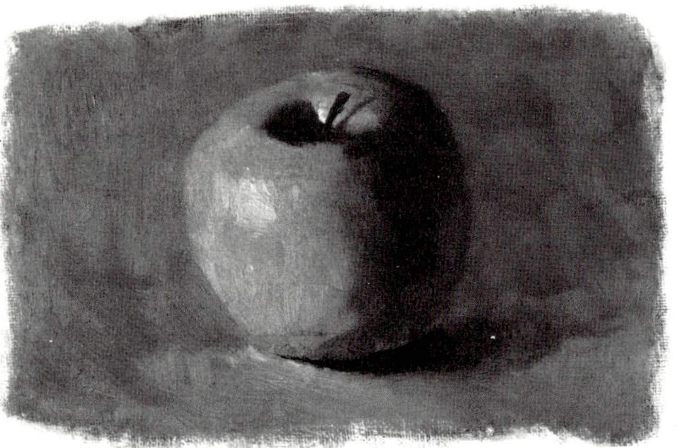

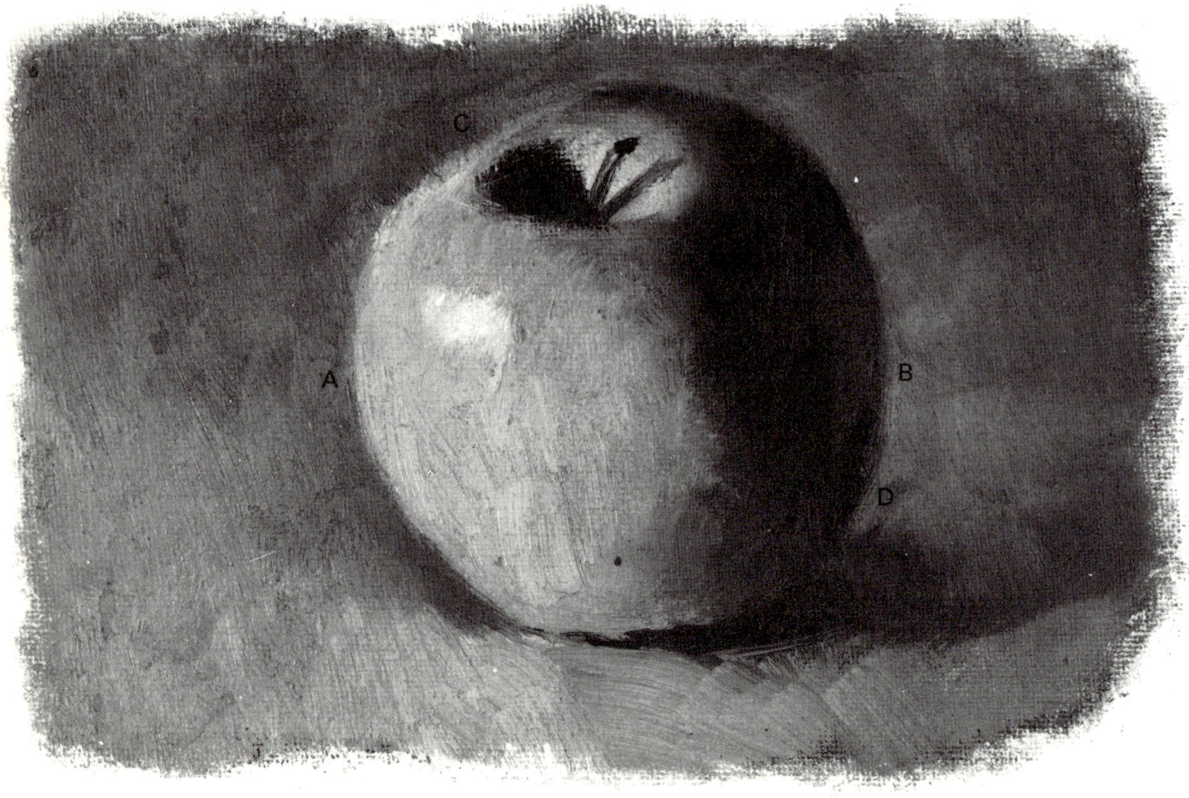

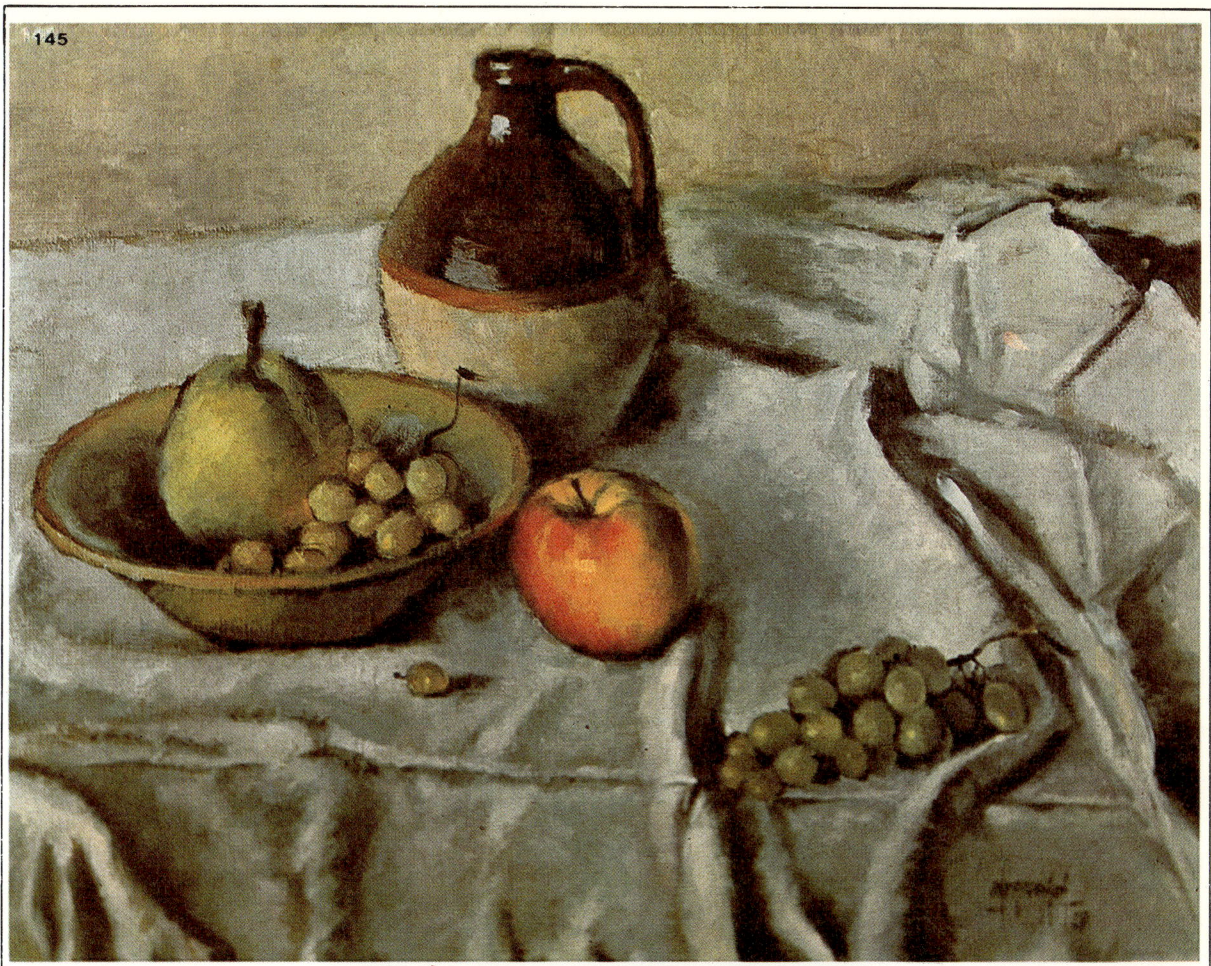

An example of the use of light and shade

I have painted this still life to demonstrate what I've said about light and shade, values, contrast and atmosphere. Look carefully at these points.

146

The more distant areas should be less sharp than the nearer ones. Note here that the back line of the cloth is a vague, indistinct line.

In order to separate and distinguish shapes, you sometimes may need to emphasize an outline, as in these illuminated parts of the jar and the pear.

Shown-up contrasts, reflected light, deep shadow, highlights, shadow and projected shadow... all the effects of light and shade are manifested in this little grape.

The effect of deep shadow is clear in this fold of the cloth, helping to show up its volume.

This reflected light on the part of the apple in shade did not exist in the model, but I made this contrast in order to show where the apple ended and separate it from the background.

The rendering of this bunch of grapes is a good example of reflected light.

from theory to practice

A popular exercise in art schools and one that can be done anywhere by any artist is the drawing and painting of folds of fabric, like the cloth in the still life we've just seen. Cézanne, for instance, painted tablecloths, curtains and fabric in nearly all his still lifes.

A carefully arranged piece of cloth, either white or in a plain, light colour, is a really excellent subject from which to study the modelling —the effects of light and shade— of objects in general.

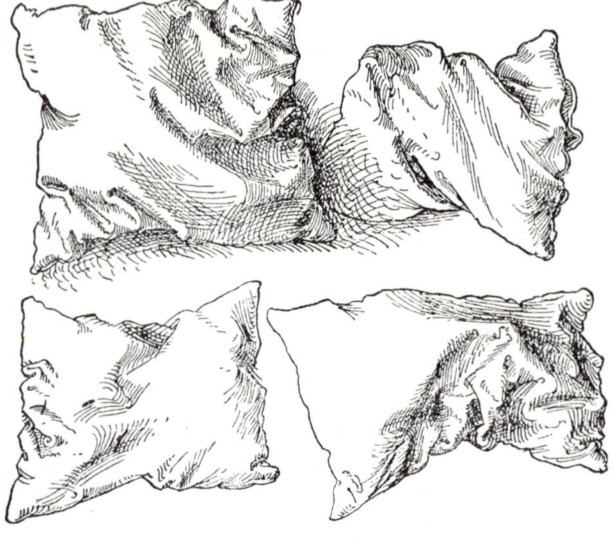

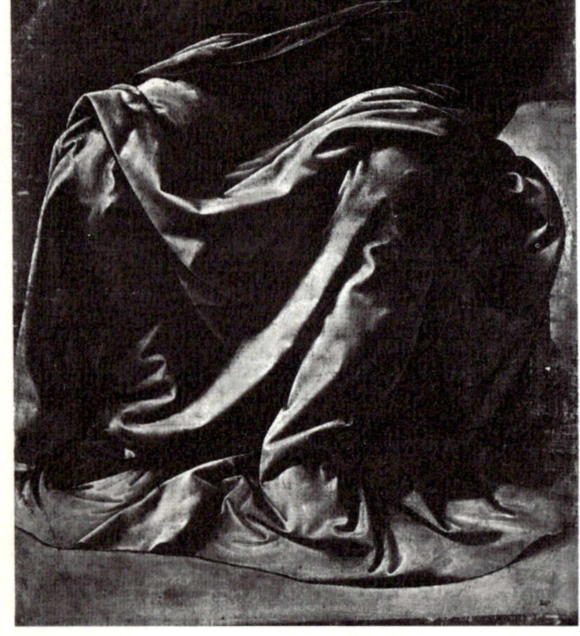

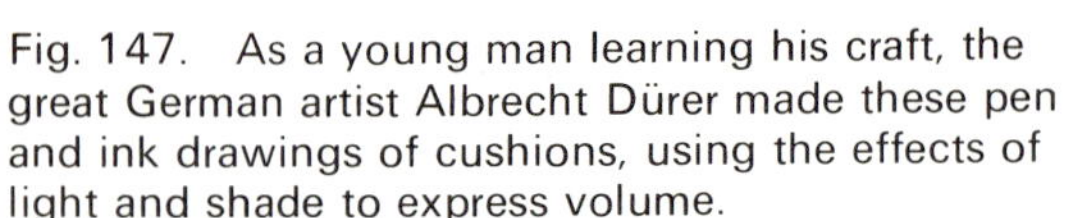

Fig. 147. As a young man learning his craft, the great German artist Albrecht Dürer made these pen and ink drawings of cushions, using the effects of light and shade to express volume.

Fig. 148. A useful exercise done by the young Leonardo da Vinci: *Study of drapery in a seated figure.* He used chalk and wash or white pastel on grey paper.

Fig. 149. Now have a go yourself. Put a piece of fabric or a tablecloth over something on a table, or let it hang over the side, giving unevenness and folds. Then paint directly, without making a drawing. This is a really valuable exercise, as you will discover.

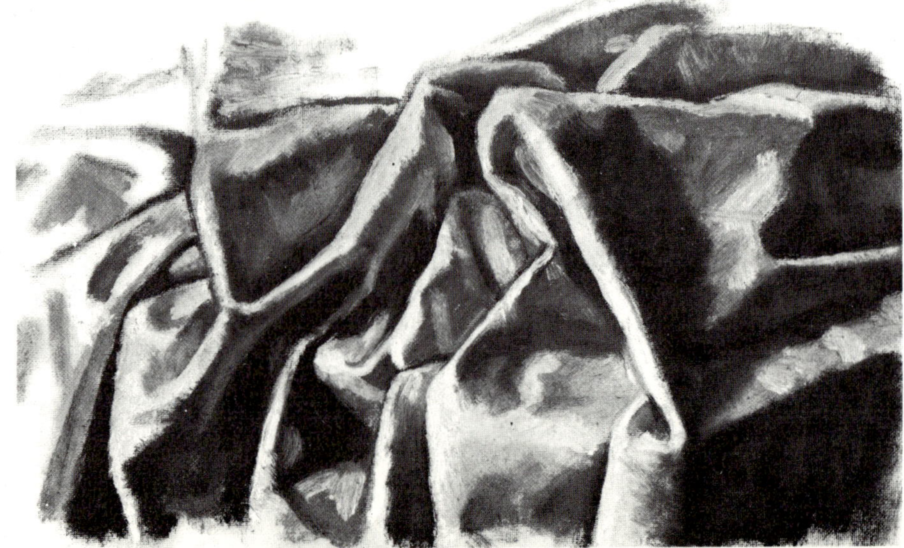

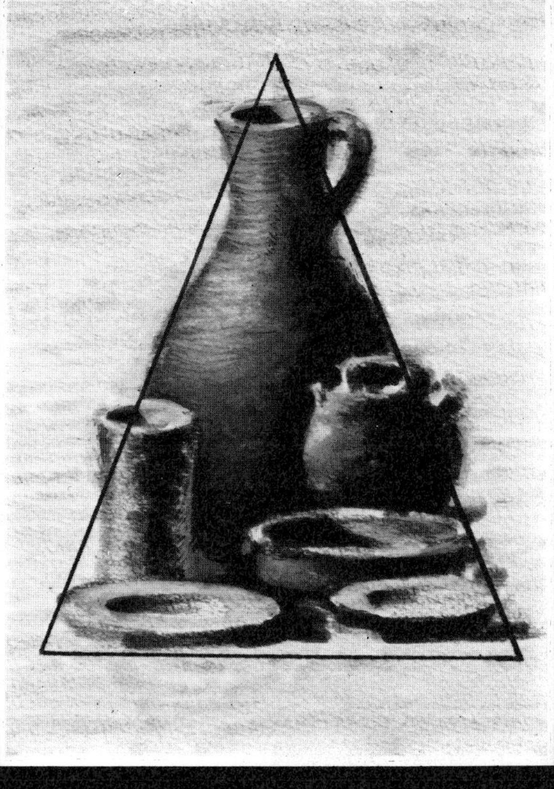

choosing your subject composition

a question of imagination

It seems unnecessary to go and search for a still-life subject. In the dining-room or living-room there'll probably be books, an ashtray or two, some pottery and perhaps a vase of flowers —all that before going into the kitchen and opening cupboards full of bottles, pots and pans, dishes, glasses and cups and saucers. In the refrigerator there'll probably be fruit, vegetables, fish, eggs and so on.

So the simplest way of choosing a model seems to be that of going from room to room and having a look round in the hope that the sight of one object will suggest another.

The professional doesn't work this way! If he wants to paint a still life he'll start in his mind, thinking of a subject and its various parts, considering shapes, structure and lighting. At this point he may even make a preliminary sketch. At the same time he tries to visualize colour, tonal values and harmonization. Only then may he search for a choice of objects to provide new shapes and colours which may enrich his original idea.

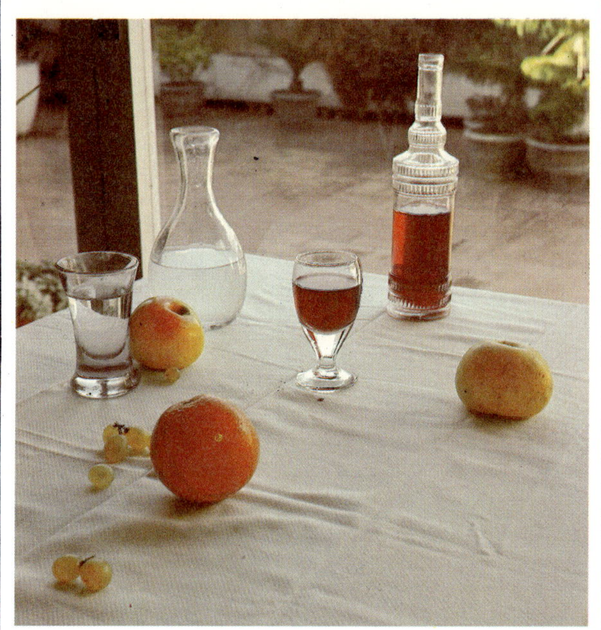

Fig. 151. Some modern artists have claimed that the problem is not a matter of choosing or looking for a model but of discovering one, as in Picasso's well-known comment: "I don't search, I find!". Things left on the table after a meal can make up an excellent subject —and the chances are that their colour, lighting and unstilted arrangement will produce a picture in contemporary mood.

Fig. 152 (A). Other things —a vase, a jug— which have been sitting neglected in the corner of a cupboard can make excellent subjects for a still life.

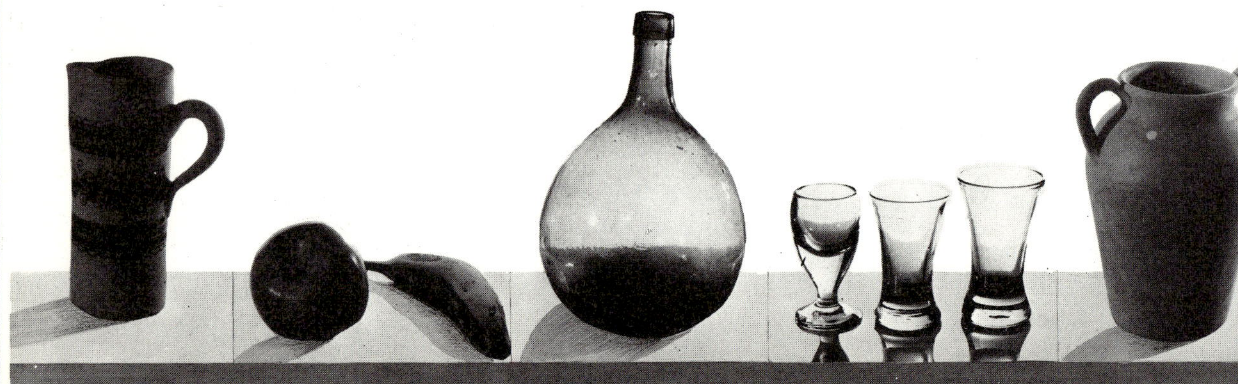

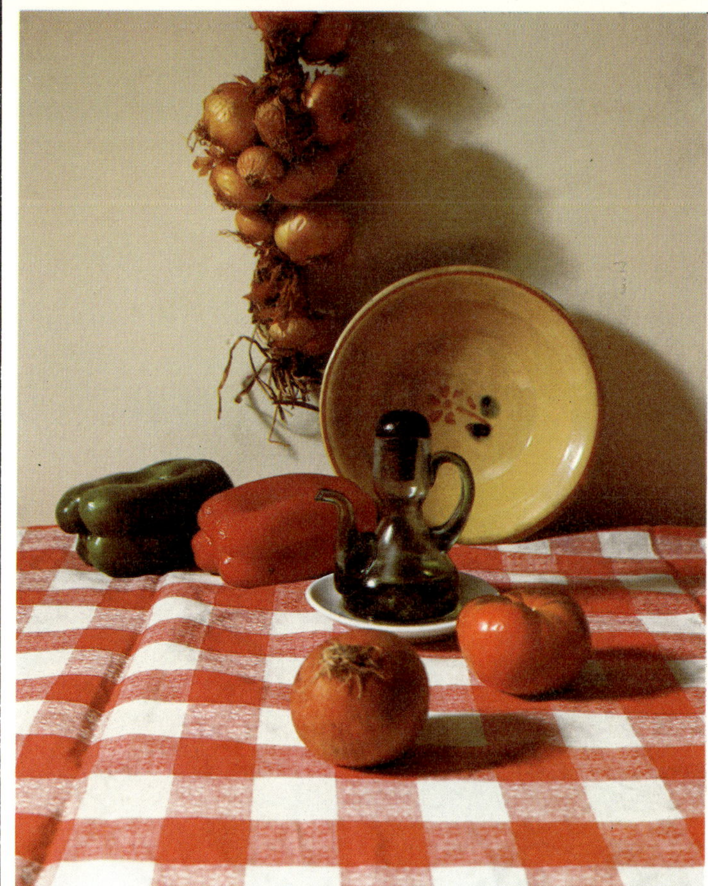

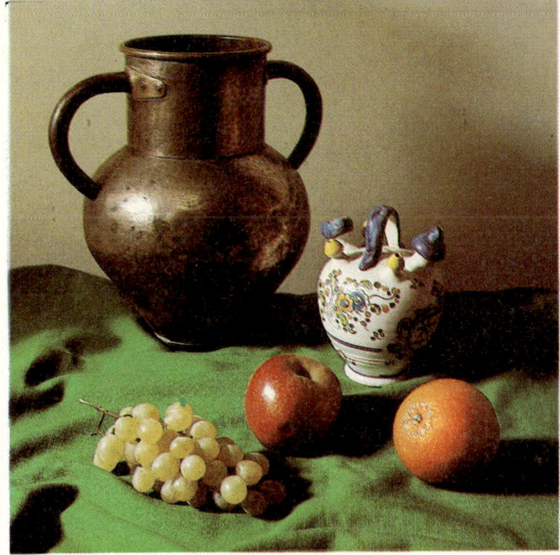

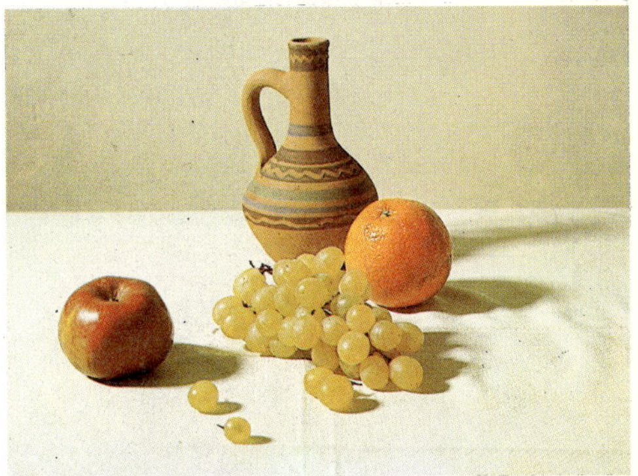

Fig. 153. You don't need to rack your brains to find a subject like this. Sometimes it may involve looking at an object carefully and finding others in the same category.

Fig. 154. Above: a case where choice of the model has been determined by colour. Below: ordinariness and simplicity make this a good subject.

Fig. 152 (B). When choosing objects to paint, try to find things with something in common —use, shape and colour. These will help the picture's theme and composition.

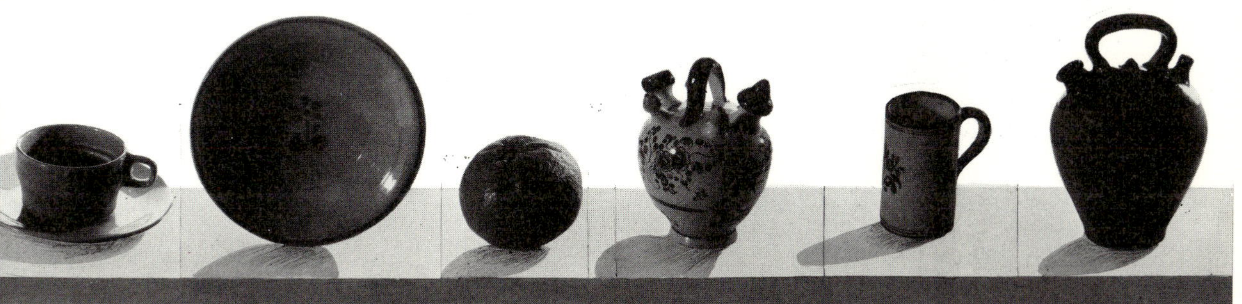

grouping

Paul Cézanne wrote a letter to his son about choice of subject: "The range is infinite; the same subject matter seen from different angles can provide such an interesting variety that I think I could work for months on end without moving from my place, just leaning a little to right or left." Cézanne was simply saying that a subject could be found anywhere or, as Renoir declared, that any object is suitable for painting: "Subjects I can manage with one or two odds and ends of any kind!" All the same, it's certain that Cézanne and all the Impressionists who painted still lifes *did* consider the theme beforehand, searching for things with some affinity and cogitating on a title which could sum up the painting's content. They tried to find related objects for components of their still lifes.

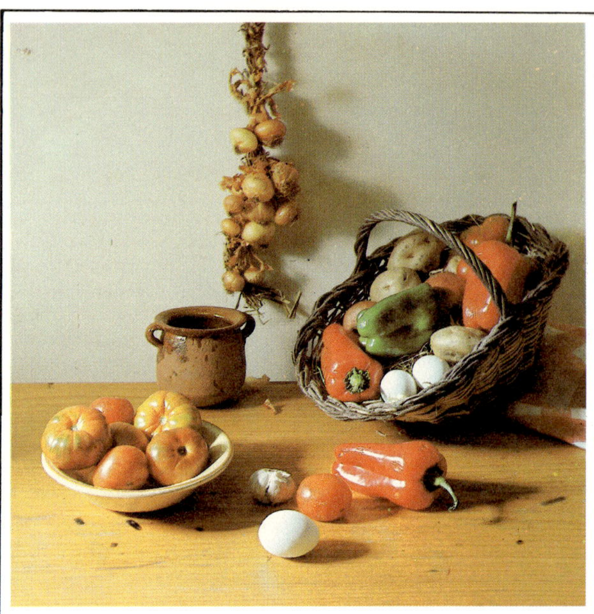

Fig. 155. In this composition, affinity of components shows the subject and the artist's intention.

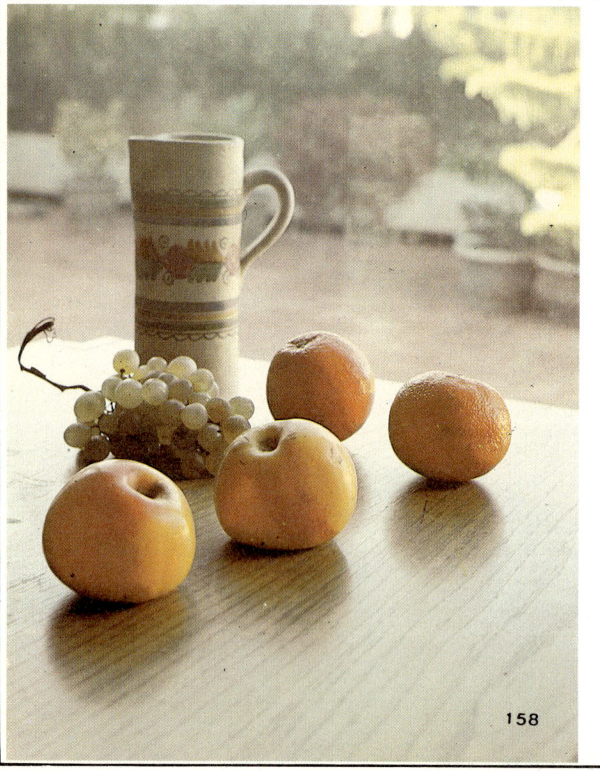

Figs. 156 and 157. Right hand page *"Still life with fruit"* might be the title of the upper picture, while the still life below might be called *"Music"* or *"Still life with flute"*. The unity of content in the two works is further enhanced by the range of *warm* colours in the still life with fruit and of *cold* colours in the still life concerned with music.

Fig. 158. Affinity of the components of a still life, in an attempt to express a particular idea or mood, may be relative, as in this picture of fruit with a jug, treated in a more modern idiom with simplicity of lighting.

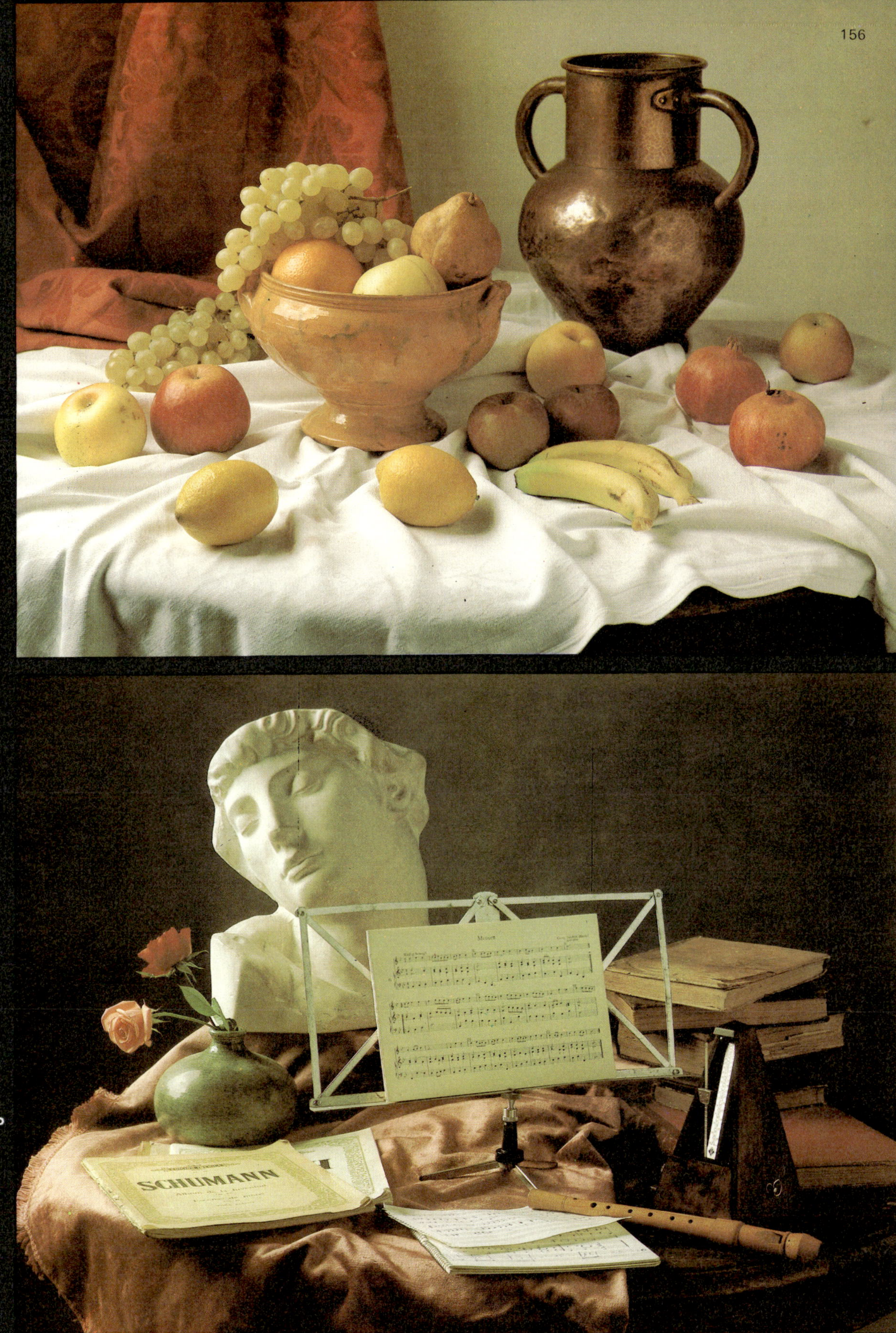
SCHUMANN

colour planning

In the paintings of the great masters, even the most modern, colour is obviously planned very carefully. This planning usually stems from a tone or dominant colour which expands into a range of colours to make a set of perfectly gradated colours or shades.

We speak of *warm colours, cool colours* and *broken tones,* referring to the colours and ranges described below:

a) **range of warm colours** (dominant colour: red) comprising light green, yellow, orange, red, carmine, purple and violet;
v) **range of cool colours** (dominant colour: blue) comprising light green, green, viridian, luminous (Prussian) blue, cobalt blue, dark (ultramarine) blue and violet;
c) **range of broken tones** (dominant colour: grey). These are formed by mixing complementary colours in unequal proportions (plus a greater or lesser amount of white). This gives a variety of shades and colour gradations and a wealth of tones.

As I've described earlier in this section, when an artist conceives and selects a subject, he is also thinking of a particular colour range, which may be warm, cool or broken.

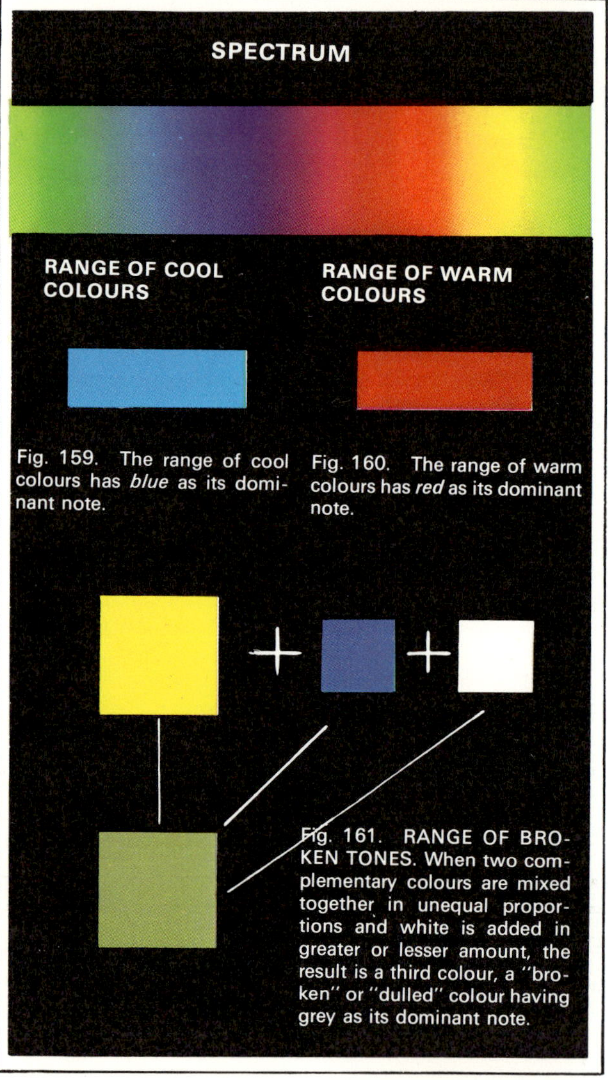

Fig. 159. The range of cool colours has *blue* as its dominant note.

Fig. 160. The range of warm colours has *red* as its dominant note.

Fig. 161. RANGE OF BROKEN TONES. When two complementary colours are mixed together in unequal proportions and white is added in greater or lesser amount, the result is a third colour, a "broken" or "dulled" colour having grey as its dominant note.

Fig. 162. The still life shown on the next page, top right, has colours consistent with a warm colour range. This range is the result of a deliberate choice of dishes and fruits, etc., in colours centred on reds, oranges, siennas, ochres and yellows. This warm colour tone is enhanced by the lighting —natural light and a slightly yellow artificial light.

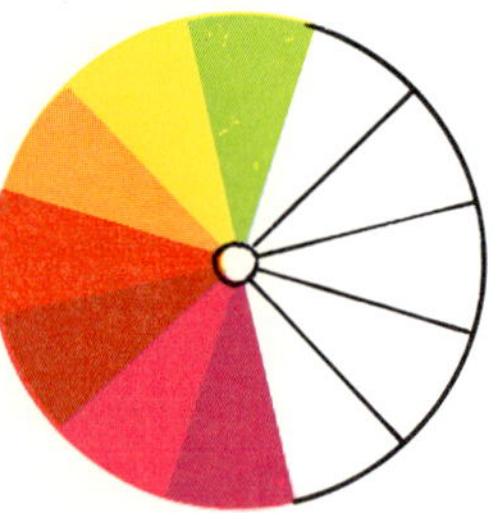

Fig. 163. To suit a still life conceived in a range of cold colours, the artist selected components with either a neutral colour or a bluish tinge; the fish, table and parsley, the cloth in the foreground, the dish and the glass demijohn. The photograph shows only a slight bluish tinge, but the artist would probably accentuate this when painting.

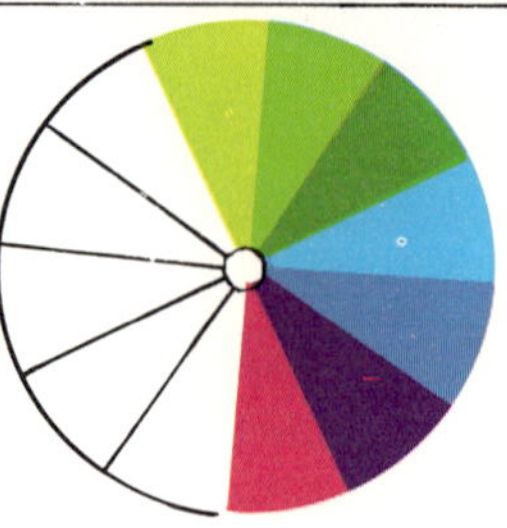

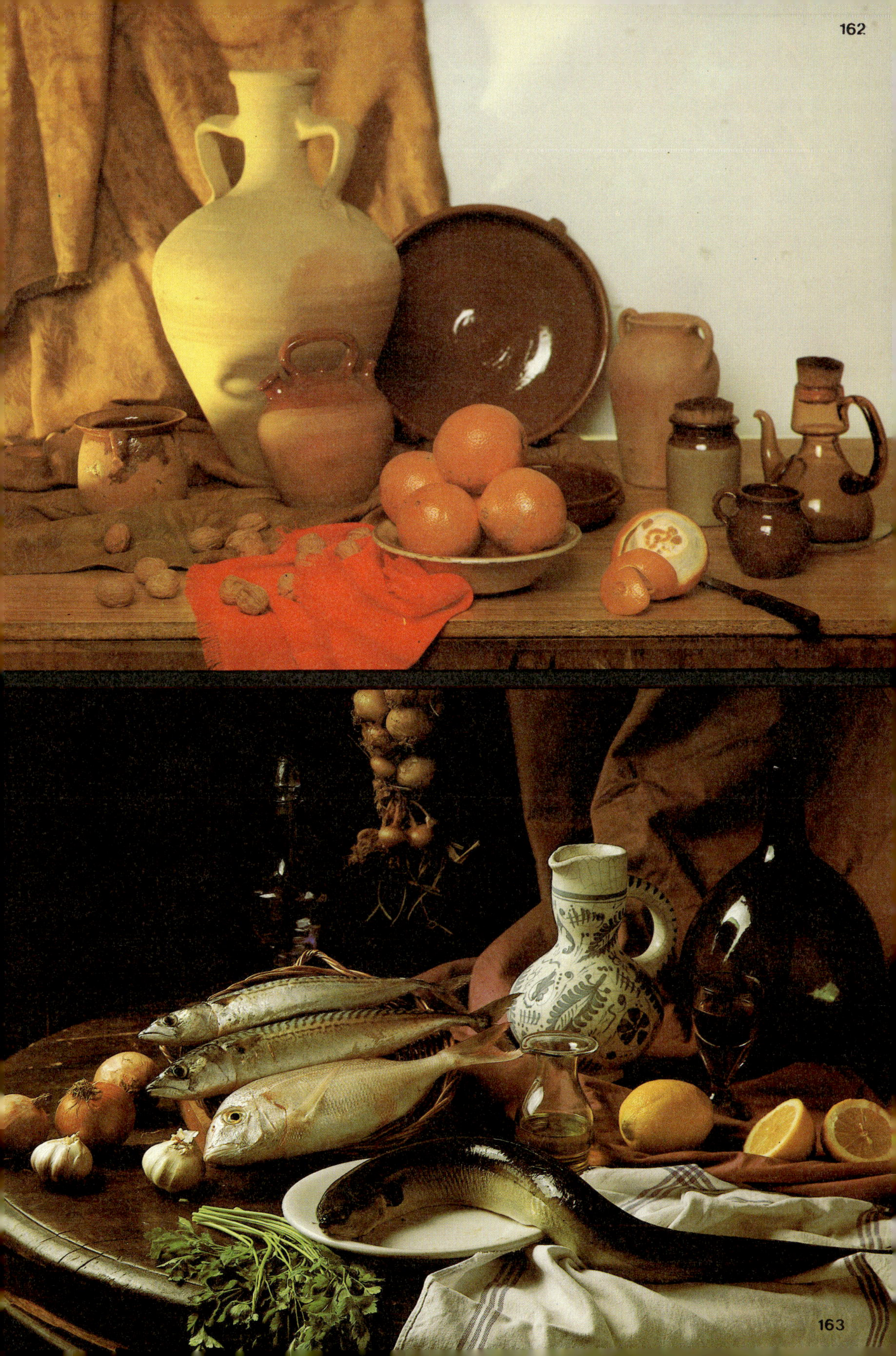

162

163

colour planning

Fig. 163. To complete this set of examples (Figs. 162 and 163). Fig. 164 shows a *range of broken tones* comprising an unequal mixture of complementary colours, with the addition of a greater or lesser amount of white.

Fig. 165 (below). Conventions and laws of art are never absolute. Artistic genius often lies in exceptional, unconventional works. In this still life we see how a note of cool colour is perfectly acceptable in a picture conceived entirely with warm colours —with red, ochre and yellow dominant. Here, a flask containing blue liquid can be set without difficulty into the colour harmony of the picture as a whole.

164

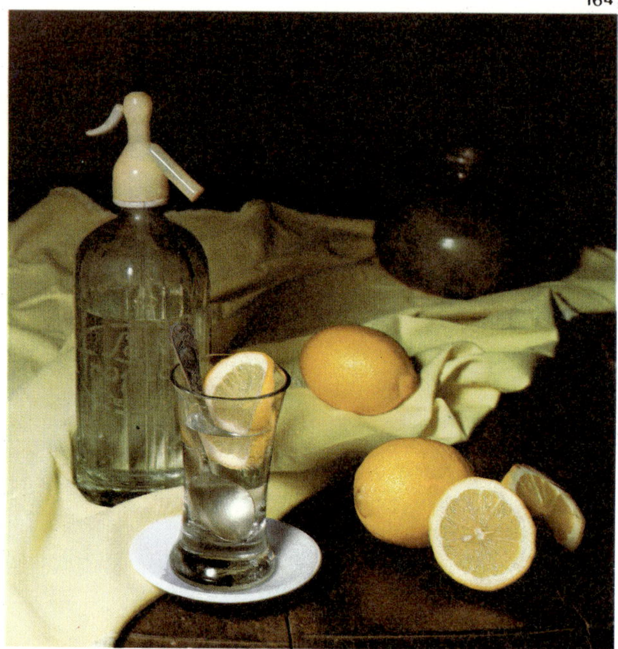

165

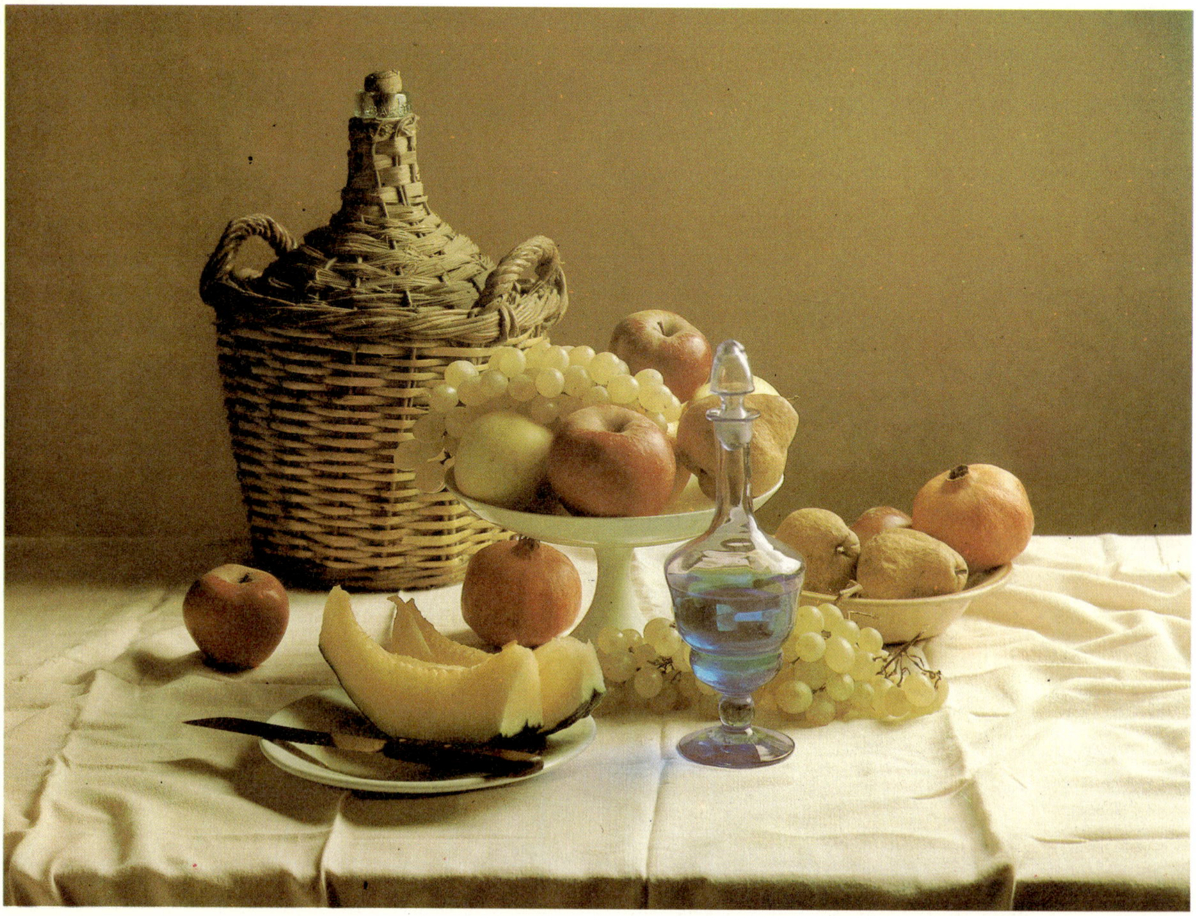

what is composition?

Composition is defined as the art of co-ordinating model, background, lighting and colour. "It means seeking balance and proportion, and therefore beauty" wrote Jean Guitton. This might mean that beauty lies in orderliness and unity. But according to René Huyghe: "There is a danger in unity: excessive unity leaves something to be desired; unity must be enriched by diversity."

The same idea was expressed thousands of years ago by Plato, the Greek philospher. Asked "what is composition" he replied with a definition which still holds good today:

Composition is the skill of finding and representing unity within diversity.

So it is, on one hand, a matter of arranging and co-ordinating model, background, lighting and colour to give a combination which doesn't turn out monotonous, uninteresting and dreary because of over-much unity and order; on the other hand, the work should not be a muddle! It's not easy to strike the happy medium. As John Ruskin said: "There are no rules for the art of composition; if there had been, Titian and Veronese would have been ordinary men."

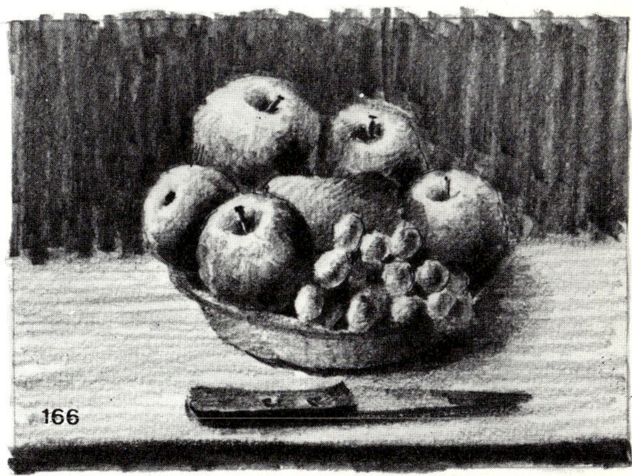

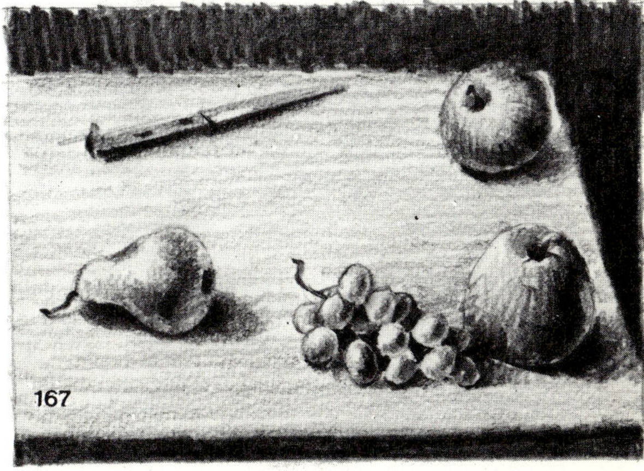

Fig. 166. BAD – over-much unity: there is no originality here; the picture is monotonous and uninteresting. The diagram (right) shows the emphasis on the horizon which divides the picture in two, with the dish and the fruit forming a single block.

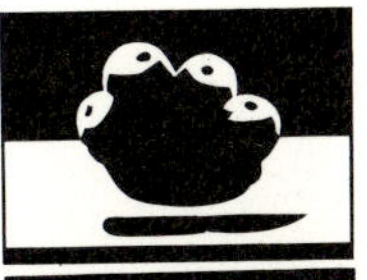

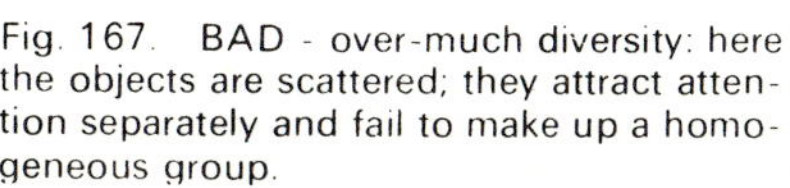

Fig. 167. BAD - over-much diversity: here the objects are scattered; they attract attention separately and fail to make up a homogeneous group.

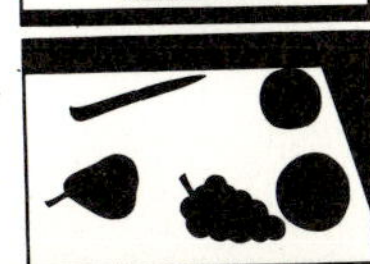

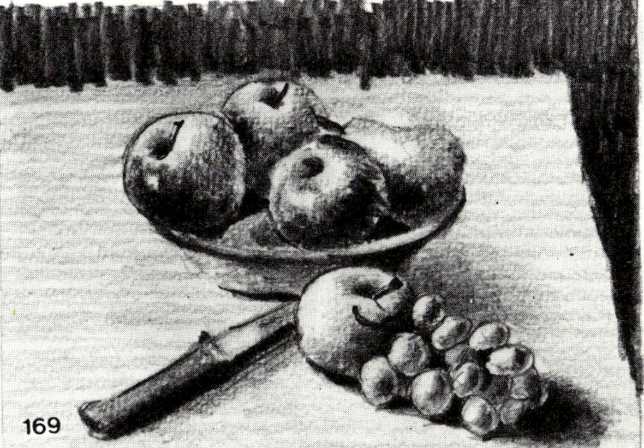

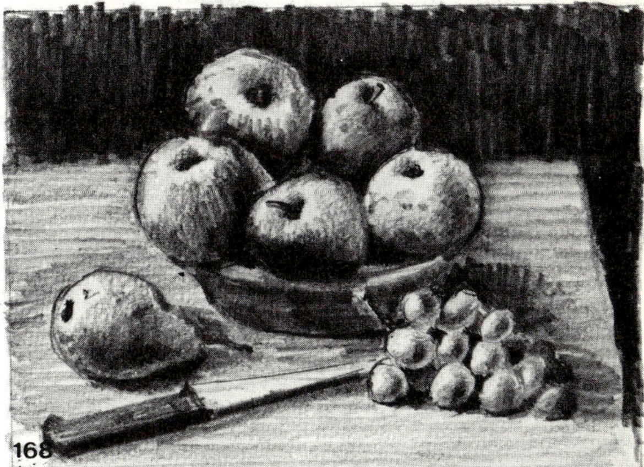

Fig. 168. BAD - over-much unity: the excessive orderliness is masked by a little variety, but this doesn't really exist as the diagram here reveals. It is a picture with too many geometric similarities.

Fig 169. GOOD - This is a good example of unity within diversity; just compare this diagram with the others and you'll see the *unity* stemming from the arrangement of the components as a whole. You'll also find *diversity* created by the positioning and lighting of the picture's different components.

the rule of the golden section

Suppose you have a blank canvas in front of you and want to begin your sketch. Where should the main subject be placed; in the centre, towards the top, towards the bottom, towards the right or towards the left? The answer to this is given in an ancient precept handed down by the Roman architect Vitrivuis, who wrote as follows:

Rule of the Golden Section

"To obtain an aesthetically pleasing unequal division of any given space, the lesser part must be in the same proportion to the greater as the greater is to the whole."

To find this ideal division, multiply the width of the canvas by the factor 0.618 (the mathematical expression of the rule of the *Golden Section* is the ratio 1:0.618).

Example: Fig. 173A shows a rectangle 40 millimetres in width; multiplication of 40 by 0.618 gives a round figure of 25 millimetres with 15 over.

Apply the same dividing figure to the length of the canvas and you will find the **Golden Point** (fig. 173B). This is the precise position for the picture's centre of interest. Finally, Figure 173X shows that there are four Golden Points in every two-dimensional space.

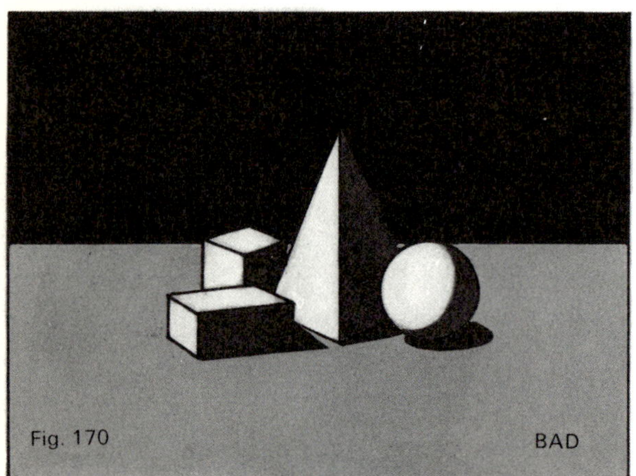

Fig. 170 BAD

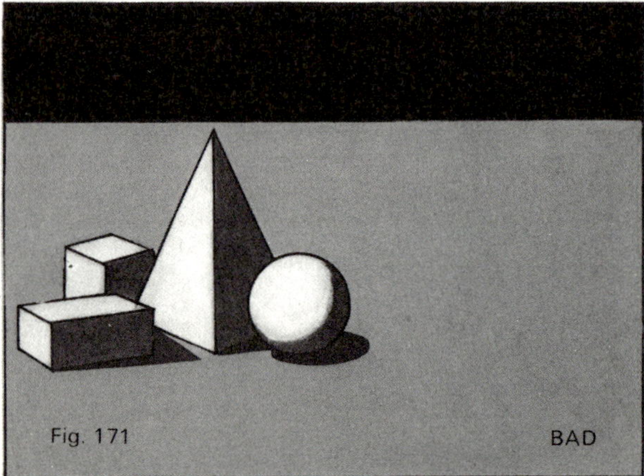

Fig. 171 BAD

Fig. 173

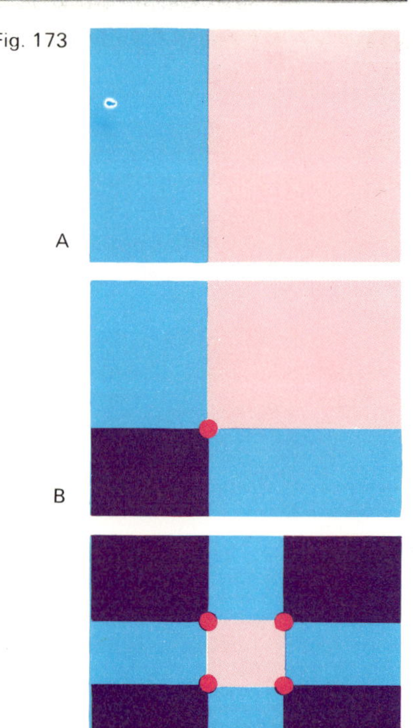

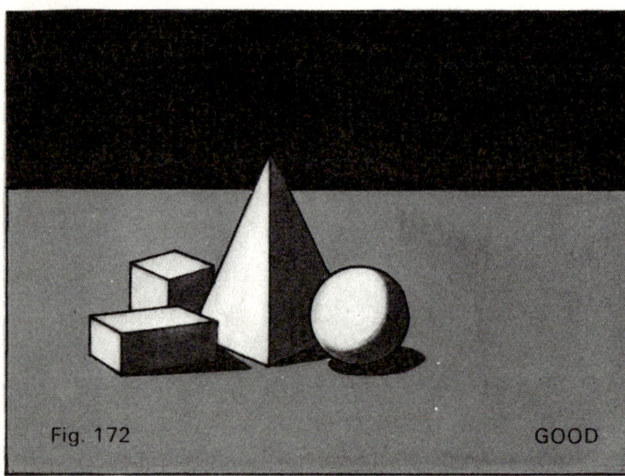

Fig. 172 GOOD

Fig. 170. It's not a good idea to put the model in the middle of the space with the horizon cutting the picture in half.

Fig. 171. Nor is it wise to push the principal element over to one side in order to obtain diversity from asymmetry.

Fig. 172. Using the rule of the Golden Section almost automatically gives a better spatial arrangement.

design

In every picture there is a more or less definite shape pattern. The pleasantness of the composition depends on the nature of this design. In this connection one could say that the success and acceptance of a given shape is directly related to its simplicity. Experimental studies carried out by Fischer have demonstrated that, of three sets of different shapes (abstract, natural and geometric, Fig. 174), his subjects tended to prefer those that were geometric. Fischer attributed this to a nihilist attitude ("maximum enjoyment with minimum effort"). René Huyghe arrived at the same conclusion when discussing the enormous predilection for geometric forms in art: "The more geometric the shape, the more enthusiastic the mind becomes, as a result of its ability to grasp the complexity of reality reduced to a basic shape".

Long before all this, in the seventeenth century, Rembrandt laid down for his pupils a basic formula for composition using the triangle as the foundation.

So try to work out a basic geometric design when you start thinking about the composition of your pictures. Have a look at the basic designs shown on this page.

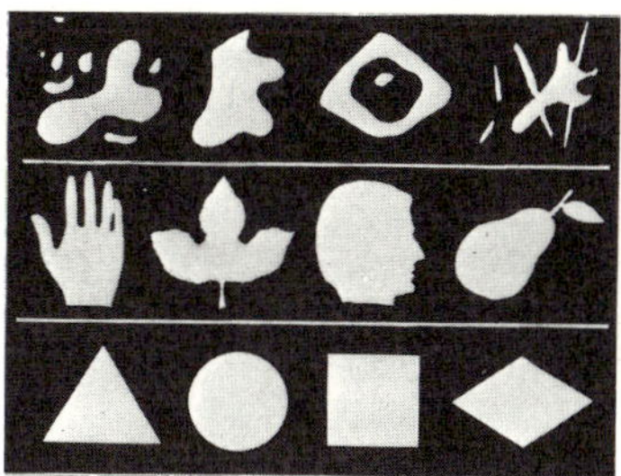

Fig. 174. Fischer found that, out of these three sets of basic shapes, the geometric set scored highest.

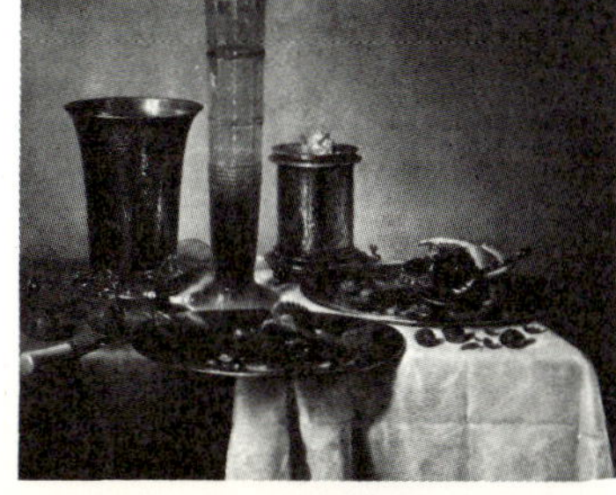

Fig. 175. This is Rembrandt's formula for composition: a triangle or diagonal line dividing the picture into two equal parts, usually into a pale and a dark area.

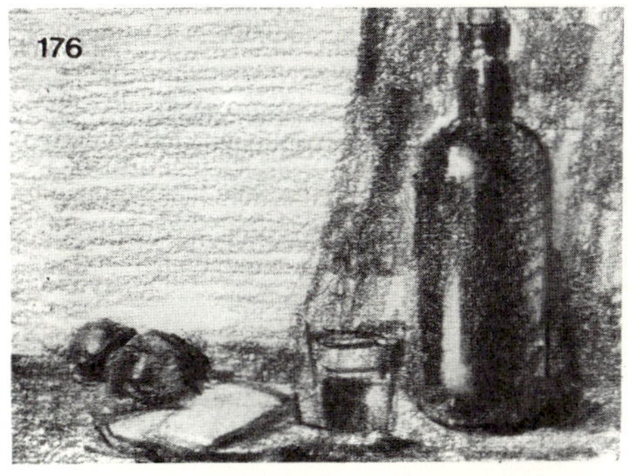

Fig. 176. L-shaped composition, a variant on Fig. 175; its asymmetry presents greater diversity.

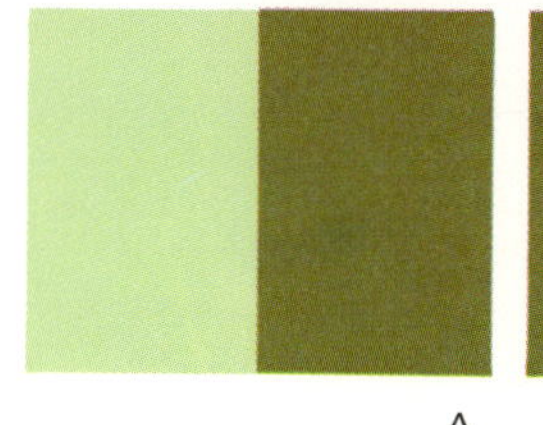

A

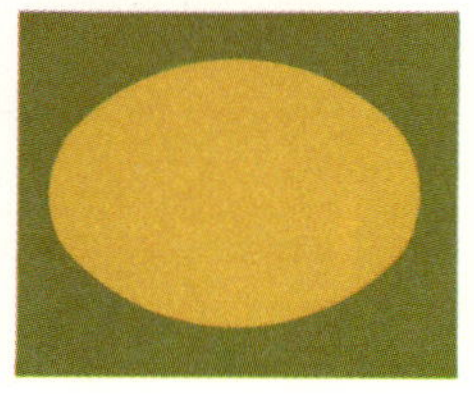

B

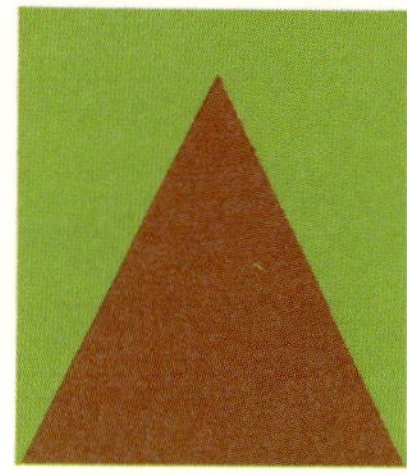

C

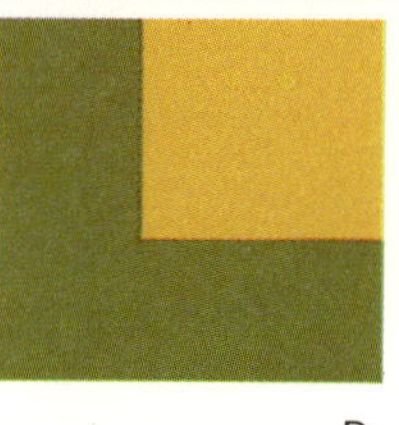

D

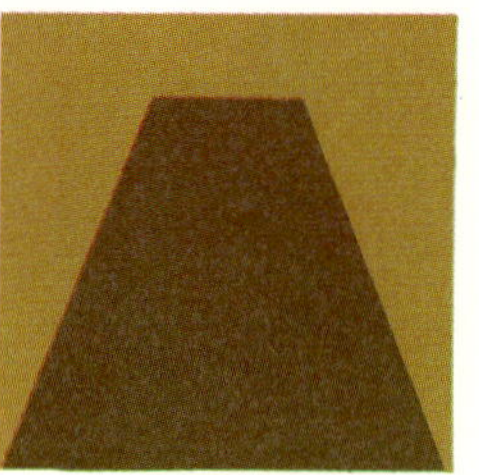

E

Fig. 177. A rectangular or vertical division of the picture by light and shade (A); an ellipse on a dark background (B); a pyramid (C); an L shape (D); a truncated cone (E): these may also provide satisfactory formulae or patterns for basic composition.

symmetry and asymmetry

You'll know that a symmetrical composition presents all the components of a picture on either side of a central point so that the two sides correspond. It's clear that *symmetry is virtually synonymous with unity,* whereas *asymmetry,* or free and intuitive positioning, even when balanced, *is synonymous with diversity.*

Most artists prefer asymmetrical composition —it's more dynamic and immediate and provides greater opportunity to express creativity. But bear in mind that there are many examples of both types of composition. Symmetry can work well when used rather rigidly for the naïf style of painting; it can also be used more flexibly, so that the artist can shift objects around, emphasizing the overall unity and still allowing the desired variety to emerge clearly.

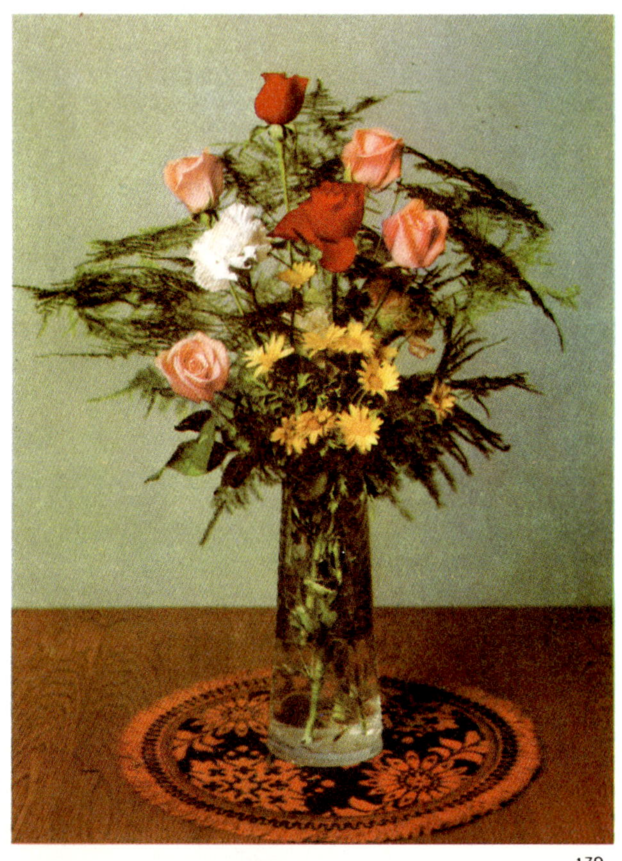

178

179

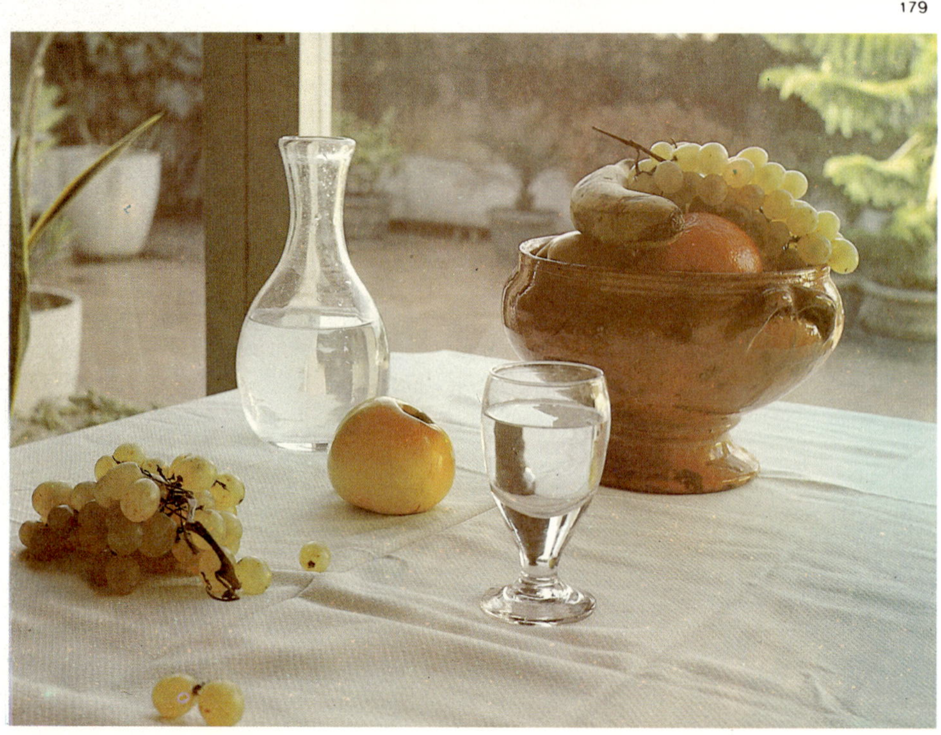

Fig. 178 (above): it's difficult to avoid symmetry with a bunch of flowers in a vase, but the artist may choose to place a flower or some other object at the foot of the vase to break up the too completely symmetrical result.

Fig. 179 (right): asymmetry is synonymous with variety and is closer to freedom of expression, hence innovation and experiments. In this example the arrangement looks fairly random; in fact it took a great deal of thought and concentration.

symmetry and asymmetry

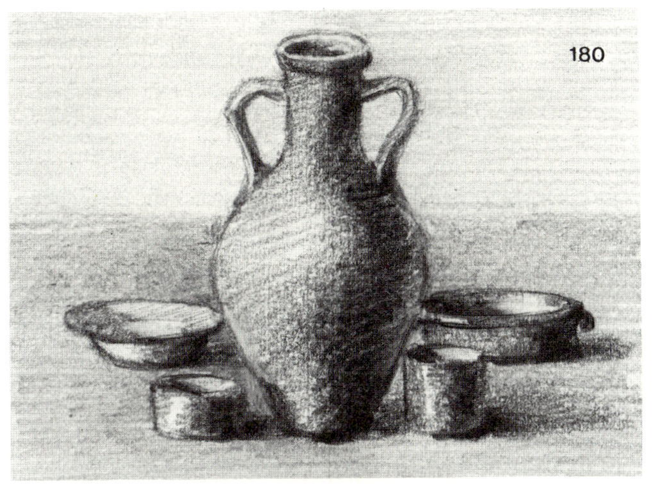

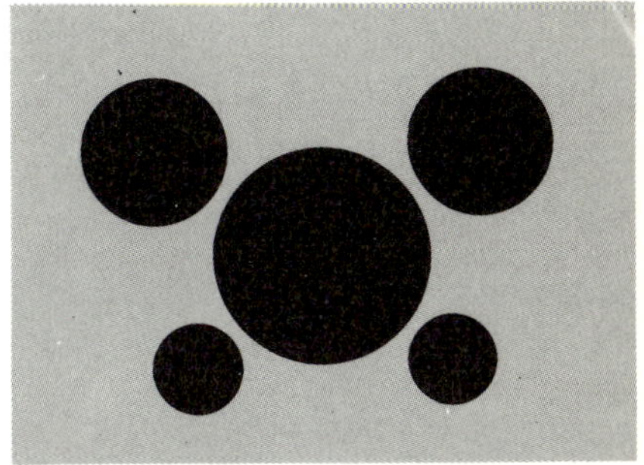

SYMMETRICAL ARRANGEMENT
Fig. 180. Placing components evenly on either side of an imaginary central point in a painting may give an impressión of symmetry even though those elements are not particularly alike.

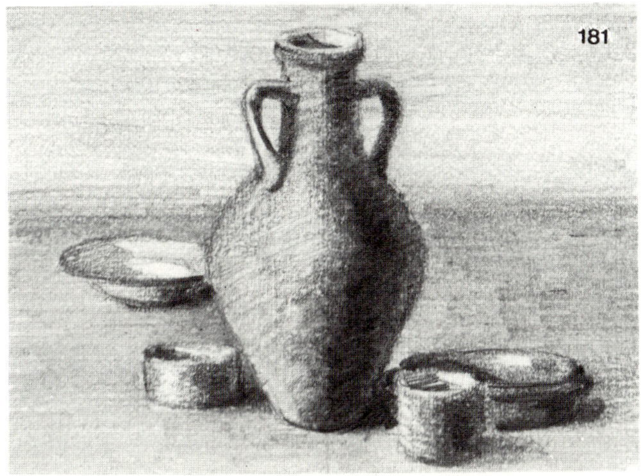

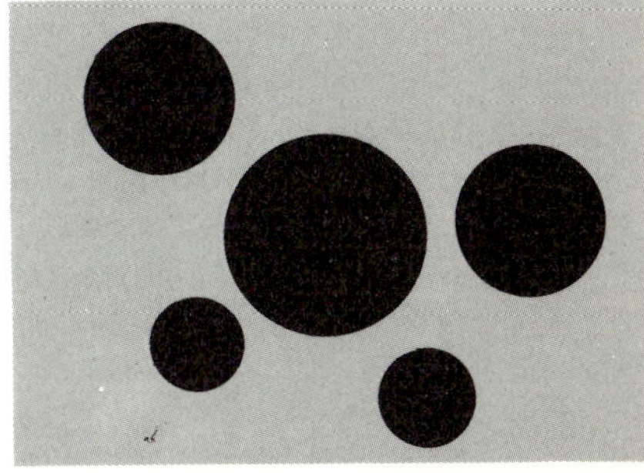

ASYMMETRICAL ARRANGEMENT
Fig. 181. It's easy enough to get away from an impression of complete symmetry by introducing diversity into your arrangement of the same objects shown in Fig. 180.

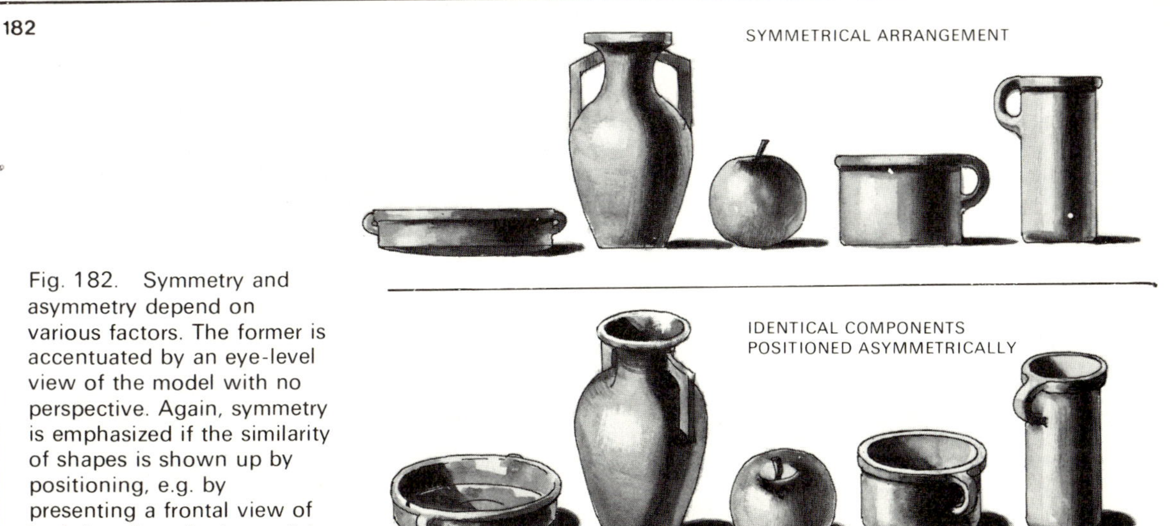

Fig. 182. Symmetry and asymmetry depend on various factors. The former is accentuated by an eye-level view of the model with no perspective. Again, symmetry is emphasized if the similarity of shapes is shown up by positioning, e.g. by presenting a frontal view of both handles of a jar or dish.

choose your lighting

When composing a still-life painting you are able not only to choose and arrange your subject as you wish, but also to choose your kind of lighting —its quality, type and direction.

The type of lighting can be either natural or artificial. In principle, it's easier to paint by natural light, with its greater quantity and consistency and its greater diffusion. Daylight is softer; it doesn't produce troublesome highlights and generally provides a better quality. It also makes for more authentic colour. Artificial light produces a slightly orange tint but the disadvantage is relative since, apart from the fact that it may yield a stupendous range of colours (remember the case of Picasso painting by the gaslight which produced his "blue" period) the artist can easily modify or correct this tendency. The greatest advantage of artificial light, apart from using it deliberately to obtain special effects, is the opportunity to paint at any time of day or night; this, of course is important, especially in the shorter days of winter.

The quality of light may be described as diffused or direct. Daylight falling upon a model indoors will give a diffused light unless the sun is shining directly on the model. If the sun *is* shining directly on the model it's not a good idea to paint at all, because there will be excessive contrast. Artificial light always gives direct lighting, which is usually harder, diminishing the effects of light and shade. However, this effect may be useful when painting in a particular style.

Finally, **the direction of the lighting** is another important factor from the artist's point of view. Frontal lighting is essentially a Colourist's lighting —lighting appropriate for painting rather than for drawing. By comparison, frontal-lateral lighting goes well with careful, descriptive work which makes shape and volume absolutely clear, while light from behind the model (counter-light) conveys better than any other an atmosphere of delicate intimacy or passionate lyricism, depending on the lightness or darkness of the background.

So choose your lighting carefully, bearing in mind the different effects we have discussed and will illustrate here, and remembering that different kinds of lighting have very different effects on a finished painting.

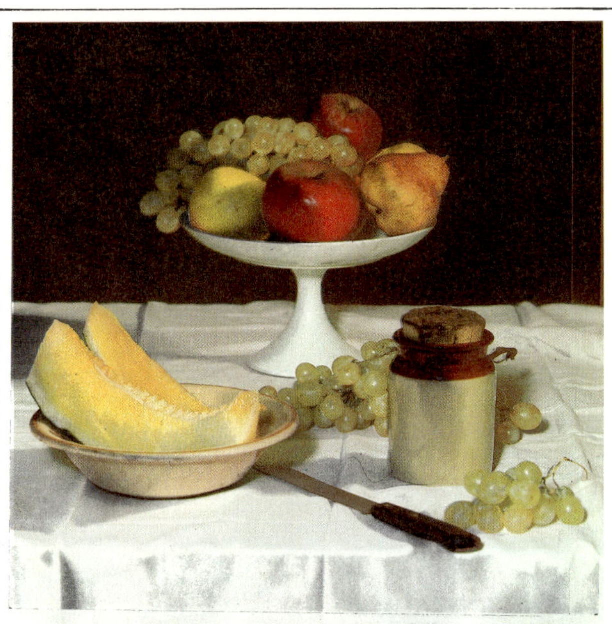

Fig. 183. **Frontal lighting:** this is very much a Colourist's lighting and was taken up by Fauvists who thought that the use of colour alone was enough to express form and outline and that shadow and volume were unnecessary. Many of the Post Impressionists, including Van Gogh, Gauguin, Vlaminck and Matisse used this technique at some time. There is still a use for it today.

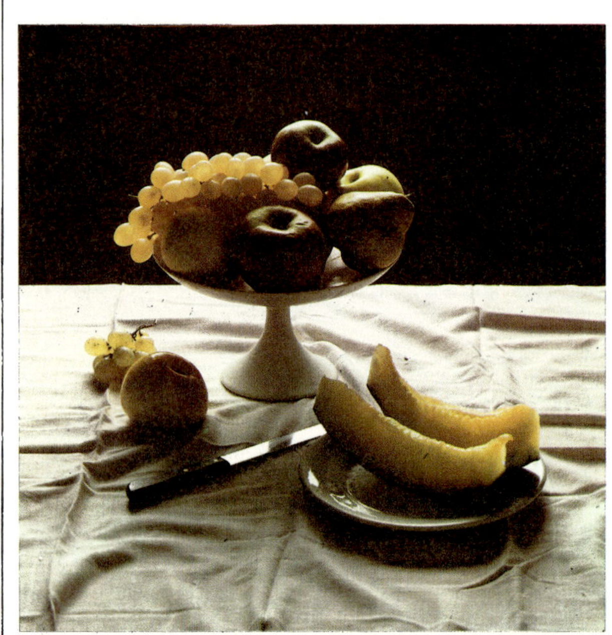

choose your lighting

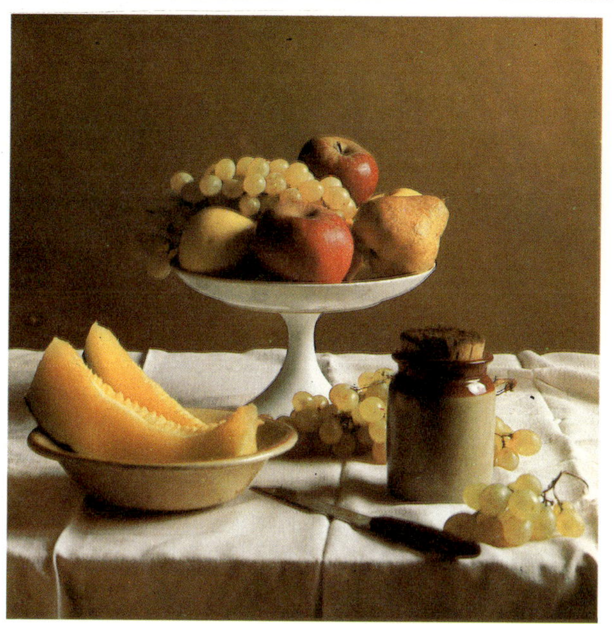

Fig. 184. **Natural side-lighting:** a type of lighting which conveys shapes mainly through the effects of light and shade; this provides an example of the effect of diffused light from a window —natural light. You'll notice that the outlines of projected shadows are imprecise, e.g. on the tablecloth. This is a classic kind of lighting but not in vogue at present, since most modern painters use the effects of chiaroscuro.

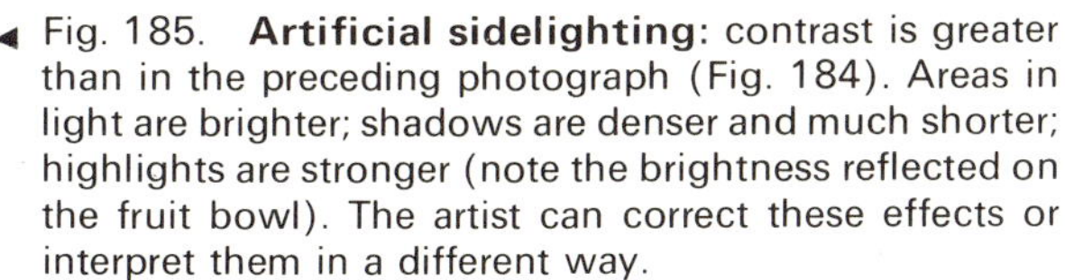

◄ Fig. 185. **Artificial sidelighting:** contrast is greater than in the preceding photograph (Fig. 184). Areas in light are brighter; shadows are denser and much shorter; highlights are stronger (note the brightness reflected on the fruit bowl). The artist can correct these effects or interpret them in a different way.

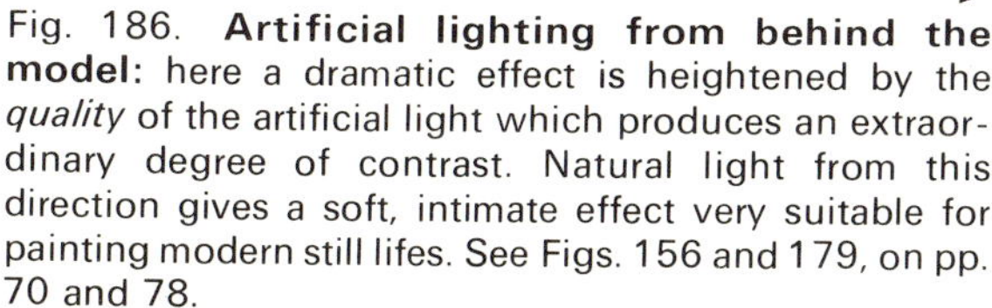

► Fig. 186. **Artificial lighting from behind the model:** here a dramatic effect is heightened by the *quality* of the artificial light which produces an extraordinary degree of contrast. Natural light from this direction gives a soft, intimate effect very suitable for painting modern still lifes. See Figs. 156 and 179, on pp. 70 and 78.

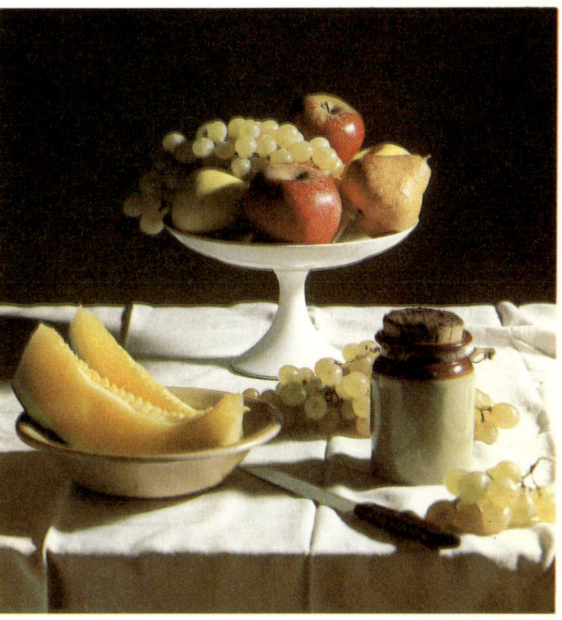

Fig. 187. **Artificial lighting from behind the model, using a reflector screen:** still life illuminated by a table lamp, the same lighting as in Fig. 186 but with the addition of a reflector screen, which could be the white surface of a blank canvas in a No. 20 stretcher (as used here) placed in front of the model and opposite the lighting. This produces overall reflection and softens the excessive contrast seen in Fig. 186.

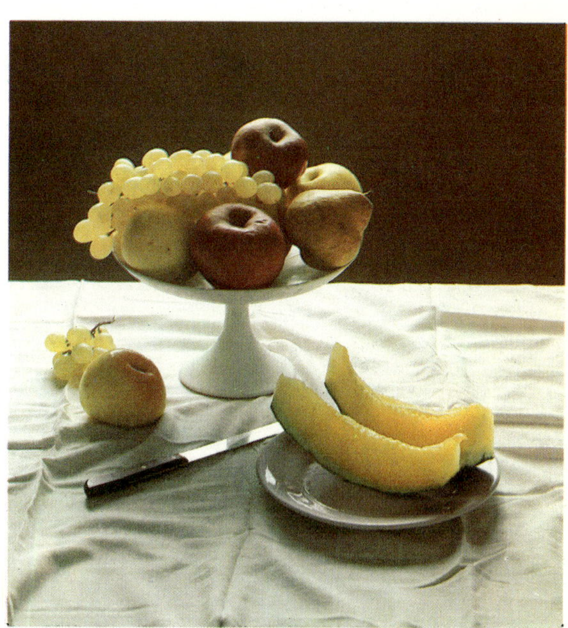

creating different planes

If the components of a still life —and this applies to any subject— are scattered all over the place, you will get too much diversity. As you know, this can be put right by grouping the picture's components and setting them in different planes. This emphasizes the feeling of depth. Putting one piece of fruit in front of another, with a jug behind it, produces evidence of the existence of a front, a middle distance and a back. The illustrations on this page show up some really vital points on how to achieve the "third dimension" in a still life.

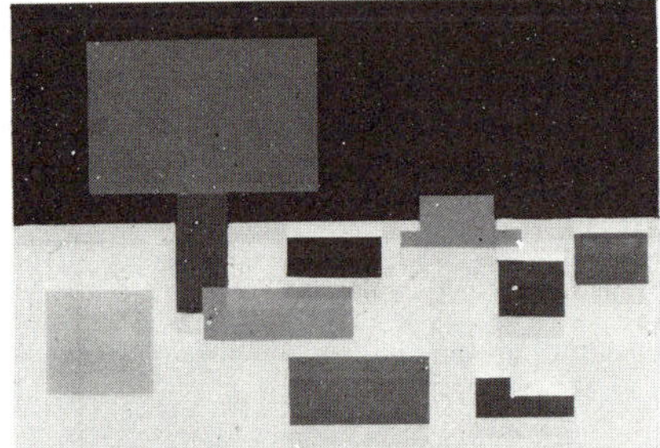

Fig. 188. Imagine that these planes are components of a still life. You will find that, if they are set one beside the other, there will be no feeling of depth.

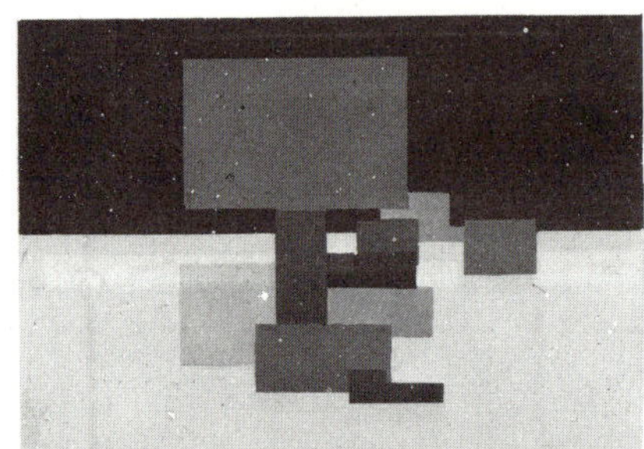

Fig. 189. By grouping these components, the painter manages to concentrate interest, but the third dimension or depth is partly lost.

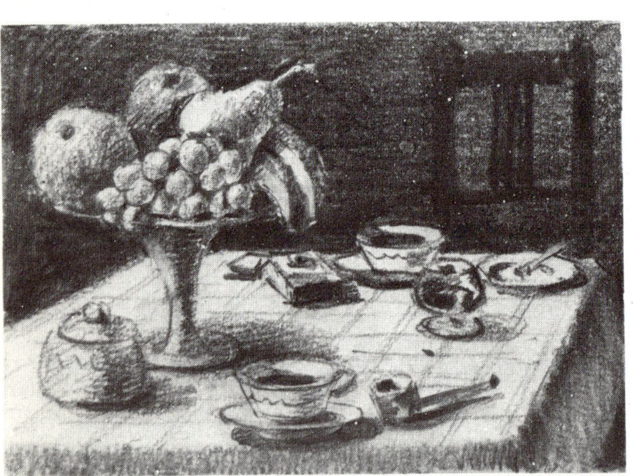

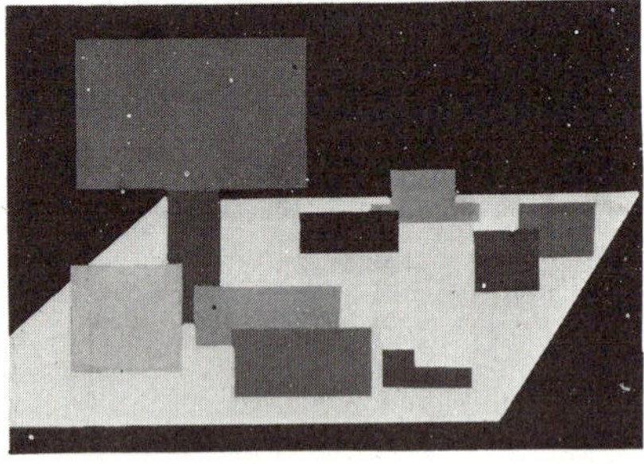

Fig. 190. If each component is placed very carefully, with some objects set in front of others, trying for *unity* at the same time as *diversity,* you'll get a clear impression of front and back, creating the illusion of the third dimension.

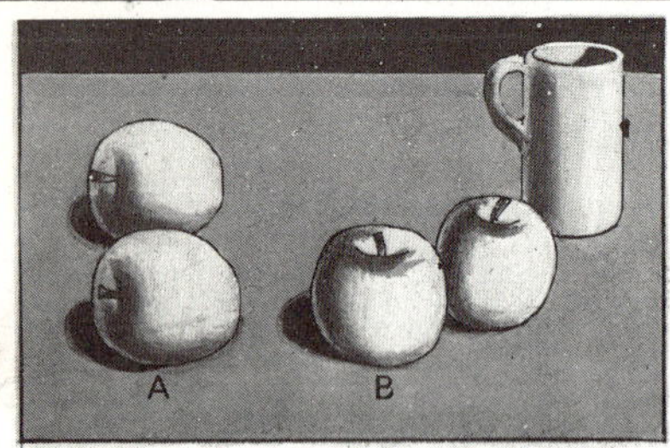

Fig. 191. Every artist has his own method of creating planes —there are no set rules. In this example the placing of apples A and B does not give enough impression of depth.

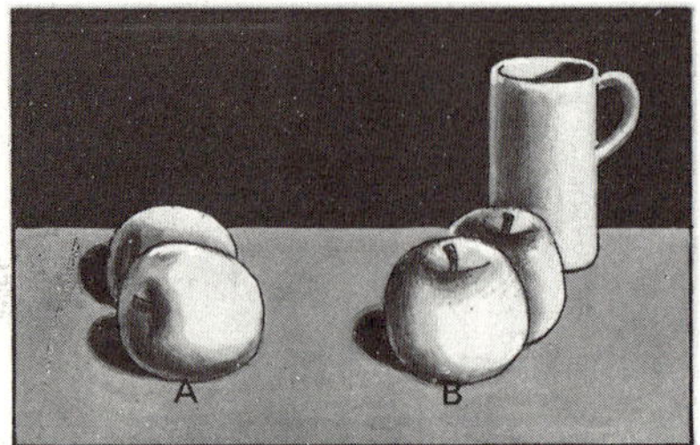

Fig. 192. The opposite applies here: apples A and B in the foreground have been placed right on top of the ones behind, in the second plane; the positioning of the jug in the background illustrates the same fault. Also, this type of grouping divides the objects into two sets, so that unity is not achieved

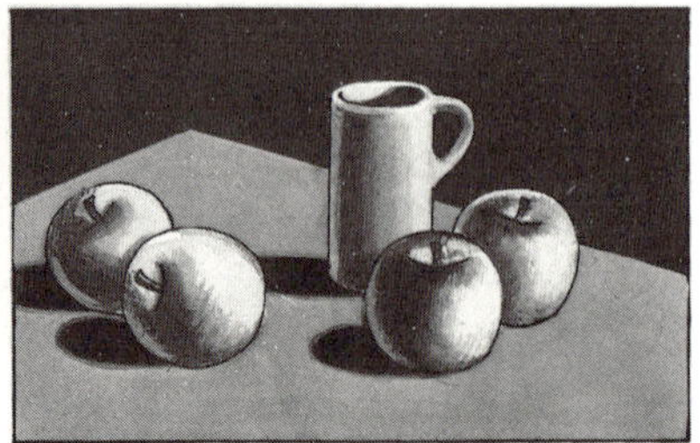

Fig. 193. Perfect treatment of depth —just right. Lateral lighting emphasizes the shadow of the jug, joining the groups to make a single cluster.

background

There is a problem in choosing and painting the background of a still life. I think it was the film producer René Clair, discussing film background music, who said he thought it should be discreet and that: "The best background music for a film was the type not listened to by the viewer." The same could be said of the background in a painting. It has to be there, emphasizing outlines and shapes by its tone or colour; it's needed to harmonize colours in a work, perhaps completing the setting or the atmosphere, but always as a secondary part of the picture. Don't use brilliant colours or disturbing shapes; nearly always use greyish tones with blurred and indefinite shapes, as long as they exist in your subject.

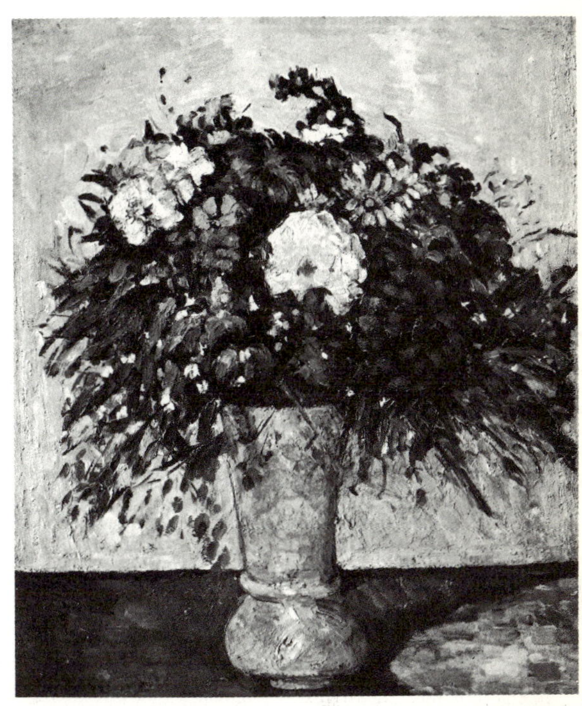

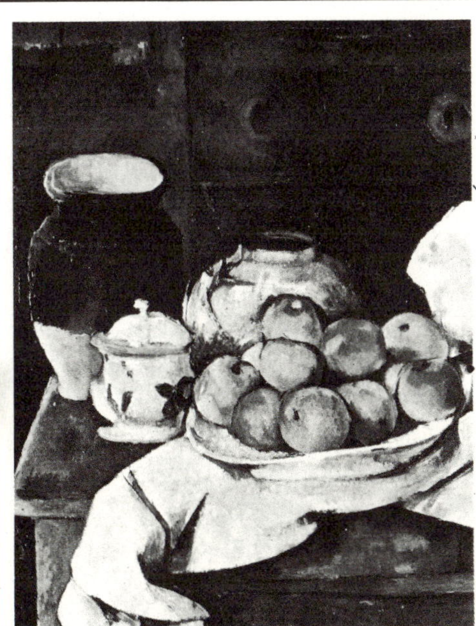

Fig. 194. The background can accentuate contrasts, define shapes and show up contours. It should very rarely be completely uniform; it needs slight variations in shade and sometimes in colour itself.

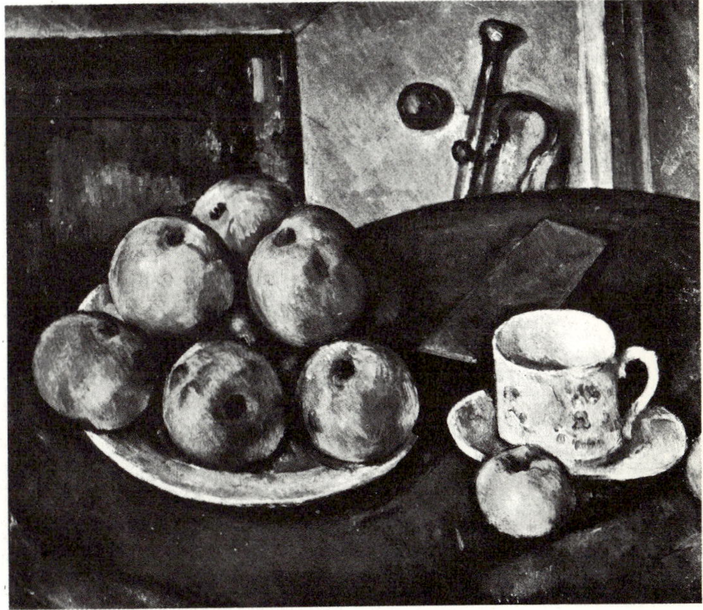

Fig. 185. Like Cézanne, you can use a background comprised of furniture or domestic bits and pieces. It may be painted in a lighter colour than the subject, as above. But it should always be set in the furthest plane, blurred and indefinite.

contrast and atmosphere

By "contrast" we mean the comparative effects of tone in any model. Contrast usually depends on the type of lighting, but it's also affected by distance: a large tree a few yards away presents light greens and dark greens, almost black; the same tree seen on a distant hilltop from a distance of several miles looks a rather light bluish or grey colour and has very little or no contrast. Hengel points out in this book *System in the arts* that, in the real world, "all objects undergo difference in coloration according to the ambient atmosphere". It's true that a still life is not a subject presenting great distances; its components are assembled in a fairly small space. Yet the effect of contrast can certainly be brought out more strongly in the objects in the foreground, since the "front" of the picture has greater definition than the "back". It is the same as when one focuses on an object, leaving everything behind it out of focus. Photographers use this method to create depth simply copying the way our eyes work.

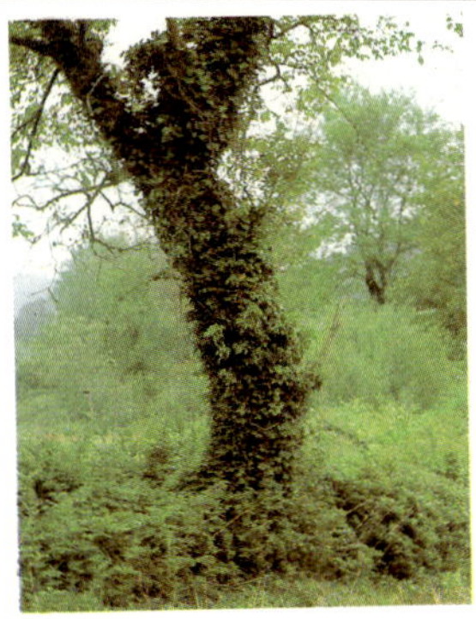

Fig. 196. Objects in the foreground here a tree present great contrasts in tone and colour.

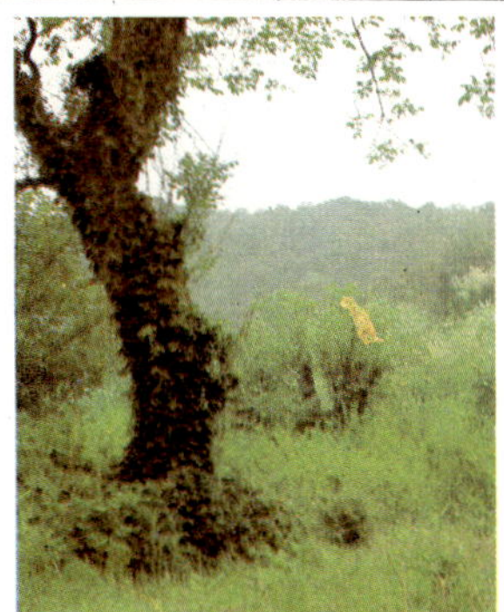

Fig. 197. Objects at a distance become paler and greyer, with no contrast.

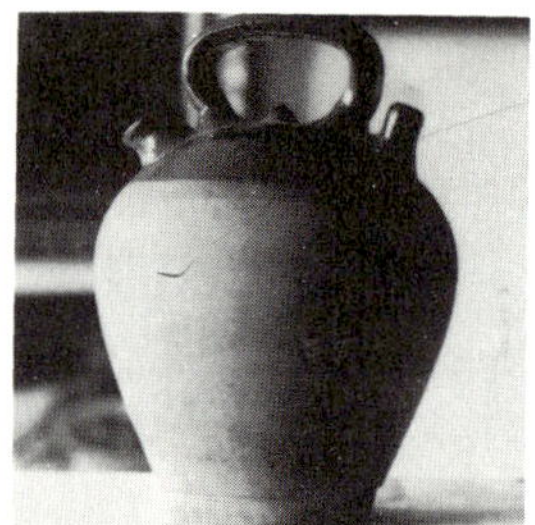

Fig. 198. When we concentrate our vision on something near us, the thing behind it appears blurred.

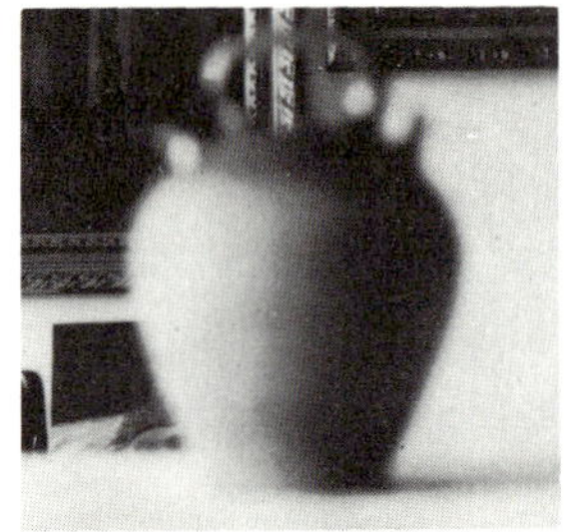

Fig. 199. When we look carefully at something at a distance, an object in front of it appears blurred.

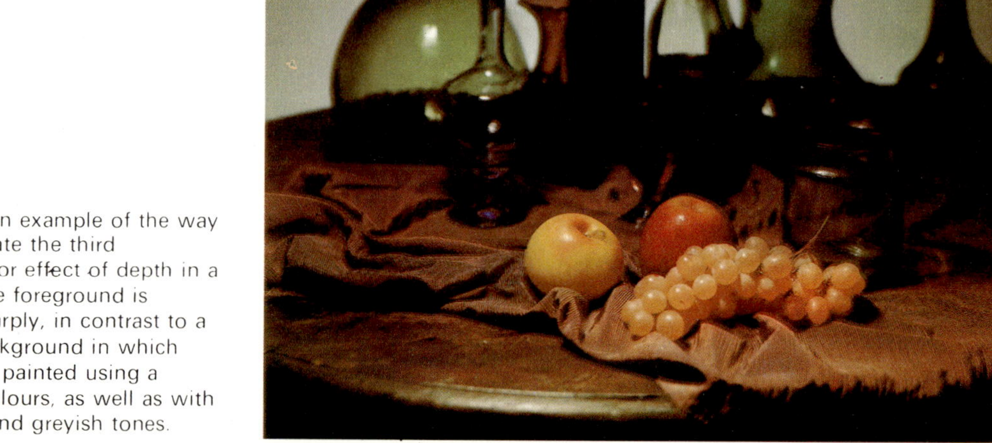

Fig. 200. An example of the way to accentuate the third dimension or effect of depth in a picture. The foreground is defined sharply, in contrast to a blurred background in which objects are painted using a range of colours, as well as with indefinite and greyish tones.

colours which advance and recede

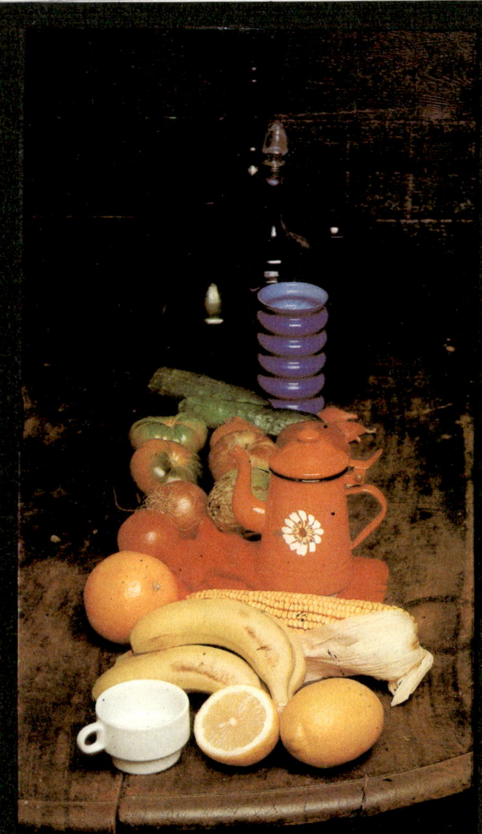

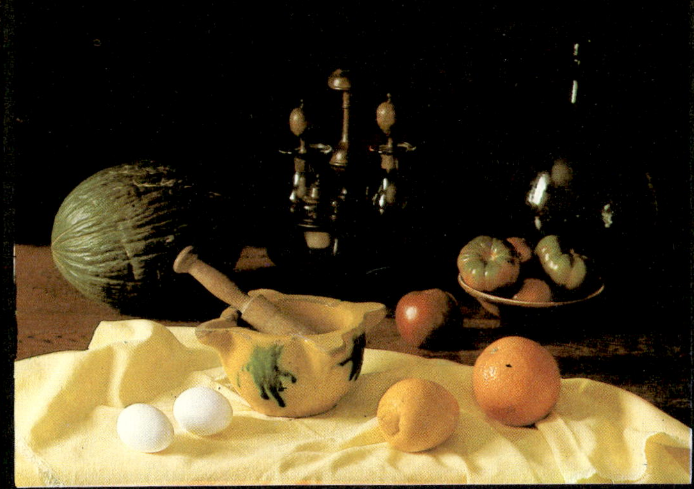

Figs. 201 and 202. White, yellow, orange and red, in that order, "bring things nearer"; green, blue, violet and dark grey "make things seem further away". If we apply this theory to the composition of a still life, we enhance the feeling of depth and help to illustrate the third dimension.

Fig. 203. The theory of advancing and receding colours can be applied in any still life, even if the components are not *precisely* yellows greens and blues. In this still life the pure whiteness of the egg provides a very definite first plane, while, simply because of their colour, the loaf and the bacon look further away, in more distant planes.

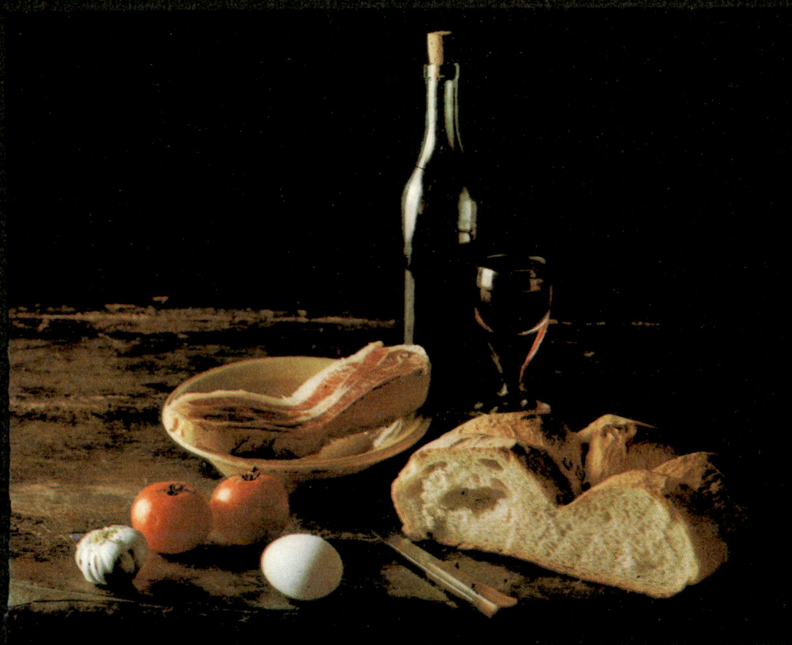

from theory to practice

Louis le Bail, a young French painter at the beginning of this century, was lucky enough to be with Cézanne when he was composing a still life. Le Bail comments:

"He went to and fro between table and easel, continually looking from easel to model; he worked a little on folds in the tablecloth, on which he placed three or four peaches and a jug decorated with flowers. Deep in thought, he returned to the easel, took a careful look, cast down his eyes for a moment and looked again; he returned to the model to add a few green pears, to study the green of the pears and the red of the peaches; he made the complementary colours vivid and used a few boxes to raise the level. What a time it took to achieve that higher level! Then he turned to the fruit, raising or lowering the position of each peach, using a coin or two as wedges. He worked lovingly and meticulously, subjecting each new arrangement to patient scrutiny."

Then, according to his friend Bernard, also a great artist, "he would contemplate the model for a long time, see it "in his own way" and create from this vision something permanent." But that's another story which we'll discuss later in the context of *interpreting the model.* Don't forget Le Bail's description of Cézanne at work; his still lifes were arranged with total dedication, by testing, looking, trying again and again until he felt satisfied.

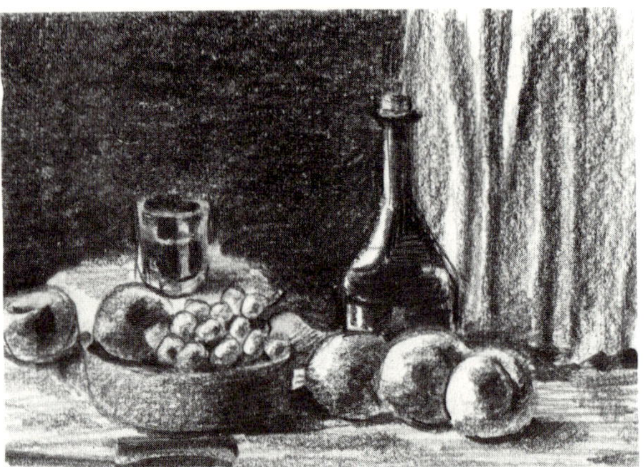

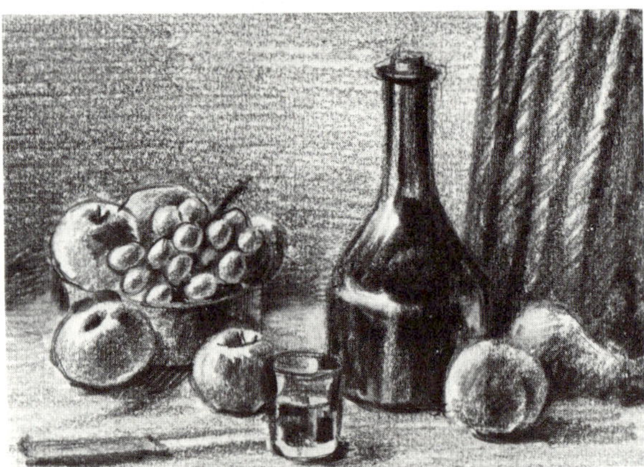

Figs. 204 and 205. It is important to spend time preparing the arrangement before you paint. With a subject which presents this kind of content and detail (above), you may, after experimenting this way and that, end up with a model like the one below.

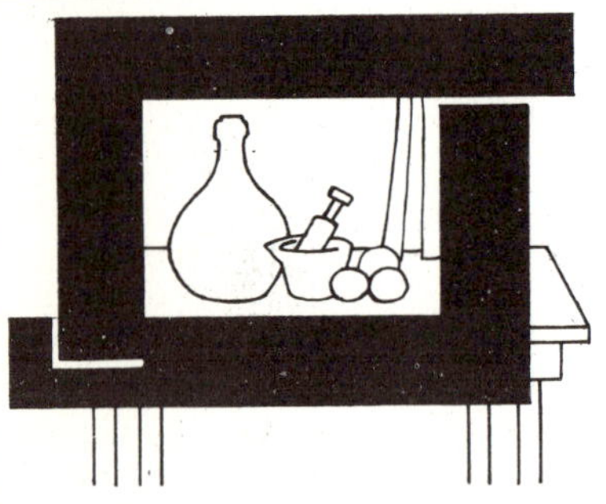

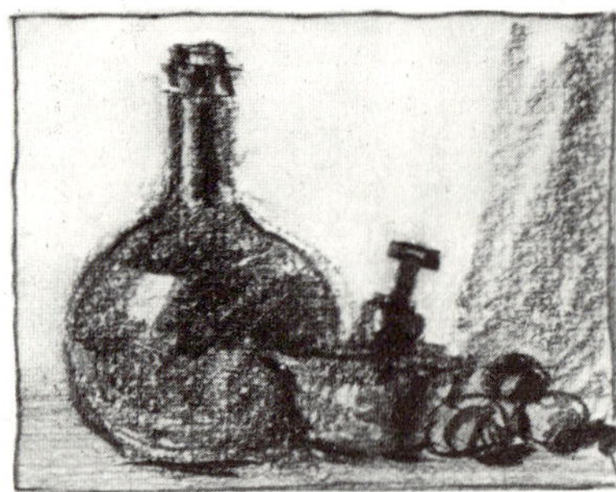

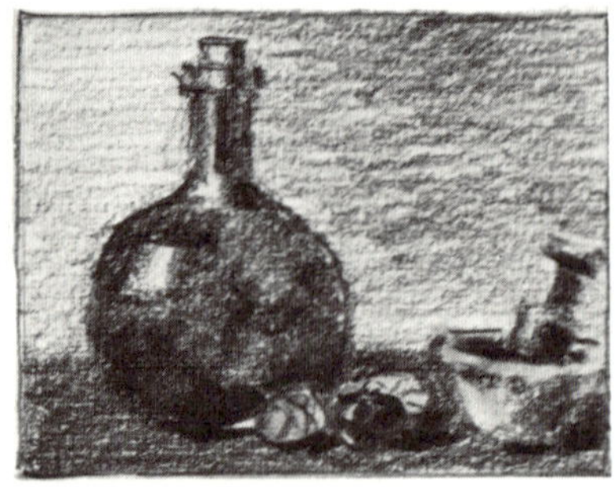

Figs. 206, 207 and 208. It's a good idea to prepare two rightangled pieces of black cardboard to use as a frame so that you can study the composition of a picture, see above. It is also useful to draw one or two preliminary sketches in charcoal, red chalk or very soft lead pencil, working to a size no greater than 12×17 cm. When you are doing this, try to work out the positions and proportions of the components of your still life in relation to your space, as well as studying the colours of background components and the type of lighting.

from theory to practice

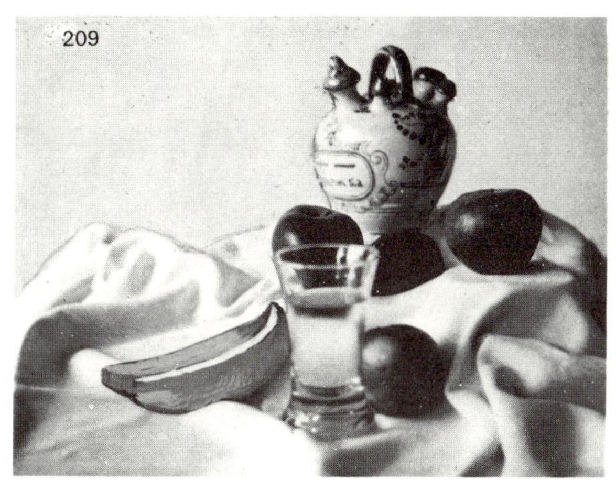
209

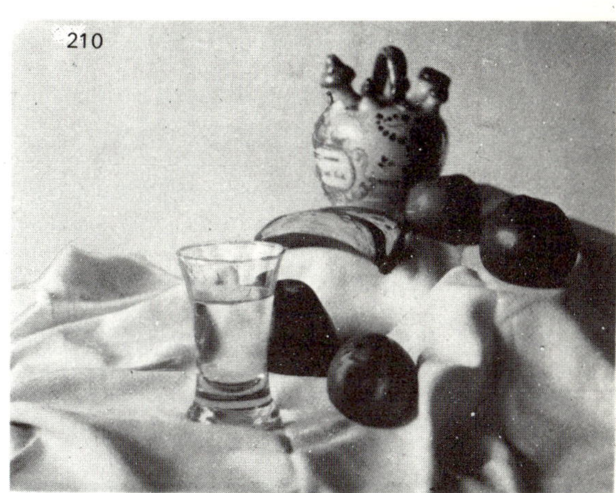
210

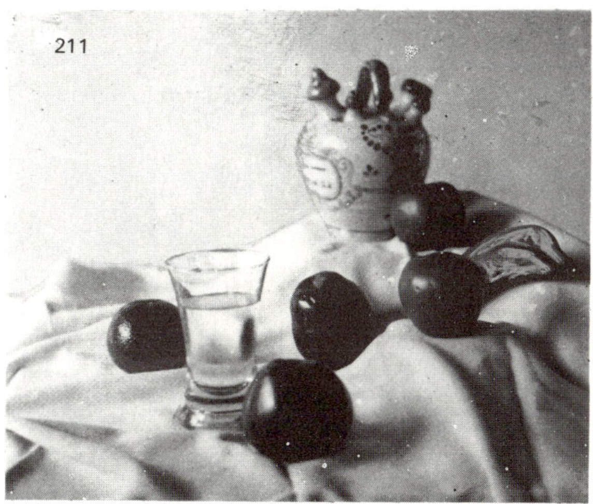
211

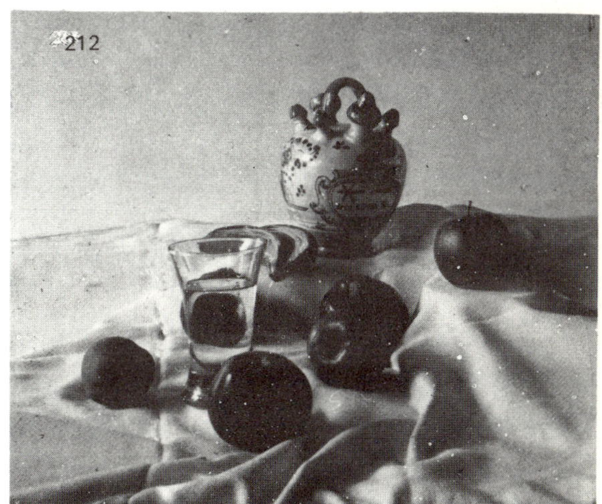
212

Here is an example of the art of composition used in a still life.

Fig. 209. First attempt: I have laid the tablecloth on boxes and in humps to create varying levels and I've put the wine-pitcher at the top; then I placed the fruit and the glass at the front. But the glass is almost directly in front of the pitcher, one piece of fruit looks as if it's partly inside the glass and another is buried and hidden in the middle...

Fig. 210. The position of the glass is better, but there are pieces of fruit in line in front of the wine-pitcher...

Fig. 211. I add an orange. It's an improvement, but the two apples piled up on the right are unsightly.

Fig. 212. Bad: the position of the pitcher, the foreshortening of the bananas, the apple "inside" the glass...

Fig. 213. Better: the overall arrangement is more harmonious; the composition looks good; the spacing is alright and the outlined shapes, including the folds of the tablecloth are better.

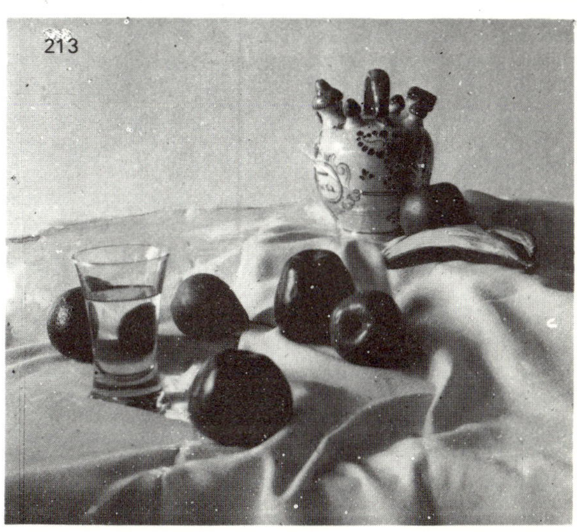
213

from theory to practice

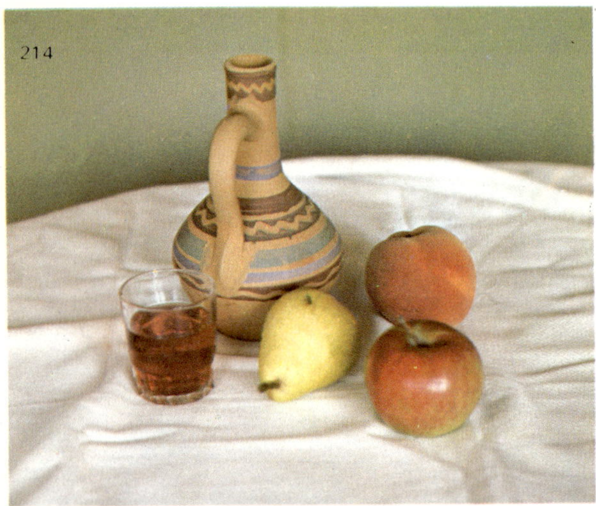

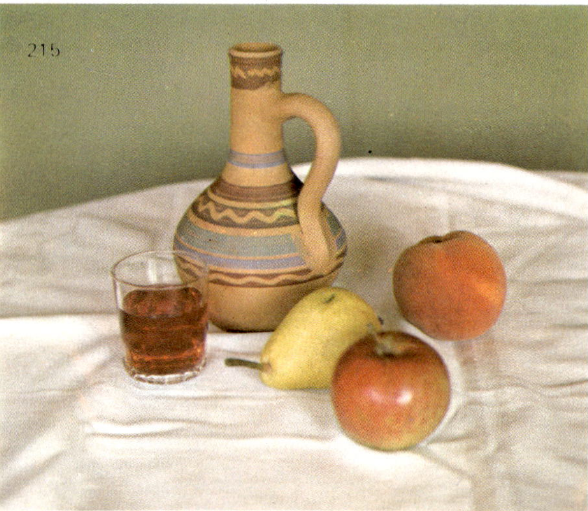

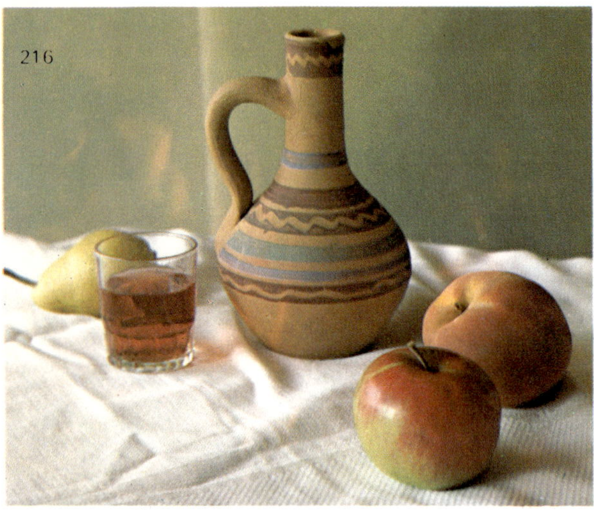

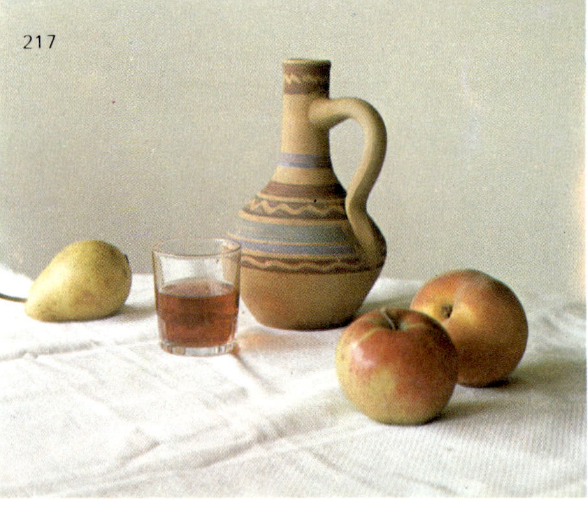

Here's an example of the art of composition used in a still life.

Fig. 214. Bad: too much unity; the position of the pitcher makes the handle too foreshortened; there's a displeasing bit of arrangement —the apple and peach are exactly in line one above the other...

Fig. 215. This is better in every way; the picture could be painted now, but it would still be tedious because of too much unity.

Fig. 216. Better than the last one, but...

Fig. 217. ...this slight change is an improvement; the pear is a little further from the glass and the handle of the jar is in a more functional position. Also —and this is perhaps the most important feature— look at the horizon: from Fig. 214 onwards, the tablecloth has been lowered each time, so that it's now at a better level.

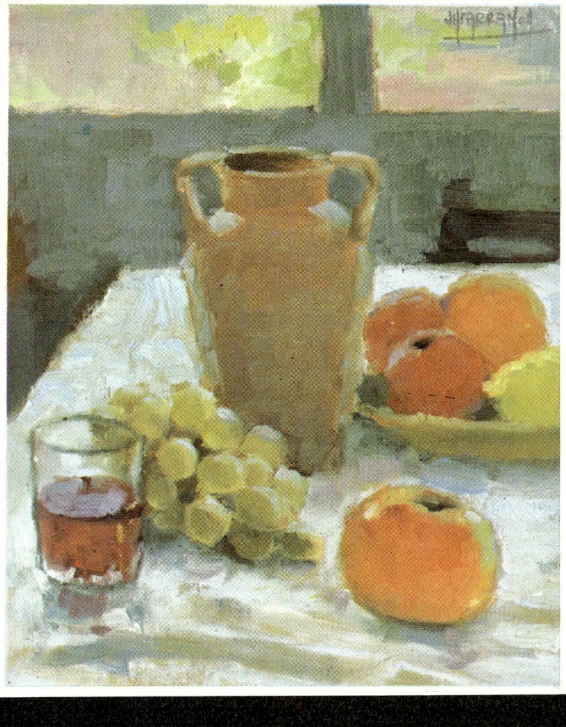

Oil painting: its craft and technique

professional tips

How far from the model?
One-and-a-half or two metres at most. At four metres a bunch of grapes becomes a splash of colour; you need to be at least two metres closer to appreciate all the different shapes, the chiaroscuro and the colours.

The painter should be not more than two metres from the subject.
What about the artist's viewpoint? Should the model be seen from a high position, a low position or somewhere in between? It's usual to take a viewpoint with an angle of vision of about 45 degrees. Figs. 221-224 should clarify this further.

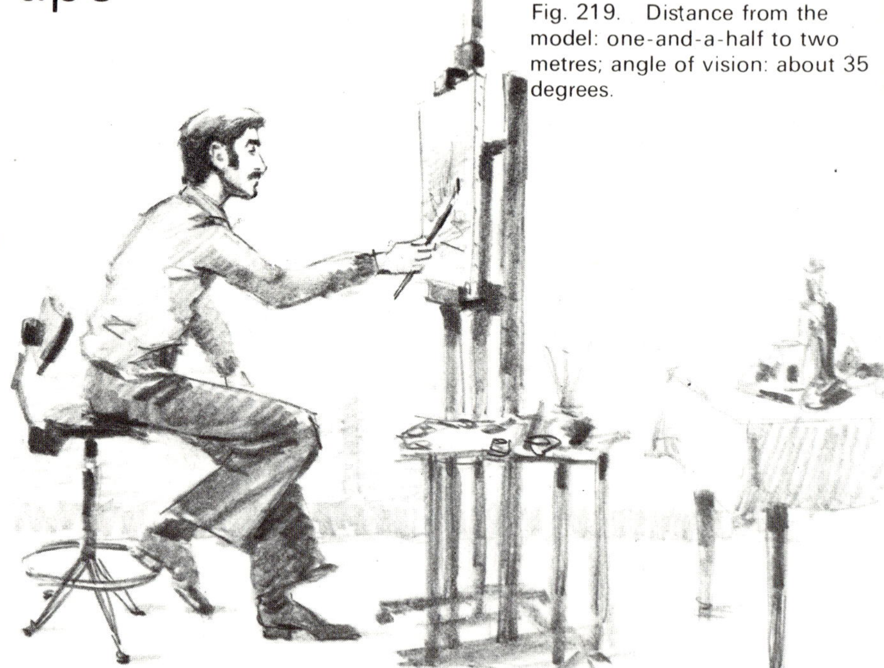

Fig. 219. Distance from the model: one-and-a-half to two metres; angle of vision: about 35 degrees.

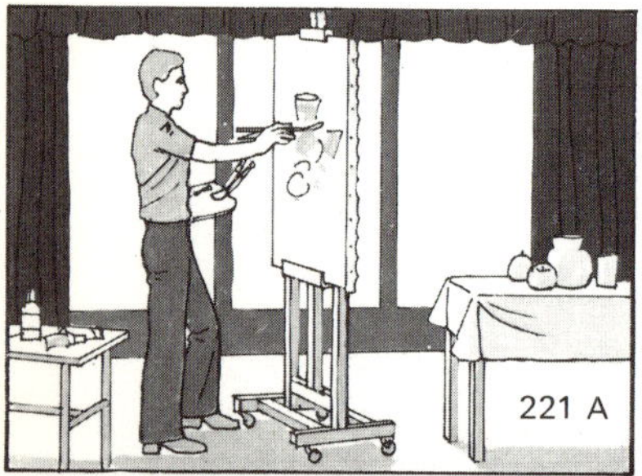

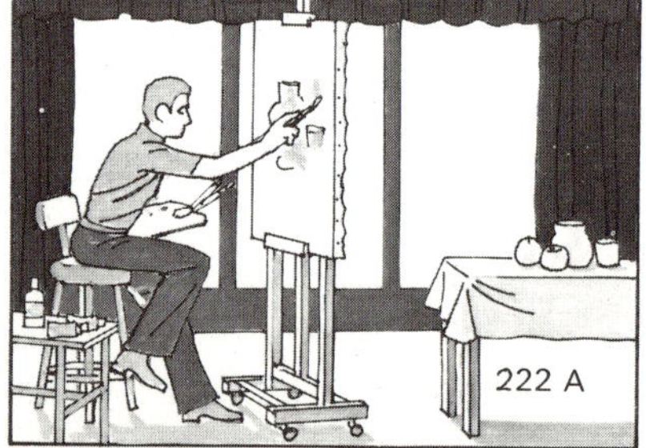

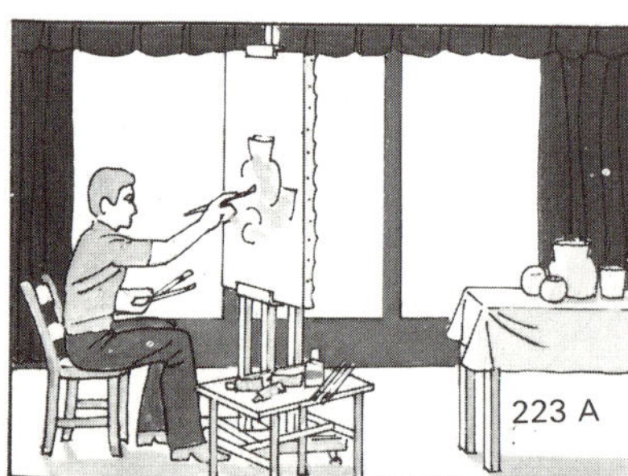

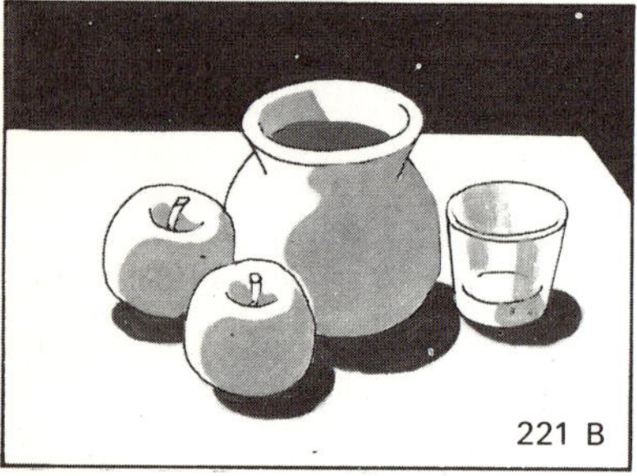

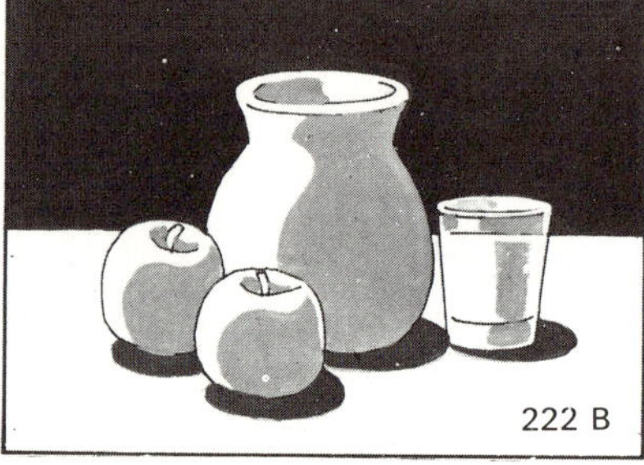

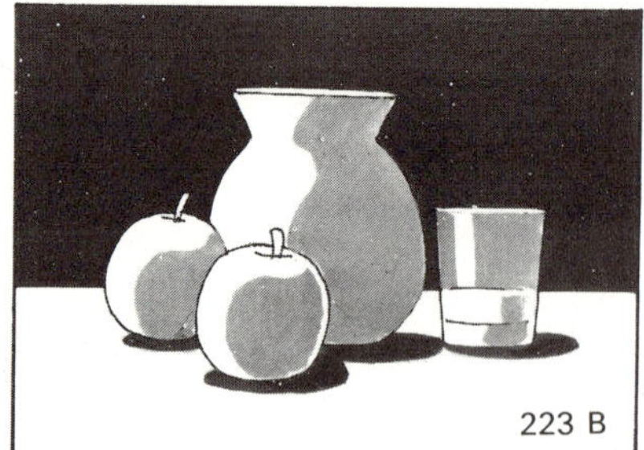

Figs. 221 A and B. If you paint looking down at the model, and too close (A), you'll get a rather peculiar and unsuitable perspective (B).

Figs. 222 A and B. If your painting stool is about 70 cm high and you are sitting about one-and-a-half to two metres from the model with your angle of vision at about 35 degrees (A), the perspective should be correct (B).

Figs. 223 A and B. If you paint from a position almost level with the model (A) you'll get a rather unusual frontal view (B), but it's up to you, as shown in Fig. 224...

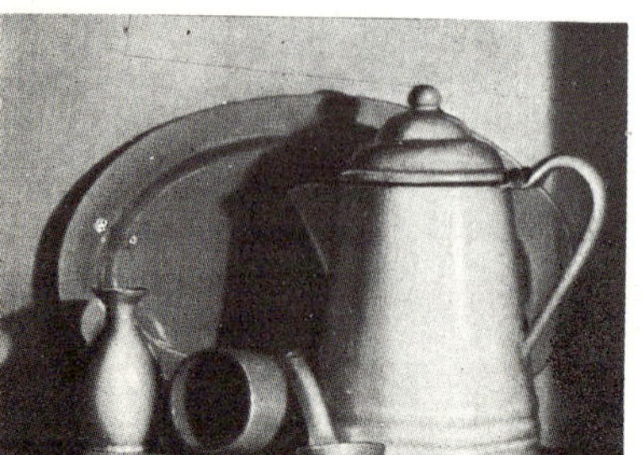

Fig. 224. ...the American artist Ken Davies often chooses a low position, level with the model; the result can if you are like Ken Davies — be similar; this still life, painted meticulously in the fashionable *trompe l'oeil* style has a characteristic Ken Davies hallmark.

professional tips

Care of palette and brushes: They should be cleaned regularly; dunk and rub them clean at least three or four times a go to get really true colours.

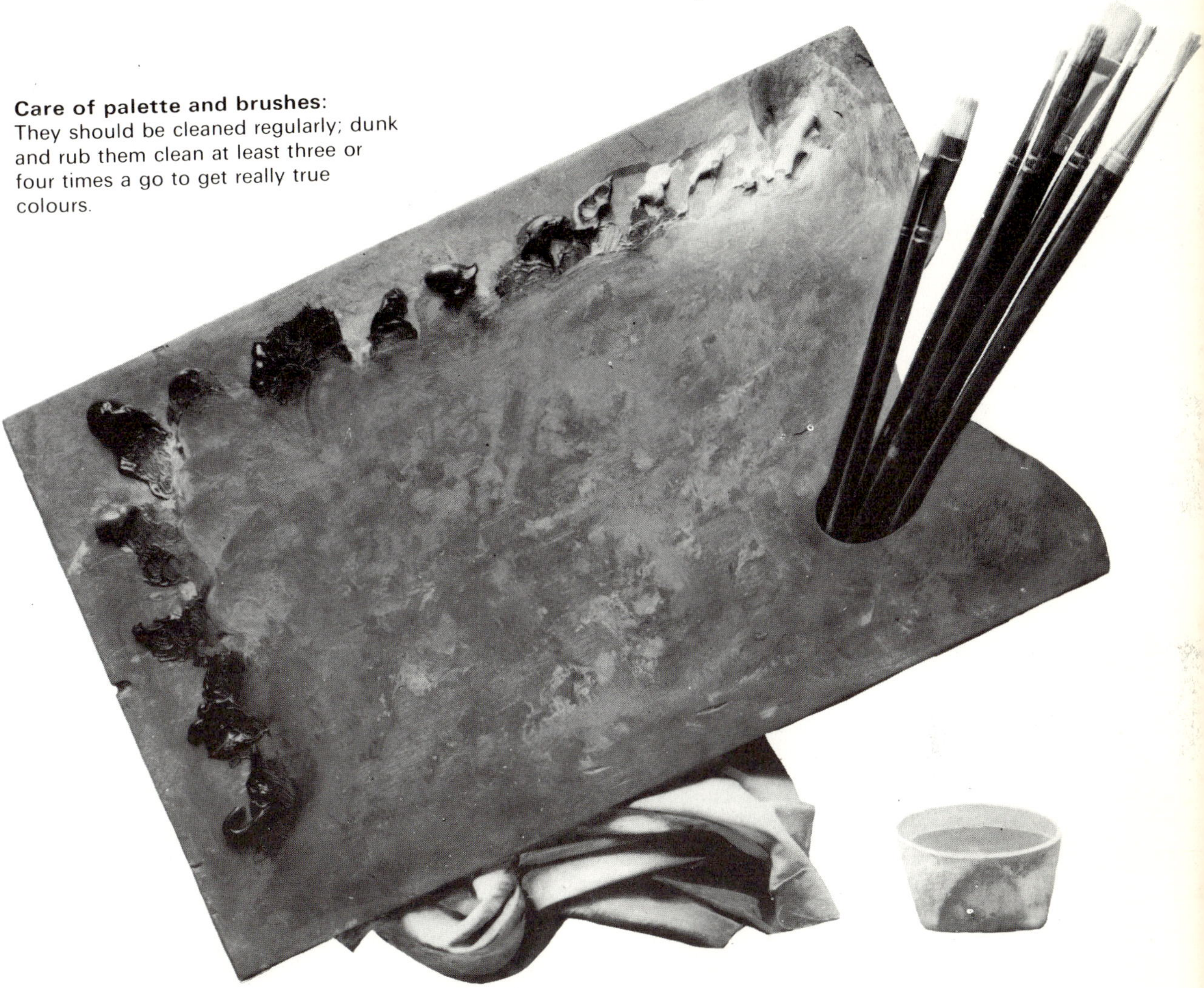

After about an hour's work on a painting you may well be short of space on your palette for mixing new colours, e.g. a special pink with a bluish tinge. This is where the crunch comes: if you are inexperienced, you may make the pink from some left-over white (which won't be very clean), using an earlier mixture of carmine and cobalt blue and perhaps something else you can't quite remember —ending up with a grey-tinged pink If you know better you'll realize that the time has come to stop, clean the palette, renew some of the colours, clean the brushes and start again from scratch.

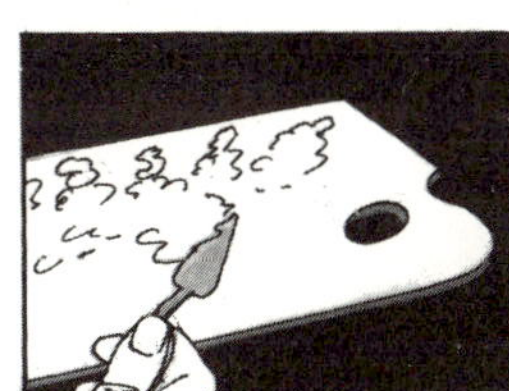

Fig. 225 A. Clean the palette with a palette knife as if you were using a trowel.

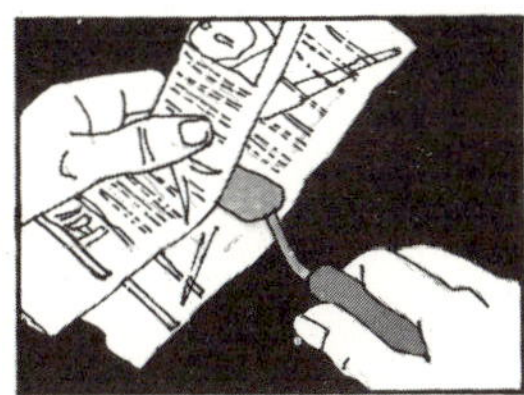

B. Then clean the palette knife with smallish (quarto-sized) bits of newspaper.

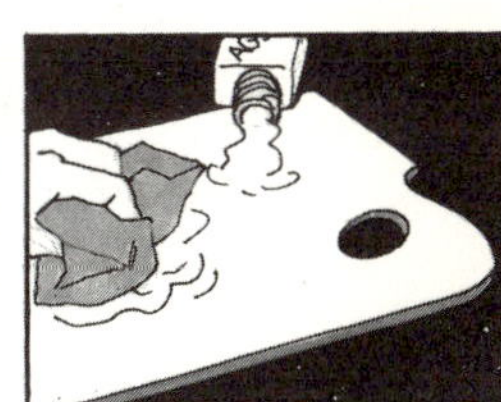

C. Now rub the palette, first with a few sheets of newspaper and then with a rag and white spirit.

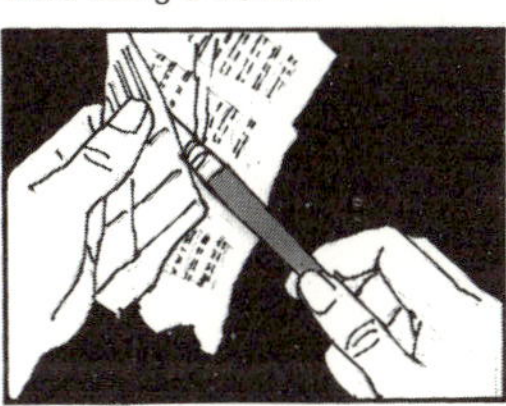

Fig. 226 A. Clean the brushes, wiping off the paint with newspaper.

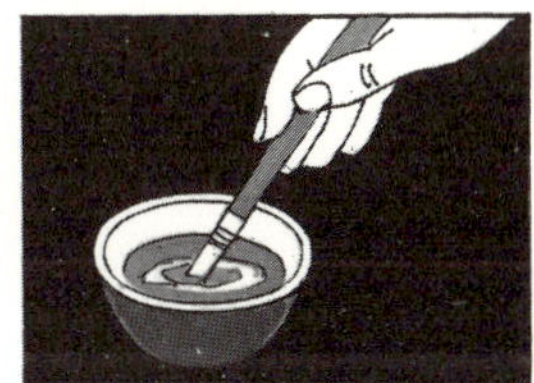

B. Then dip them one at a time into white spirit. Don't worry about the white spirit becoming muddy.

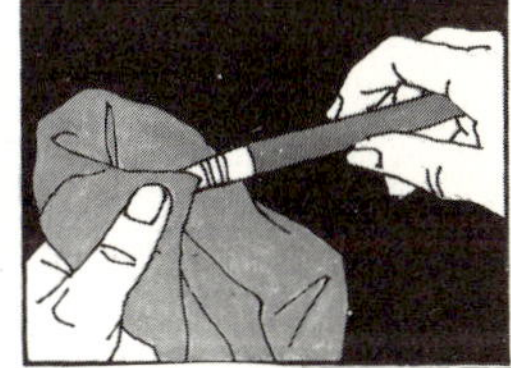

C. Finally, use a rag to squeeze the brushes clean. This is a temporary method, use it when you want to continue working.

draw first?...or paint straightaway?

So you're all set: still life carefully arranged: palette at the ready and you face a blank canvas. Beginning a work is not easy —this applies to nearly every form of art. Mallarmé described the blank canvas with feeling: "empty, defending its whiteness". And you wonder whether to begin with pencil or whether to paint straightaway. This is an age-old problem which has been debated for centuries. Way back in the 1500s, the Florentine Vasari wrote from a visit to Venice describing Titian's way of going about it: "He used colours immediately, without making preparatory drawings; he said that this was the right and proper way". At about the same date, Michelangelo, who always drew to start with slyly remarked to Vasari: "What a pity that in Venice they don't begin by learning to draw correctly."

Although both ways of working have been used over the last hundred years, it seems that there are two completely different techniques. There are artists sometimes labelled "Colourists", who paint very few shadows, lighting from the front, or using diffused lighting and generally seeing the whole subject as patches of colour. This style has been used by van Gogh, Matisse, Bernard and so on who started from scratch with paint. Then there are painters loosely labelled "Valuists" who put in all the chiaroscuro: Chardin, Corot, Manet, Nonell, Dali and others; these started on a picture by drawing. But it's not a good idea to state categorically that any particular painter does one or the other. We know that Picasso sometimes started with drawing and sometimes with painting. "To paint or to draw?" said Cézanne, "When you get colour in all its rich variety, you'll get plenty of clear shapes as well." This is true.

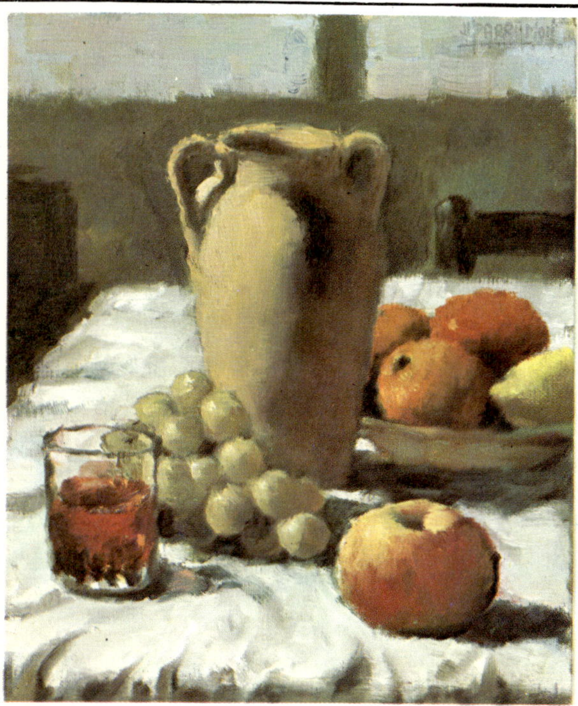

Fig. 227. You can treat any subject with either style —it all depends on your lighting. If you light from the side, you'll use the "Valuist" style; from the front, "Colourist." An artist who paints a still life with the full interplay of light and shade may well start off by drawing.

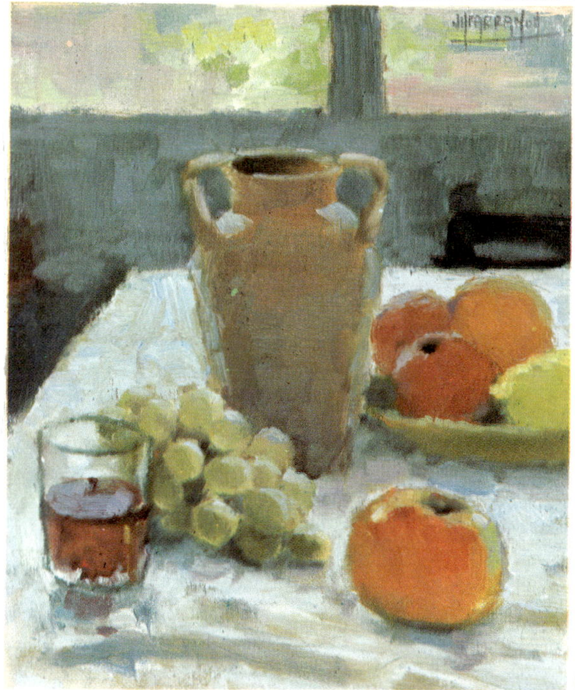

Fig. 228. A "Colourist" painter works like this primarily because he considers it more abstract, more creative and less academic, but also because he believes that colour can express everything, without the aid of volume or modelling. As Bonnard wrote: "Colour on its own can express light, represent mass and convey atmosphere."

where should one begin?

The *law of simultaneous contrasts* tells us that a colour looks paler or darker according to the surrounding colour. Given this, it would be a mistake to begin by painting a small area or an isolated object on a blank canvas, since its value might become lighter or darker acoording to the surrounding colour applied later.
So fill in the big empty spaces as soon as possible. In a still life the large empty area is usually at the back.

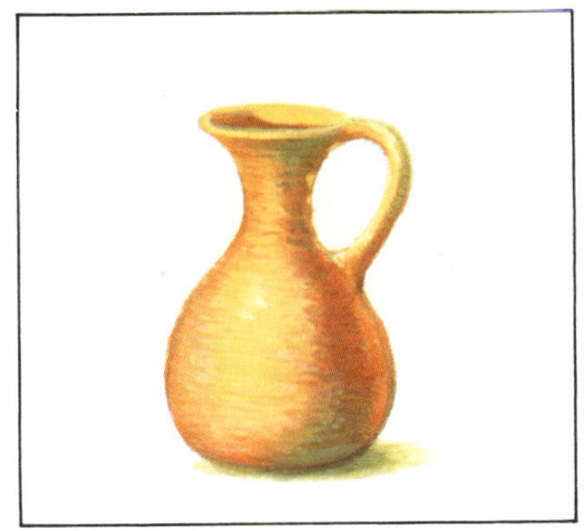

229

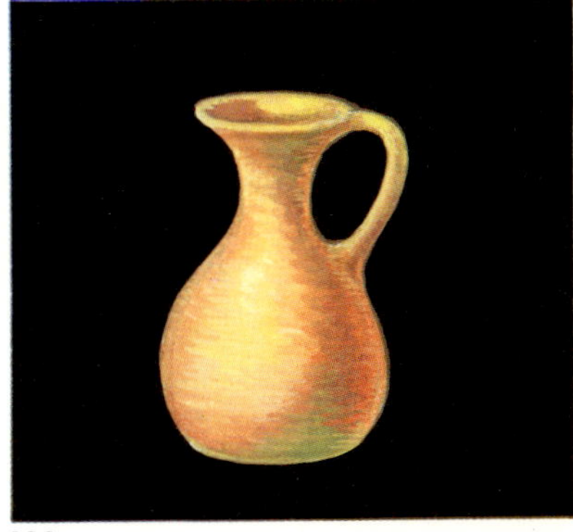

230

231

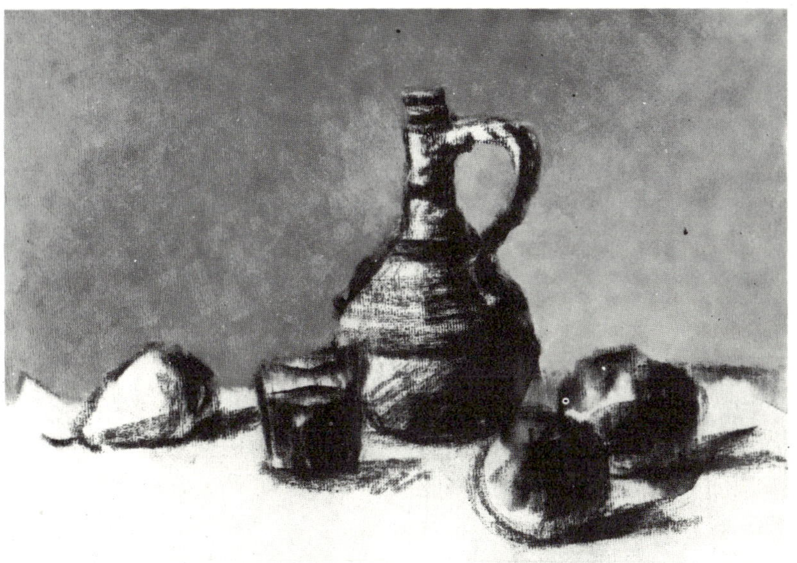

Fig. 231. Where do I begin? It's wisest to get some colour down as soon as you can —the canvas won't look so alarming and you'll eliminatc falsc contrasts. In a still life it's nearly always best to start with the background.

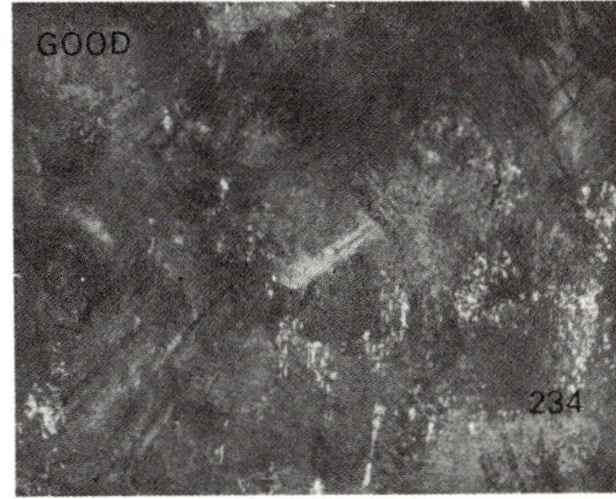

Fig. 233. BAD: even if the background is all one colour it shouldn't be completely uniform in shade.

Fig. 234. GOOD: the background should contain plenty of variations of shade, even if its only in one colour; then its true colour will be enriched and shown at its best.

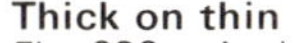

232

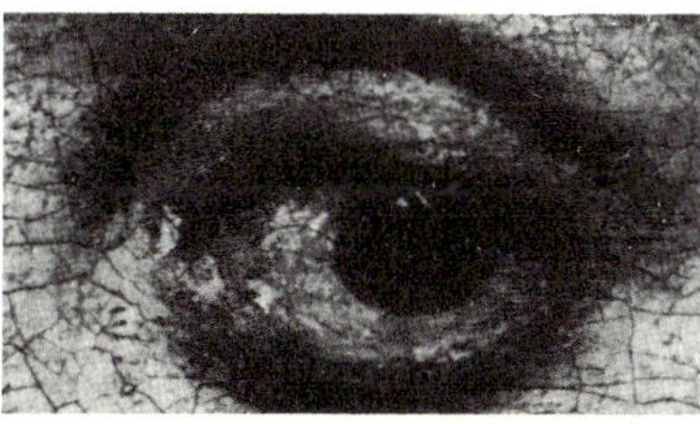

Thick on thin
Fig. 232. A tried and tested rule to remember when applying the first layer of paint to a canvas is this: to prevent a painting cracking as time goes by, you need to use more turps on the first layer. The paint as it comes from the tube is *thick* —and is even greasier if diluted with linseed oil; the same paint diluted with turpentine is *thin*. Of course, a thick layer takes longer to dry than a thin layer. If you paint thin on thick by mistake, the top layer (thin) dries more quickly than the layer beneath (thick). When the latter dries, he top layer contracts and cracks and the picture's surface will *look* cracked.

direction of brush strokes

When using oil paint and an easel, your canvas will be upright. So it may seem practical —and logical— to make up-and-down brush strokes. But, when you think about it, you'll realize that this will depend on your subject. It doesn't make sense to use vertical strokes when painting the sea, or a big bank of white clouds, or a cloth spread out on a table. Vertical strokes can provide a particular style, but the sea or a sunset should be done with horizontal strokes, clouds with circular strokes and a tablecloth with horizontal or diagonal strokes.

Broadly speaking, painters fall into two groups, those who:
(1) paint specifically to show up the "shape" of things and those who.
(2) paint diagonally.

The former is the more usual: a cylinder is painted with strokes curved to its shape; a field of grass is painted with vertical strokes; a melon is painted as it is. If in doubt about the shapes, or when painting generally, it's wisest to paint diagonally.

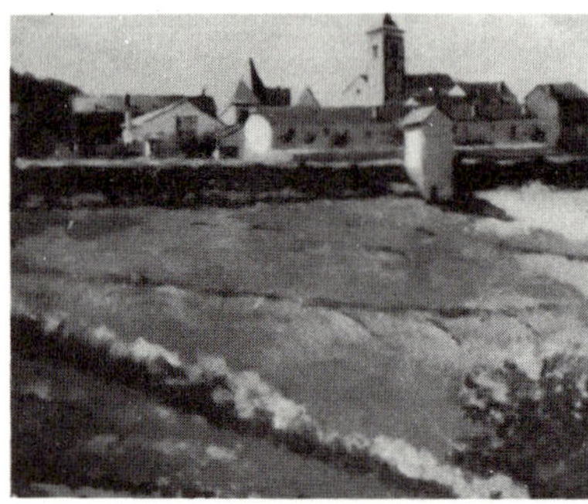

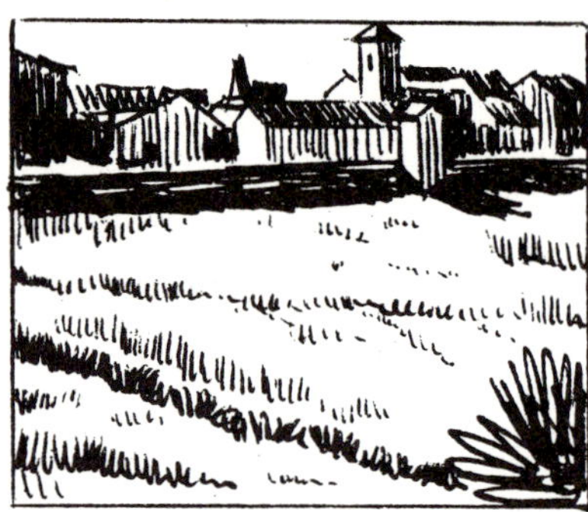

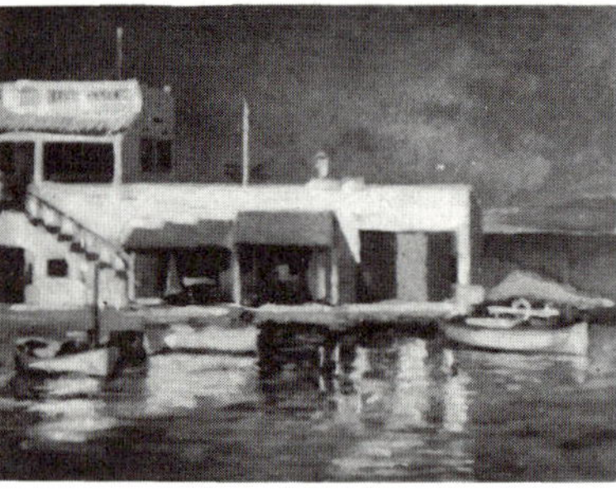

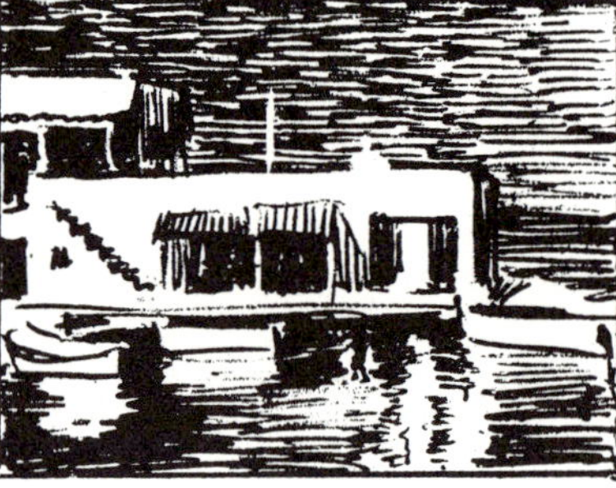

Fig. 235 (above). Some items or subjects *demand* a particular direction of brush strokes, for example a field of grass.

Fig. 236 (below). It's usually best to paint the sea horizontally.

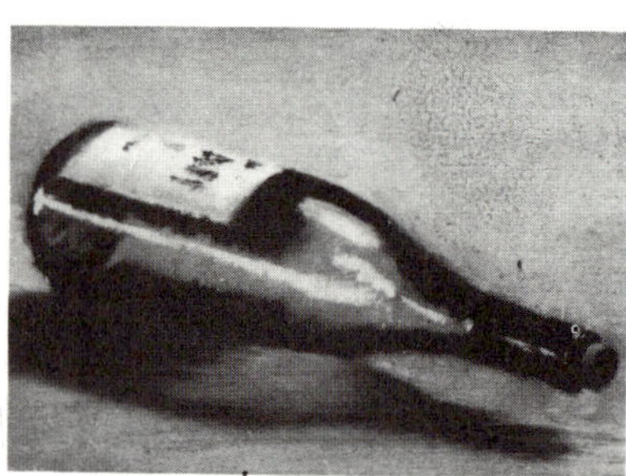

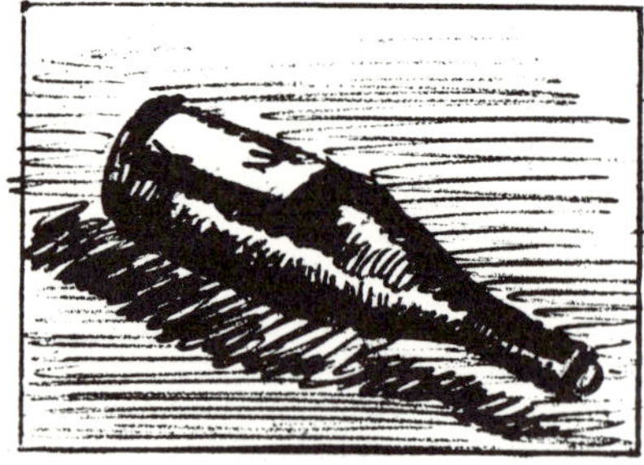

Fig. 237. If brush stroke direction follows the shape of an object or "enwraps" it, the shape is better conveyed.

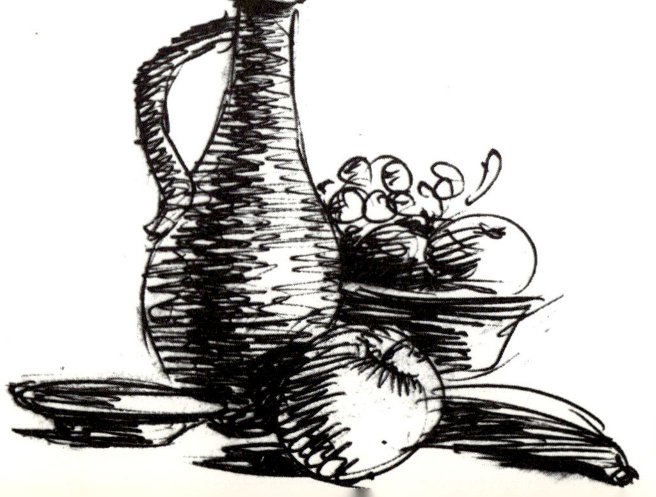

Fig. 238. The best way to learn how to cope with shape is to make preliminary sketches in pen and ink, or crayon.

synthesis

The ability to create synthesis in drawing or paintings is really a case of being able to see and draw or paint the most important parts of a subject, eliminating detail and non essentials. It is not easy and requires deep knowledge of painting technique. It also means painting with freedom, spontaneity, elegance, and with understanding of the subject and your materials. Velazquez' work is a classic example of this: any of the eyes portrayed in the faces of his *The Maids of Honour* is a perfect example of synthesis; one can count the brush strokes on one's fingers.

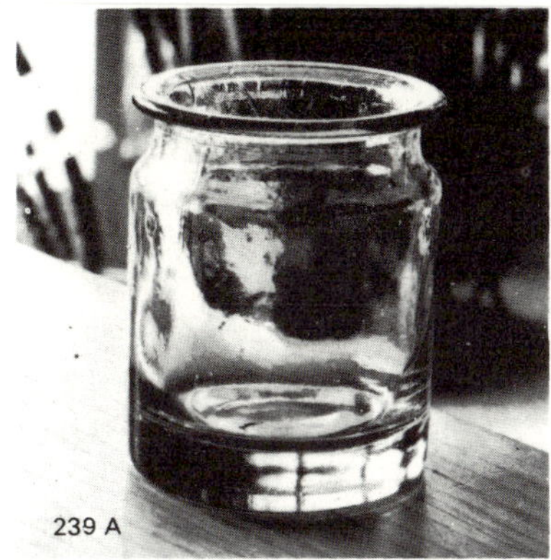

239 A

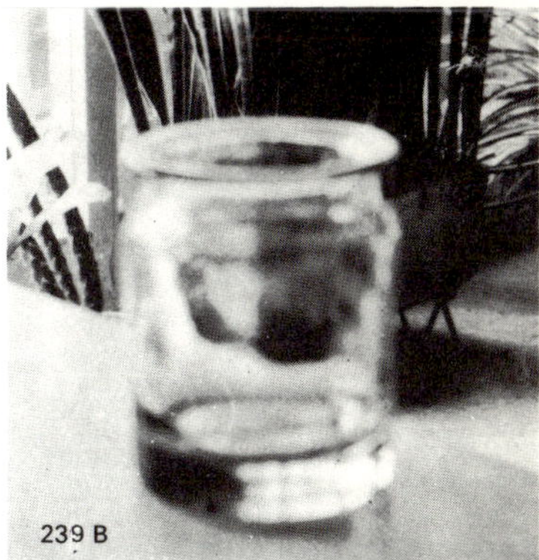

239 B

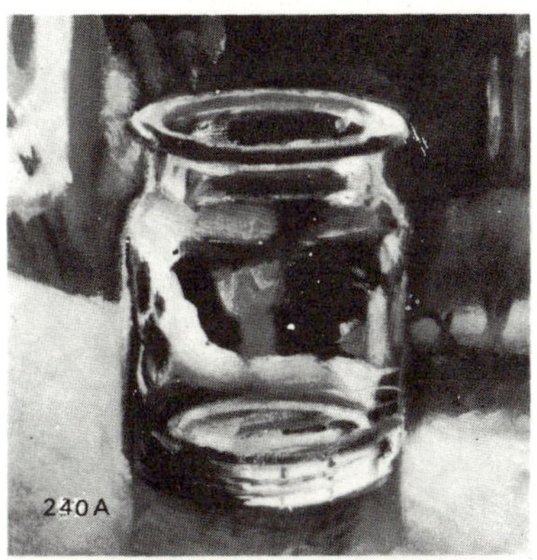

240 A

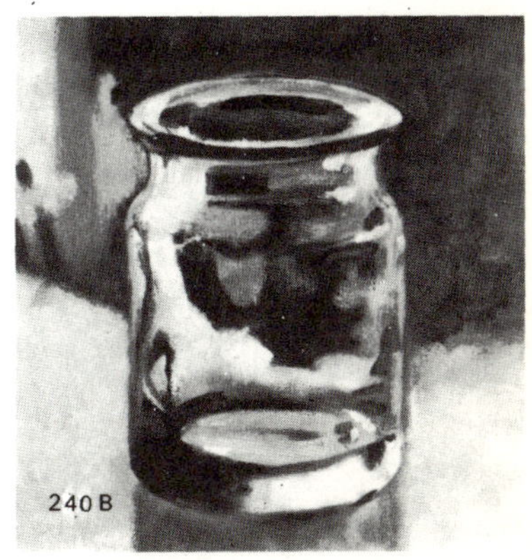

240 B

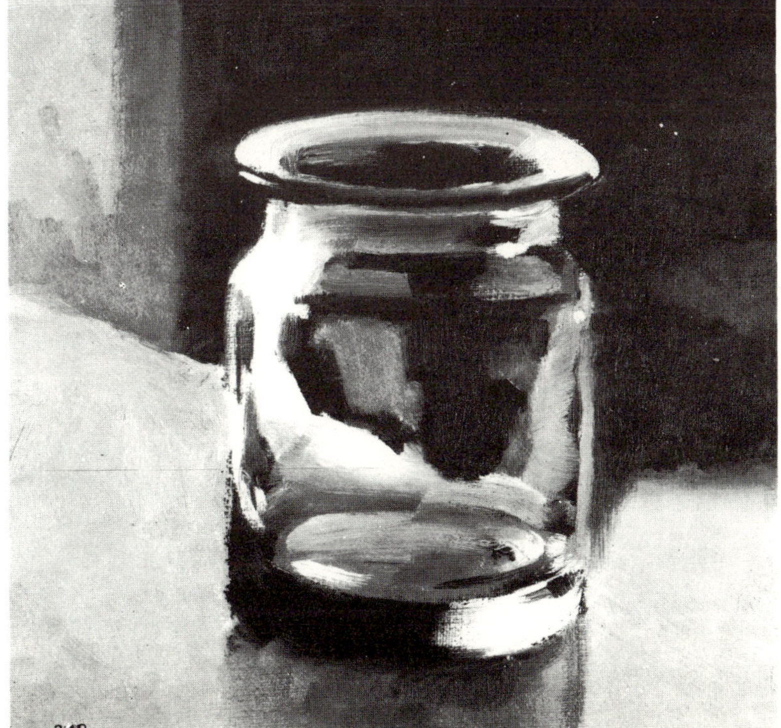

240

Figs. 239 A and B. An easy way to help you see synthesis is to look at the model through half-closed eyes. These photographs show the same glass jar, photographed with full definition, i.e. (A) as in normal vision. Fig. 239 B shows the same glass jar photographed out of focus, as if you were seeing it through half-closed eyes; this comes close to a synthesized image in that it shows only the most important lines, the shape, the areas catching the light and the highlights.

Figs. 240 A, B and C. These illustrate the step-by-step development of a synthesized painting of the jar. Note the lack of detail and shapes of secondary importance. The final picture provides a combination of all you need to convey its shape.

speed painting - painting *alla prima*

Painting *alla prima* means painting a picture in a single session. This is a frequently-used method nowadays (you hear of rapid painting competitions) which obviously requires a special technique.

Here are some important points to bear in mind when painting *alla prima:*

1. Decide upon your range of colours —warm, cool or gradations;
2. Draw your subject, but paint the biggest areas direct;
3. Using the appropriate colour, darken the parts of your subject which are in shadow with plenty of dark colour;
4. Now you can use the *alla prima* method, remembering just two basic principles;

A. Use all the creativity you possess

B. Never change your mind, stick to your first impression.

There's an exercise to help you with this further on, but here are some notes on the technique for painting *alla prima*.

Light on dark

Oil paint is opaque, so white can be applied over black, or ochre over burnt umber. You'll have plenty of paint on the dark patches and, if you use dark colours and enough turps, you'll soon have a dry dark surface on which you can work with light colours and on which you will actually find it easier to construct, draw and paint.

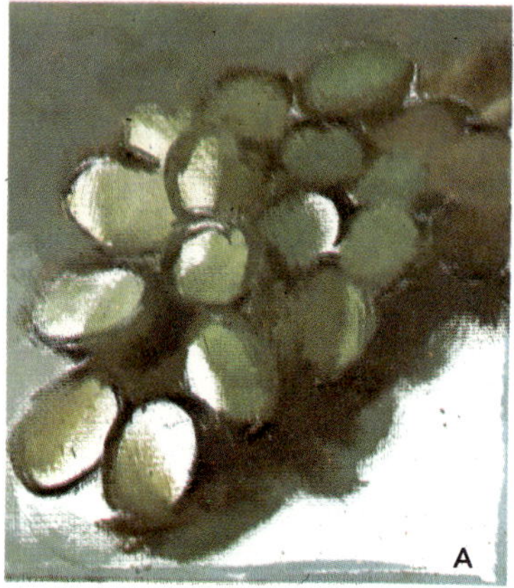

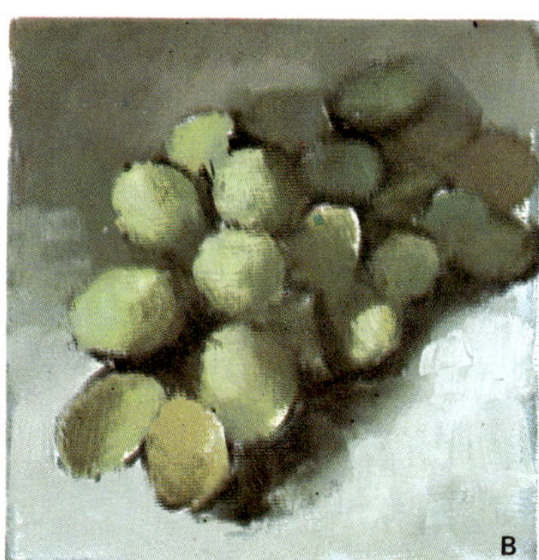

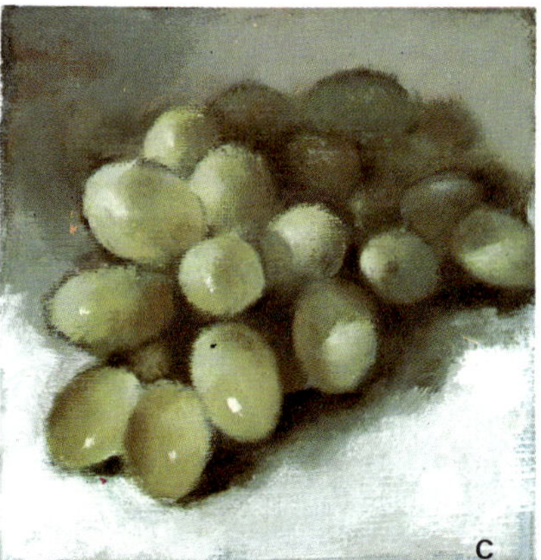

Figs. 241 A, B and C. This painted bunch of grapes shows the advantages of painting light on dark. Fig. A shows the background and the parts in shade, treated with very fluid paint as soon as the bunch has been drawn. You'll see that there are variations in colour in the dark patch; its colour is not entirely uniform. In Fig. B you can see the advantages of painting light on dark. Finally, in Fig. C, the values of each grape have been synthesized by a simple touch of reflected light and a highlight. You could still diversify and enrich the colour.

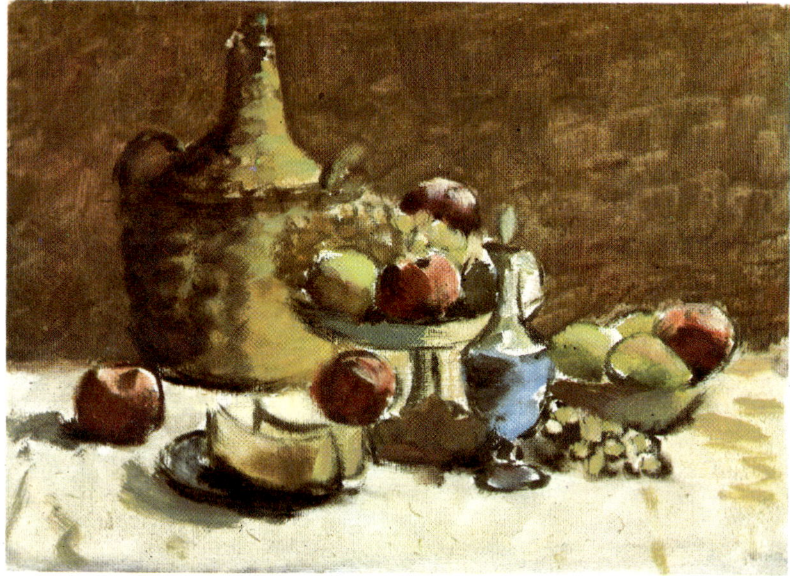

Fig. 242. When painting *alla prima* you may need a preliminary layer of general tone, using colour dictated by your subject. Turn back to the photograph on page 74 and compare it with this *alla prima* treatment of the same subject. Remember that the paint should be fluid, to dry fast and to get a *thin* layer.

speed painting - painting *alla prima*

Painting on a wet surface is basically a matter of combining delicacy with a sure touch. A light hand is needed, because you must never press on the brush, drawing it over the surface as usual; you should think in terms of *depositing one layer of paint on another.* Paint this second layer —in another colour— gently and delicately, to avoid lifting the colour beneath or, even worse, mixing the new colour with the first. You need a sure touch because, when painting on a wet surface you can't have second thoughts; you paint with a chosen colour; you construct in a chosen way and what's done is done. If you want to go back, try again, retouch, repaint or reconstruct, you'll be lost. Painting on a wet surface demands plenty of easily spreadable paint and a well-loaded brush. If the area is very big you'll just have to scrape off the paint with a palette knife and start again. Use a soft brush and diluted paint for details like lines and so on —a branch or tree trunk for example. Either way, don't put pressure on the brush. Finally, when painting on a wet surface it's essential that the brush should be cleaned every time you take up new colour, or it will mix with the previous still-wet layer of paint.

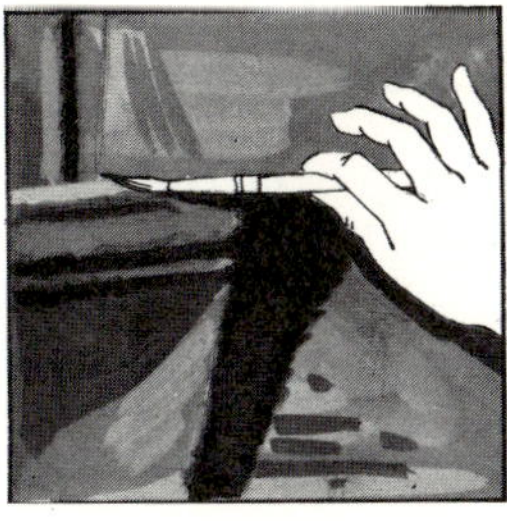

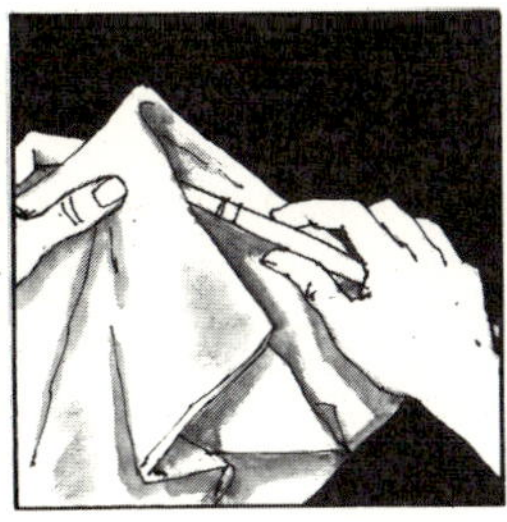

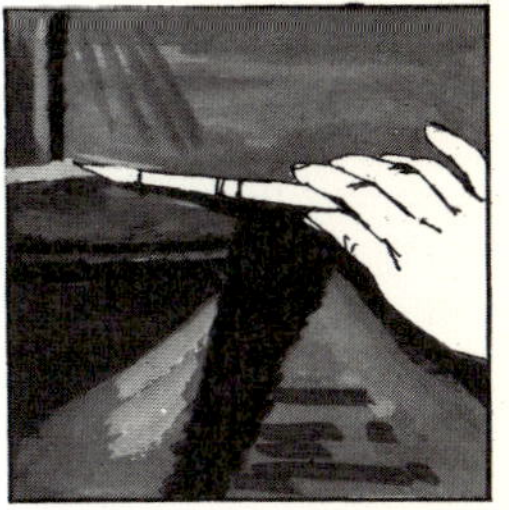

Fig. 243 A) First apply a touch of paint on top of the wet part using no pressure, slipping it gently on.

B) Next clean the brush with an old rag moistened with white spirit.

C) Take up more paint and paint again, without rubbing; apply the paint cleanly; be careful not to mix one colour with another.

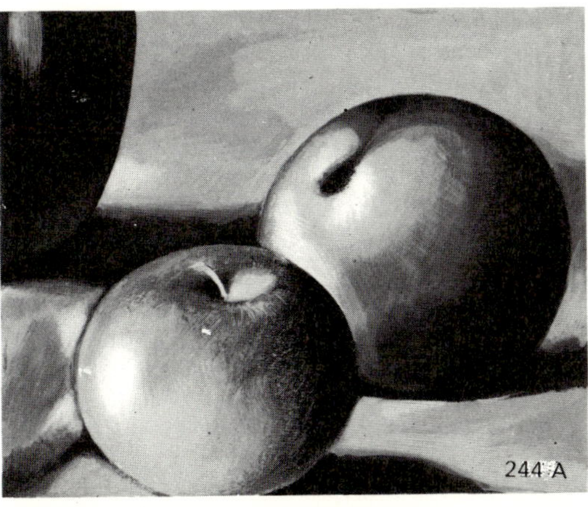

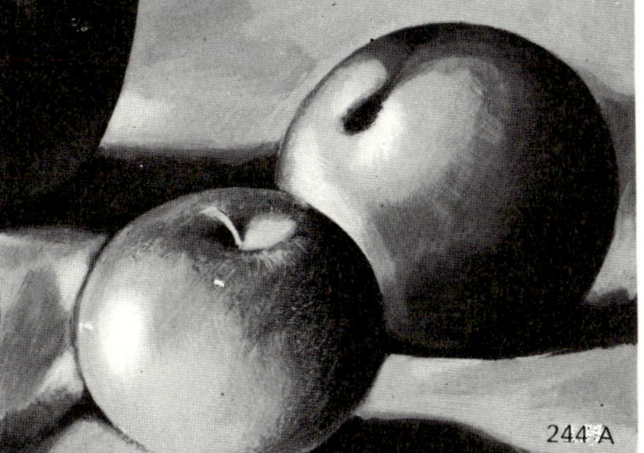

244 A

Fig. 244 A) A smooth, over-precise, too-correct finish makes the work lifeless —wax fruit and plastic flowers.

Fig. 244 B) This "unpolished" rendering is much pleasanter. It's rather imprecise, very much a quick impression, but it is fresh and spontaneous.

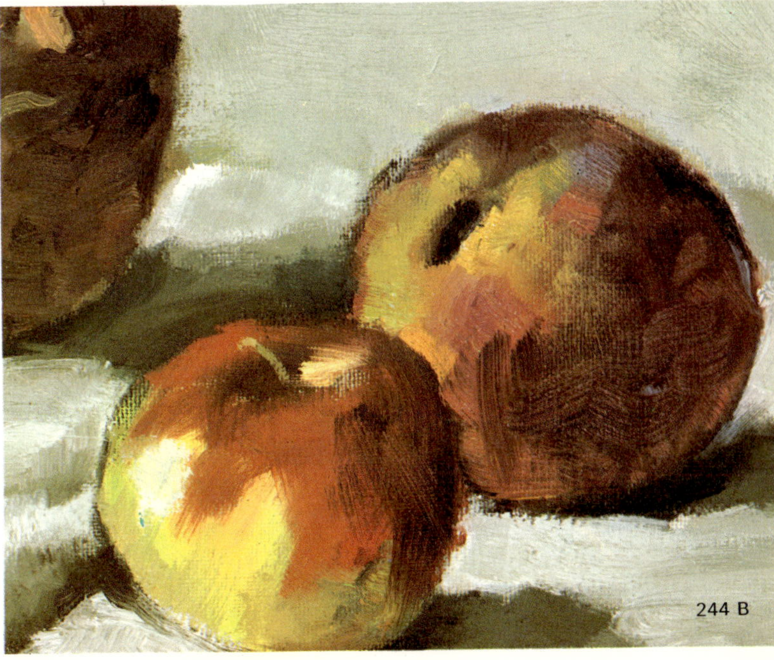

244 B

No man is perfect
I think the same applies to a picture. A "perfectly finished" picture is a lifeless picture. Absolutely perfect shaping, smoothing out, graduating shades of colour and correcting kills a work of art. Stop —don't finish it to perfection— you may finish it off! Fig. 244 B is a thousand times more agreeable than Fig. 244 A.

different techniques

Painting and drawing combined
Painting is very much more than colouring a drawing! This is especially the case with oil painting, where the initial drawing —if there was one – was lost after the first few brush strokes. Painting involves seeing colour and shape together; it's a question of painting with colour instead of with outlines and contours.

Figs. 245 A, B and C. Shape can be depicted with the paintbrush. You can use brush strokes to indicate the line of an object or to change width, height, angles or curves.

Figs. 246 A to F. The tip of the thumb applied gently or firmly is a useful means of making gradations, blending, or shifting contours. Titian used to do this. It is said that "he painted with his thumb and used his fingers to spread the paint and blend it into shades too subtle to define!" But be careful not to use this technique too much, or you may find your painting is becoming too "finished."

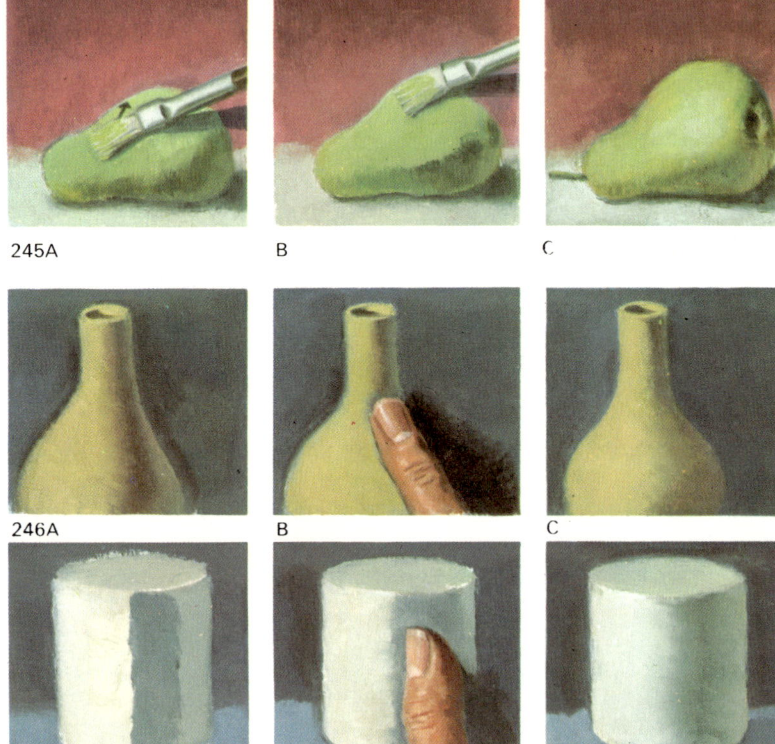

Figs. 247 A, B and C. Gradation of shades, transition from light to shade or a merging of different colours can be achieved in various ways.

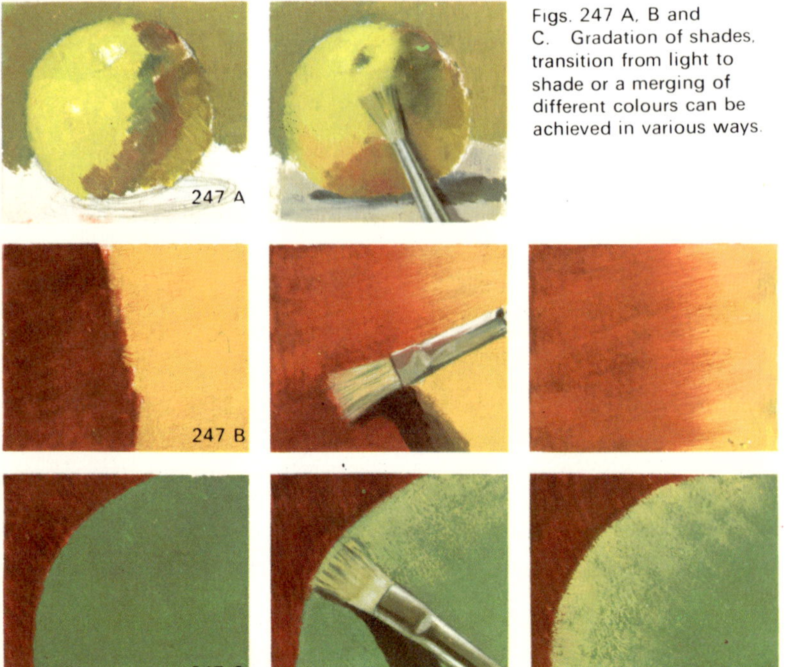

A) To merge two colours with shade variation you need a clean, unladen brush. Use it to make zigzag strokes where colours meet.
B) If the paint is very thick draw the brush from darker to lighter colour using quick, light strokes. *Warning:* after every stroke or two the brush must be dried, or the lighter-coloured paint will be marked with the darker colour.
C) If the area where you want to merge colour is dry or almost dry, you can simply take a brushful of fresh paint and rub, "scumbling" as this illustration shows.

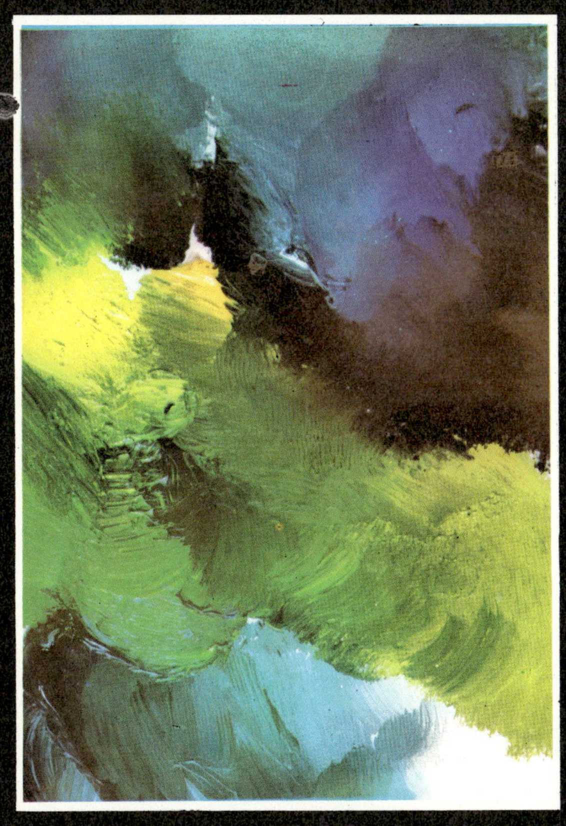

colour: its composition and its potential

mixing primary colours

Fig. 248. There are three basic colours which cannot be made from any others: yellow, magenta and blue green or cyan. These are the *primary colours* and, from mixtures of them (sometimes with the addition of white), all the colours in Nature can be obtained.

Fig. 249. In oil painting these three colours are called more precisely; 1. cadmium yellow; 2. rose madder deep; 3. prussian blue. As this illustration shows, *primary colours* mixed in pairs can make three additional colours: green, red and blue-violet or dark blue.

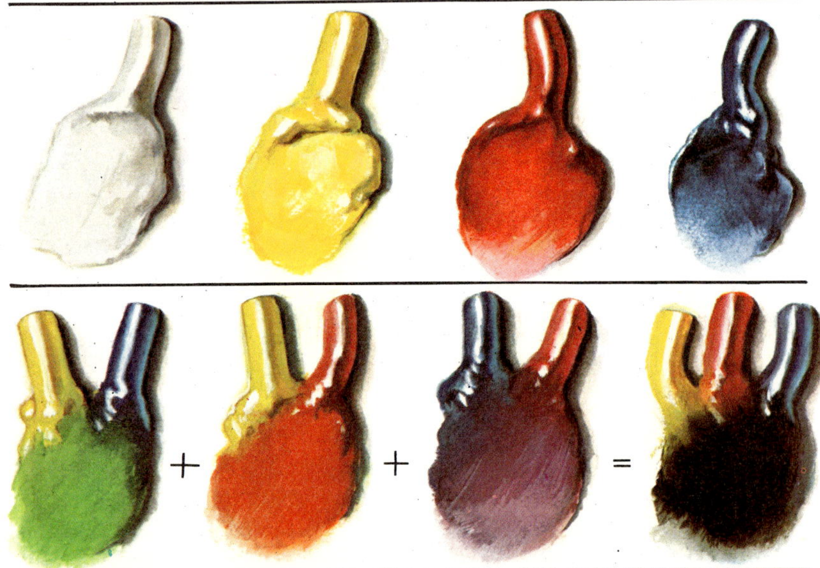

Fig. 250. Shows a range of colours based on a mixture of medium cadmium yellow and Prussian blue, giving a variety of greens.

Fig. 251. A mixture of medium cadmium yellow and dark madder lake gives a third colour, vermilion or vivid red, as well as a wide variety of pastel colours: pinks in warm and cool tones.

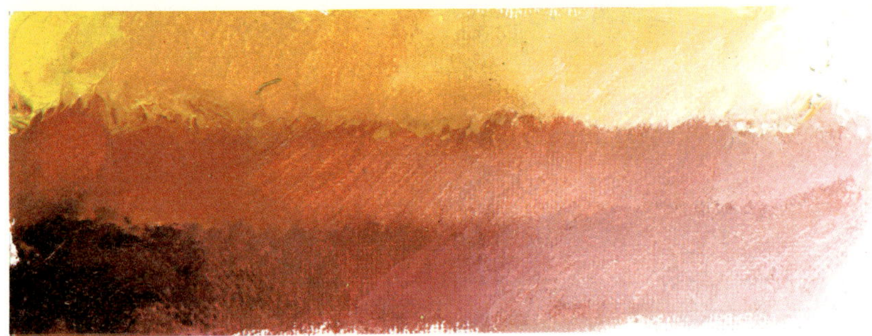

Fig. 252. Finally, by mixing Prussian blue and dark madder lake with white, we obtain a broad, rich range of blues, violets and purples.

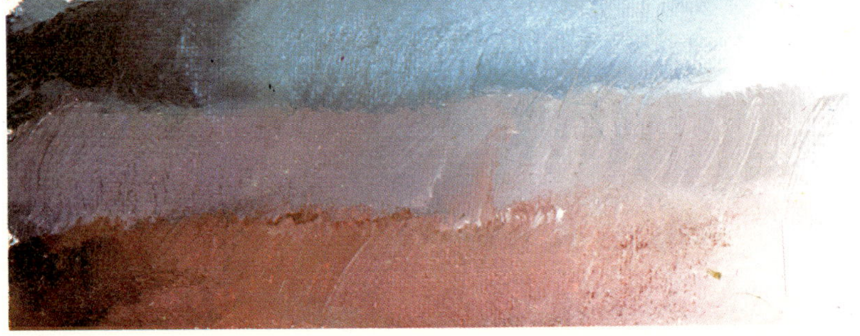

mixing primary colours

Fig. 253. This varied collection of colours has been obtained with the use of the *three primary colours* only. Try this test yourself! It will show you that all the colours in Nature can be made by mixing the primaries plus white. The illustrations below show the colours mixed for painting apples; one with broken tones.

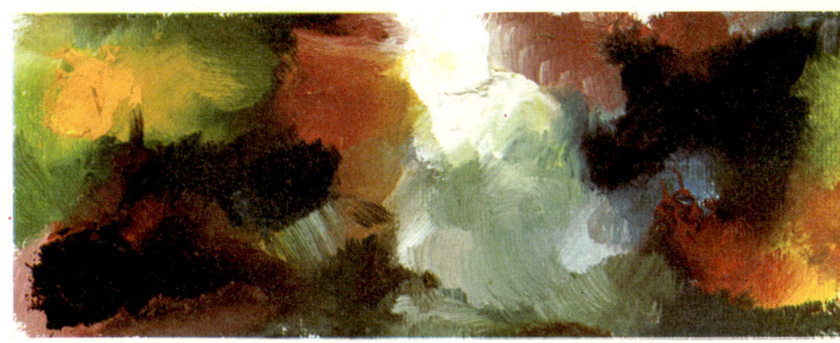

Fig. 254

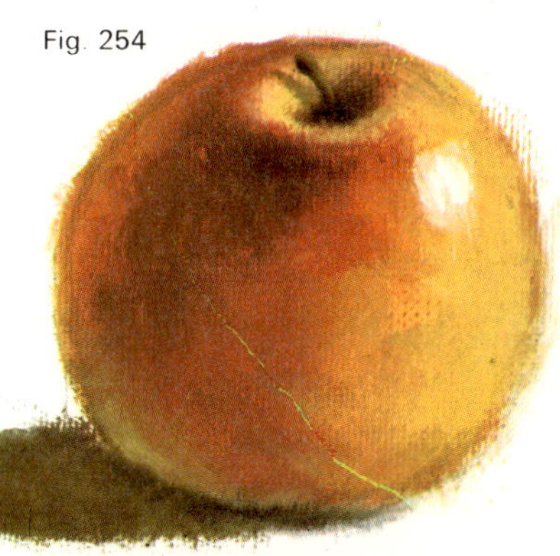

1. White, yellow, ochre, red, carmine.

2. Red, ochre, carmine.

3. Yellow, ochre, white, Prussian blue.

4. Yellow white, ochre, red.

5. Red, yellow, raw sienna.

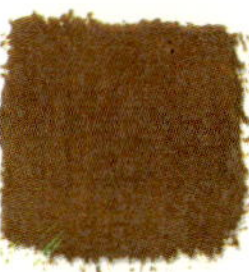

6. Ochre, yellow, red, viridian, white.

Fig. 255

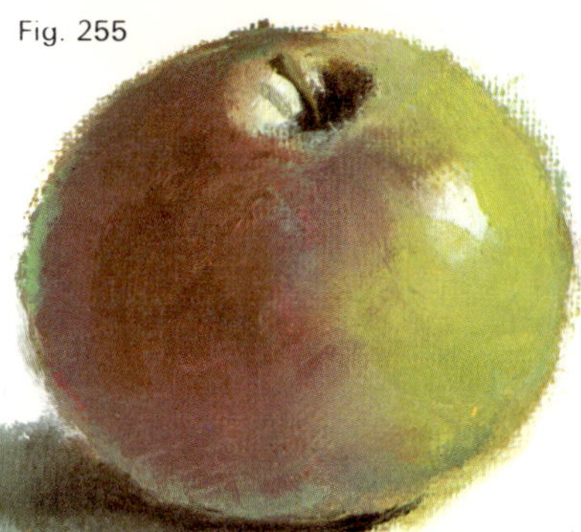

1. Viridian, white, yellow, cobalt blue.

2. Carmine, cobalt blue, Prussian blue, white.

3. Yellow, white green.

4. Mixture No. 3 with the addition of Prussian blue and raw sienna.

5. Carmine, white, cobalt blue, burnt sienna.

6. Prussian blue, umber, white.

Fig. 256

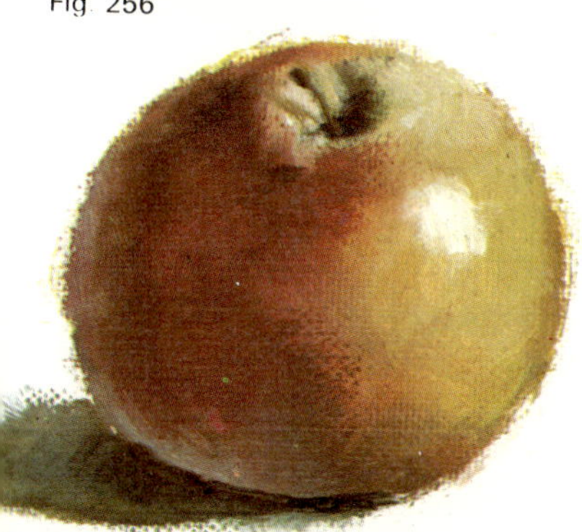

1. Burnt sienna, white, ultramarine blue.

2. Red, burnt sienna, umber.

3. Umber, lemon yellow, white.

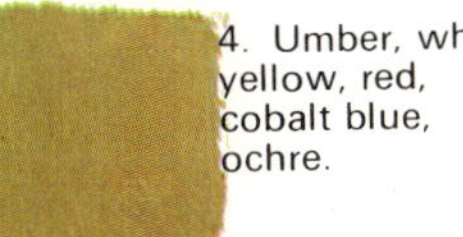

4. Umber, white, yellow, red, cobalt blue, ochre.

5. Carmine, viridian, white, Prussian blue.

6. Umber, ultramarine blue, white.

light colours and dark colours

Neutral black, cool black and warm black
Fig. 257. By mixing rose madder deep Prussian blue and burnt umber, you can make, according to proportion, a neutral black, a cool black —i.e. bluish, or a warm black— one with a reddish tinge. These shades of black are very useful, since they are right for a work painted in warm shades or cool shades.

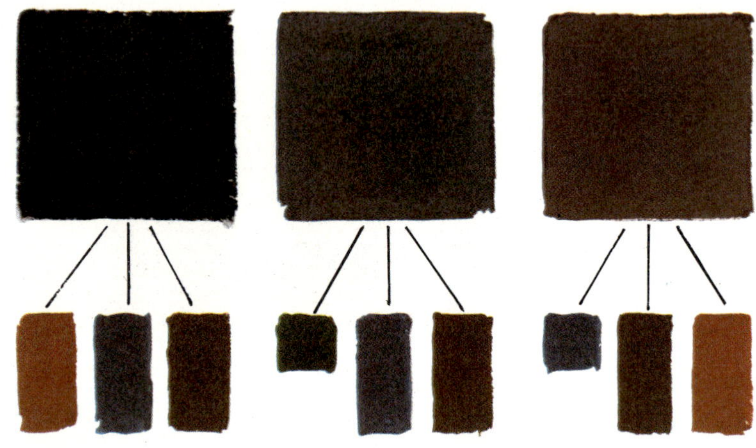

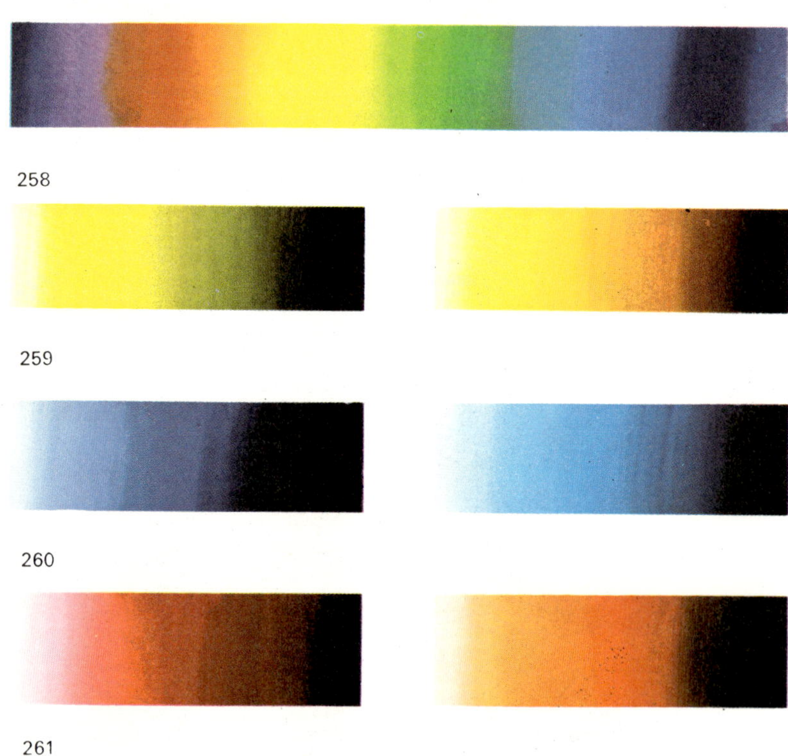

Adding black is only one way of darkening colours
Fig. 258. When you want to darken or intensify a colour, remember the rainbow in which there is no black.

Fig. 259. If yellow is darkened with black alone the result is a dirty greenish yellow; if it is darkened progressively with red, carmine, blue and black, a more natural range of intensity and change from light to shadow occurs.

Figs. 260 and 261. Similar results are obtained with the colours blue and red: the former has a marked bias towards grey when darkened with black alone; the latter loses the brilliant colours which come from lightening it with yellow and white or darkening it with carmine and violet, burnt umber and black.

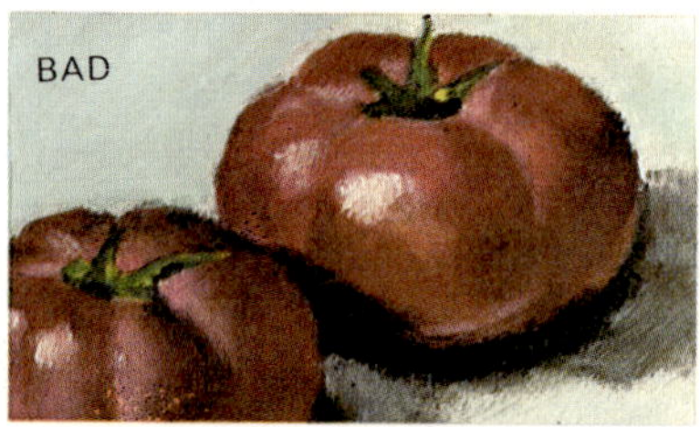

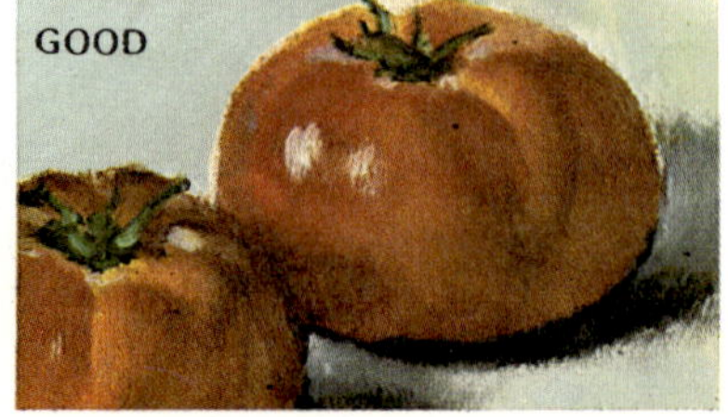

Fig. 262. Demonstration of the use and abuse of both white and black. The tomatoes on the left (BAD) have been painted with red, white and black only. In the tomatoes on the right (GOOD) more colours were added: yellow, ochre, sienna, blue, green and carmine, and just the right amount of white.

the colour of shadows

Fig. 263. **There is blue in every shadow**
Whatever the colour of your subject, there's bound to be some blue in the shadowed part. This applies even if the model is entirely bathed in light and is white, as in this cube, the shadow of which is grey —but with a blue tinge.

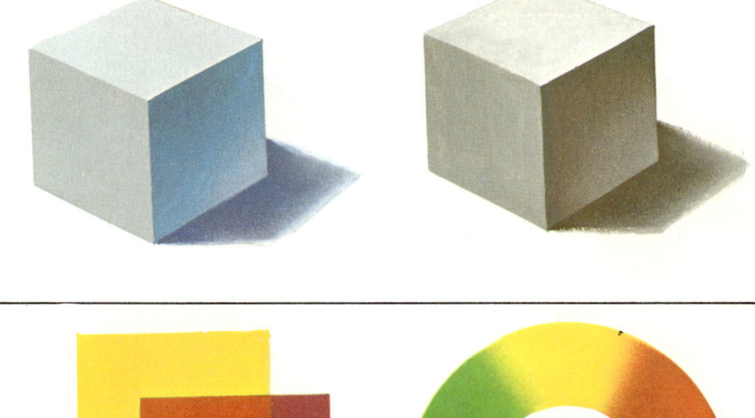

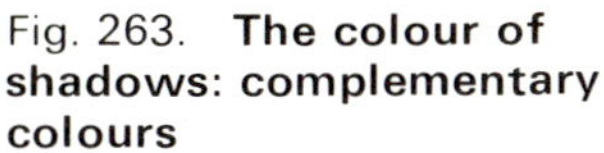

Fig. 263. **The colour of shadows: complementary colours**
The colour of shadows contains not only blue, but also the object's complementary colour. Remember that a complementary colour is one that mixed with a primary gives grey. eg. magenta is complementary to green, cyan to red, etc.

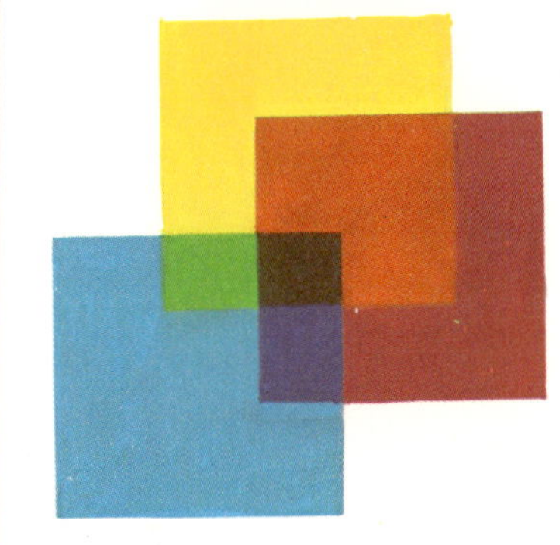

Yellow, magenta and cyan blue are primary colours. Mixed together in pairs they give the secondary colours: green, red and blue violet.

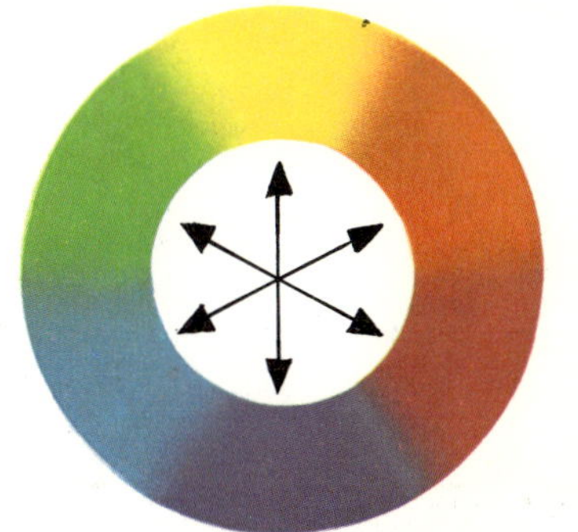

To find out which colours are complementary to which, range the six colours of the rainbow in order on a colour wheel as shown. You'll see, for example, that the complement of yellow is blue. (1)

Fig. 265. A formula for the colour of shadows:
1. The darkest colour of the object +
2. The complementary colour +
3. blue
= **the colour of the shadow.**

1 + 2 + 3 =

Fig. 266. The rule is almost infallible: The shadow colour of a red tomato is composed of dark sienna, brilliant green and luminous blue.

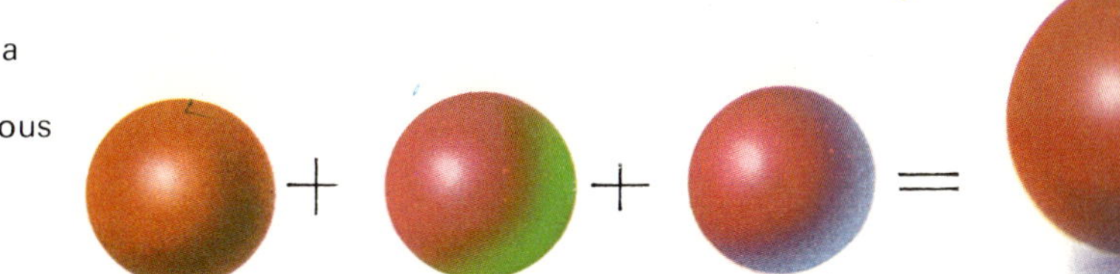

Fig. 267. The shadow colour of something blue is basically violet, i.e. the combination of cyan and magenta.

(1) For further information see *Painting* in this series.

the warm range

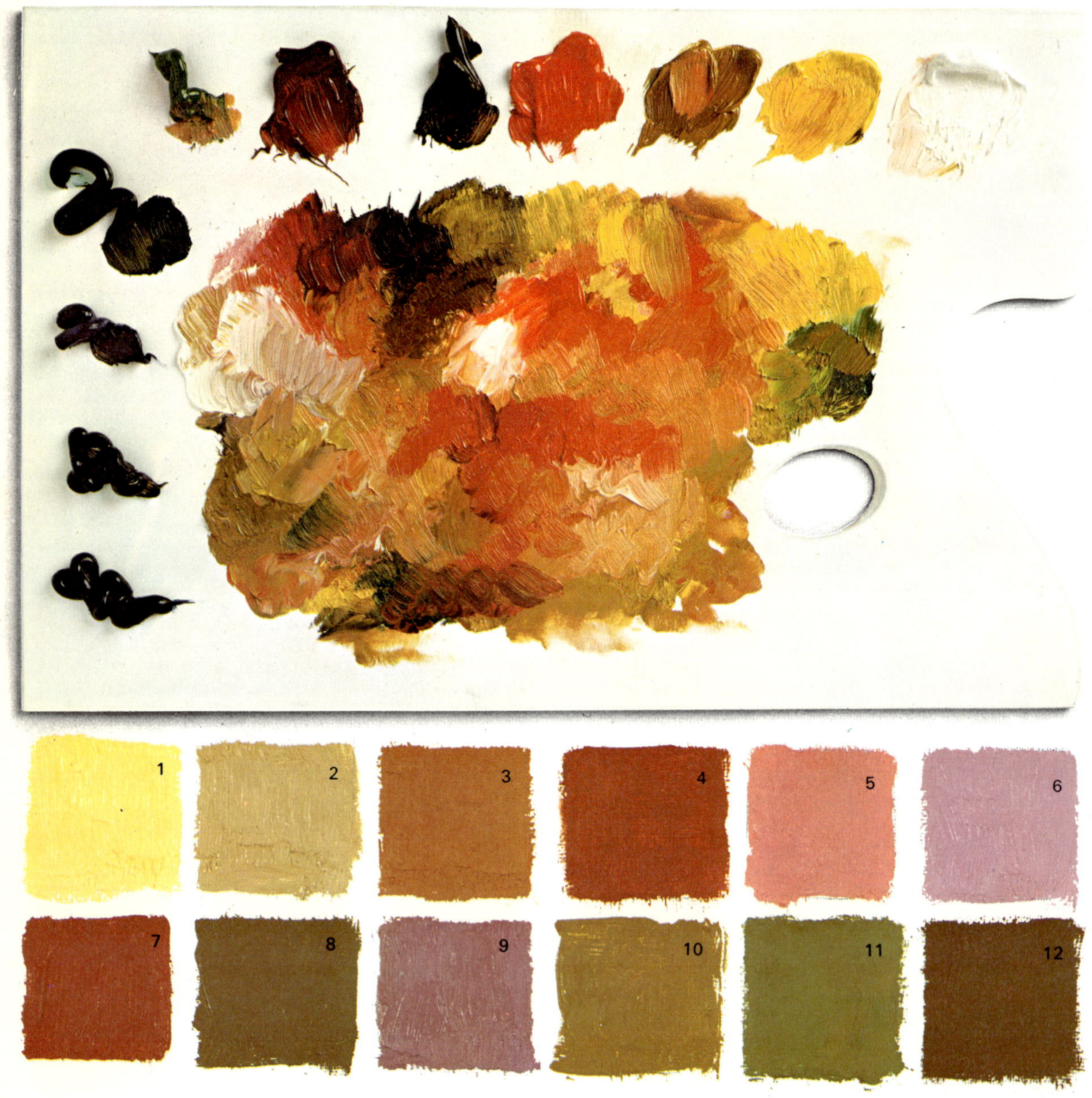

Fig. 268. Yellow, ochre, raw sienna, orange, red, carmine, burnt sienna, green... plus white: this page shows a sample of the infinite range of colours that can be composed in the warm range. See whether you can mix this set of colours.

1. White + cadmium yellow.

2. White + yellow ochre.

3. White + yellow ochre + cadmium red.

4. Cadmium yellow + rose madder deep.

5. White + cadmium red.

6. White + rose madder deep.

7. Raw sienna + cadmium red.

8. Yellow ochre + burnt umber + a touch of cadmium green.

9. White + yellow ochre + viridian + rose madder.

10. Cadmium yellow + burnt umber.

11. Yellow ochre + viridian + cadmium yellow + white.

12. Rose madder + a touch of viridian.

the cool range

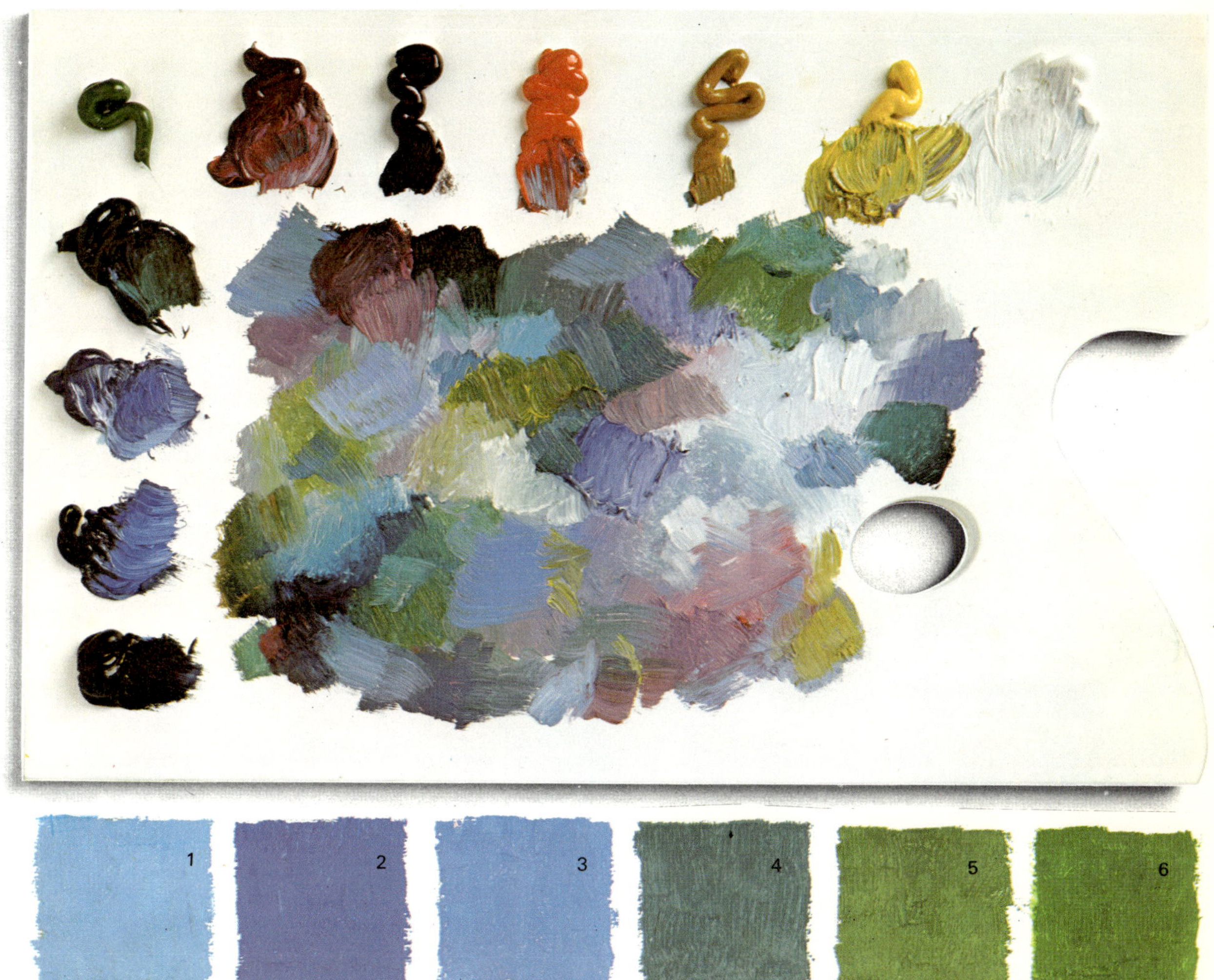

Fig. 269. **Light green, viridian, sky blue, dark blue, violet...** plus white: this page shows an example of colour mixtures, using basically greens, blues and violets.

1. White + Prussian blue.

2. White + "new" blue.

3. White + cobalt blue.

4. White + Prussian blue + viridian.

5. White + viridian + a touch of yellow ochre + a touch of cadmium yellow.

6. Cadmium yellow + viridian.

7. Cadmium yellow + Prussian blue.

8. White + viridian.

9. White + rose madder + "new" blue.

10. Prussian blue + white + rose madder.

11. Yellow ochre + viridian + a touch of white.

12. Prussian blue + viridian.

the range of broken tones

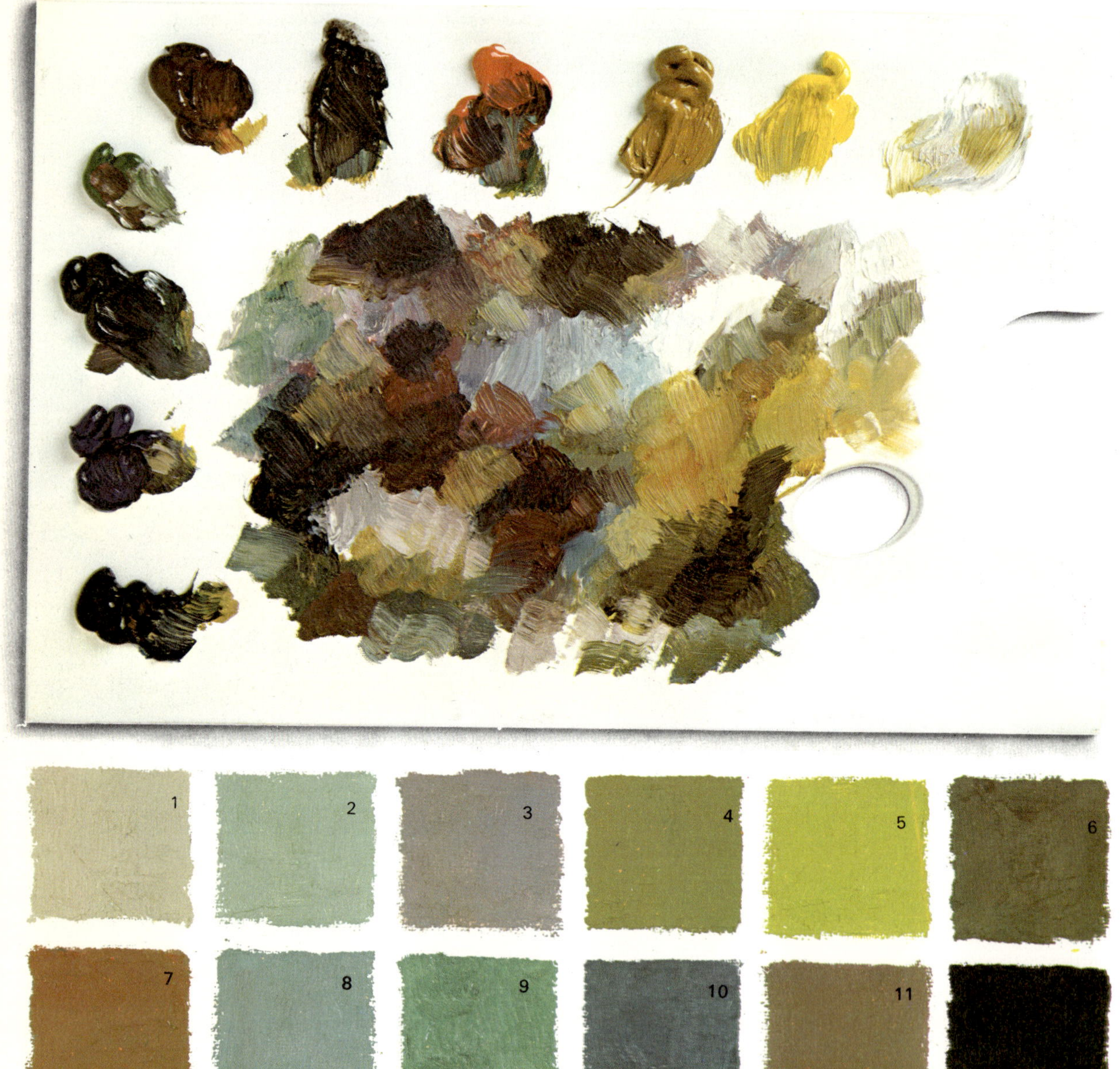

Fig. 270. ...or mixtures of complementary colours in unequal proportions... plus white. Here are some examples:

1. White + burnt umber + a tiny bit of Prussian blue.

2. Same as 1, plus a touch of viridian.

3. White + cobalt blue + cadmium red.

4. White + yellow ochre + "new" blue.

5. Cadmium yellow + white + cobalt blue + a touch of cadmium red.

6. White + Prussian blue + raw sienna + cadmium red.

7. White + rose madder + cadmium red + Prussian blue.

8. White + rose madder + viridian.

9. White + burnt umber + viridian.

10. Prussian blue + white + cadmium red.

11. White + rose madder + ultramarine blue + a touch of burnt umber.

12. Burnt umber + a touch of Prussian blue.

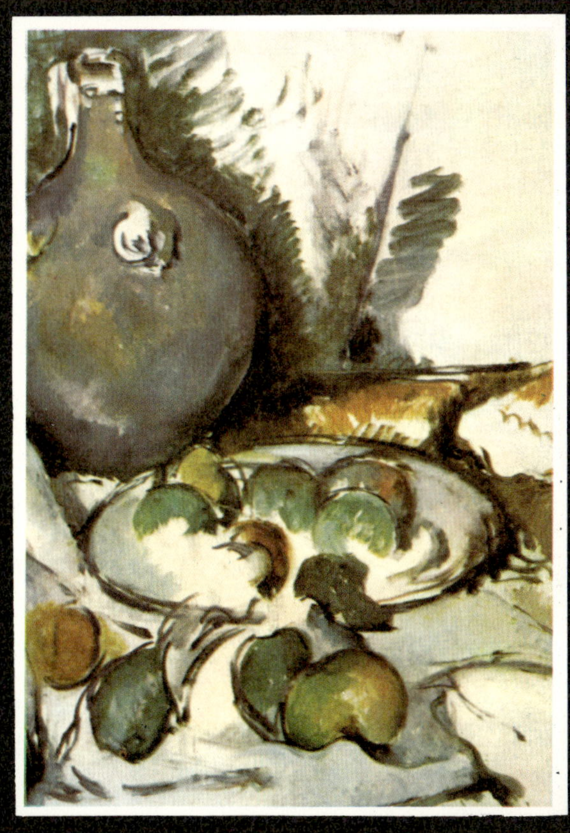

how *you* can
paint a still
life in oils

cézanne, the great master

We'll put all these suggestions into practice in a moment, but first let's have a look at some examples from the great master of this genre, Cézanne.

Any painter in this field, whether he/she be amateur or professional, can learn a very great deal from reading about Cézanne's methods and, of course, by making a study of his work. Let's analyse a few of his still lifes painted with oils and see what we can learn from them.

How Cézanne dealt with composition

Cézanne painted dozens of still lifes with fruit. He used basic items such as a white tablecloth and a plate or bowl of fruit, which he would put in the centre of his composition; he often used a bottle, some pottery or china and a pitcher, which he placed beside the fruit so that these two items would form the picture's focal point. There might be other pieces of

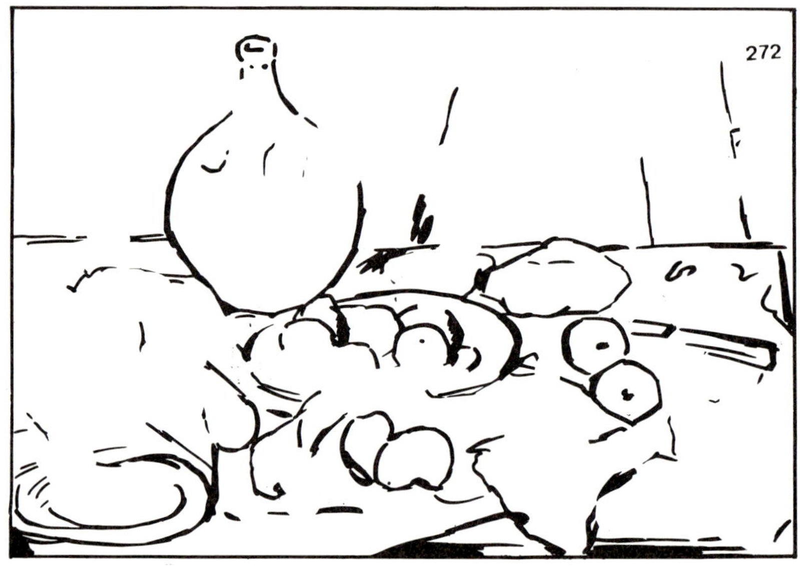

Fig. 272. It seems likely that Cézanne began his still lifes with practically no preliminary drawing. There is an unfinished painting of his *Still life with pitcher* in the Tate Gallery, London (Fig. 273, below). A reconstruction of the initial drawing indicated that this was a quick sketch in which the shapes were hardly defined at all.

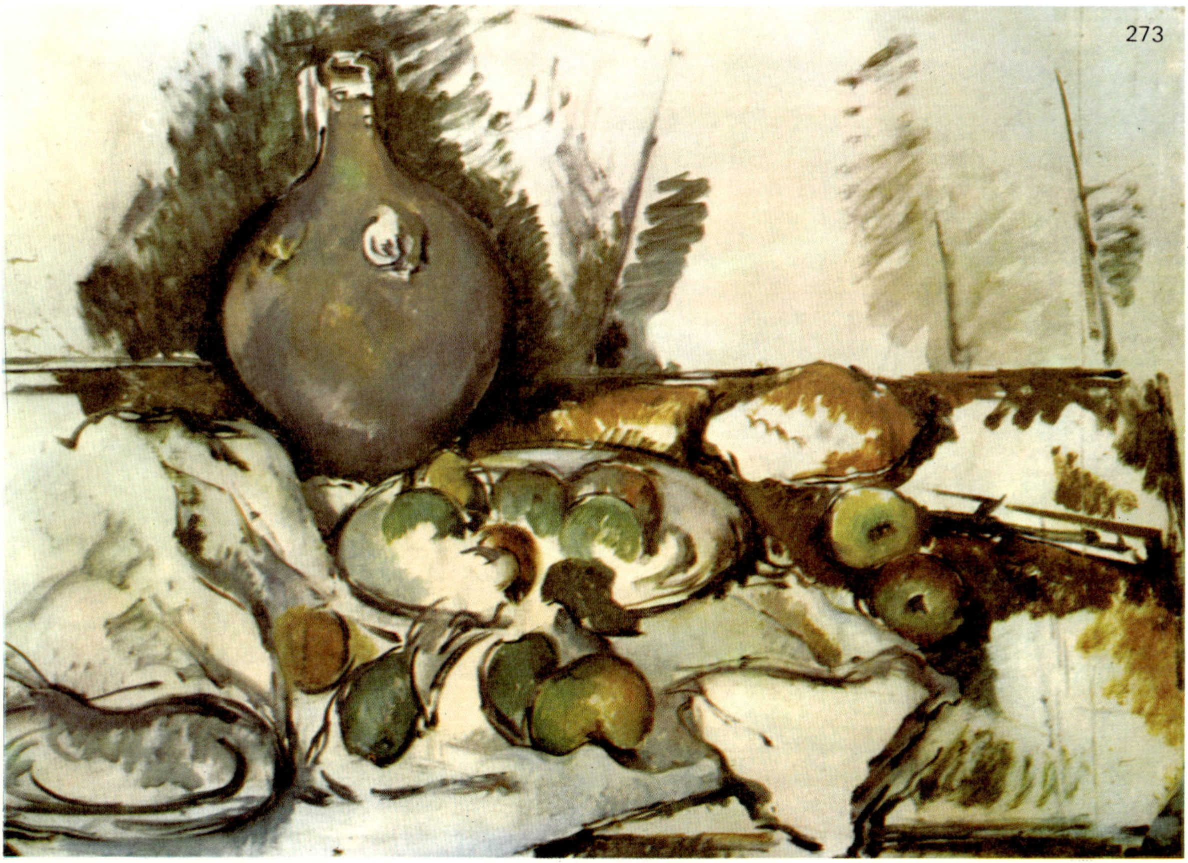

cézanne, the great master

fruit and often some fabric or a curtain as a backcloth.

His viewpoint tended to be quite high and he rendered the different shapes very freely and sometimes quite imprecisely. Cézanne took his time over the composition of a still life. "An artist cannot evoke feelings as readily as a bird sings" he commented. "An artist has to compose; it isn't easy."

Cézanne's way of painting

A farm worker who has watched both Pissarro and Cézanne at work said: "When Mr. Pissarro paints, he pecks; he does it in dabs with the paint-brush. Mr. Cézanne rubs and caresses; he paints with the brush flat."

Cézanne never lingered in one part or another of a painting, unlike many artists, who will perhaps continue working on the background until it is almost finished. He would wander about over the picture, painting here and there, not stopping to finish anything, but leaving everything incomplete, seeing and painting the picture as a whole, without rushing and without stopping.

The unfinished picture in the Tate Gallery, featuring the grey pitcher-like pottery vessel helps us to understand Cézanne's infallible way of working on the whole picture at once.

The first thing we notice is that Cézanne did not draw a precise preliminary sketch: he found it enough to put in a few rough lines for a very rapid impression (Fig. 272), moving quickly on to colour. He did not paint a first coat of colour, just a few quick touches of paint thinned with turpentine —see the plates and the tablecloth. In general, he painted from the outset with the actual required colour and with the final thickness of paint. In the grey jar, for example, there are scarcely any second touches. Using the rapid painting technique, he painted the main elements early, avoiding errors of simultaneous contrasts by balancing and adjusting colours accordingly (see P. 93 where Figs. 229 and 230 illustrate the law of simultaneous contrasts).

Looking at Fig. 273, it's quite easy to imagine Cézanne working on the plums on the dish in the middle of the table, starting to paint them, switching to the two plums on the right, moving on to the brown background of the table around those two plums,

Fig. 274. *Still life with peaches and pears.* Pushkin Museum of Fine Art, Moscow. Look carefully at the composition of this still life and compare it with the unfinished painting on the opposite page. You'll see that it adheres to Cézanne's formula for the composition of a still life —with a plate or bowl of fruit in the centre surrounded by other fruit, plus a jug, pot or some other piece of pottery or china beside the focal point.

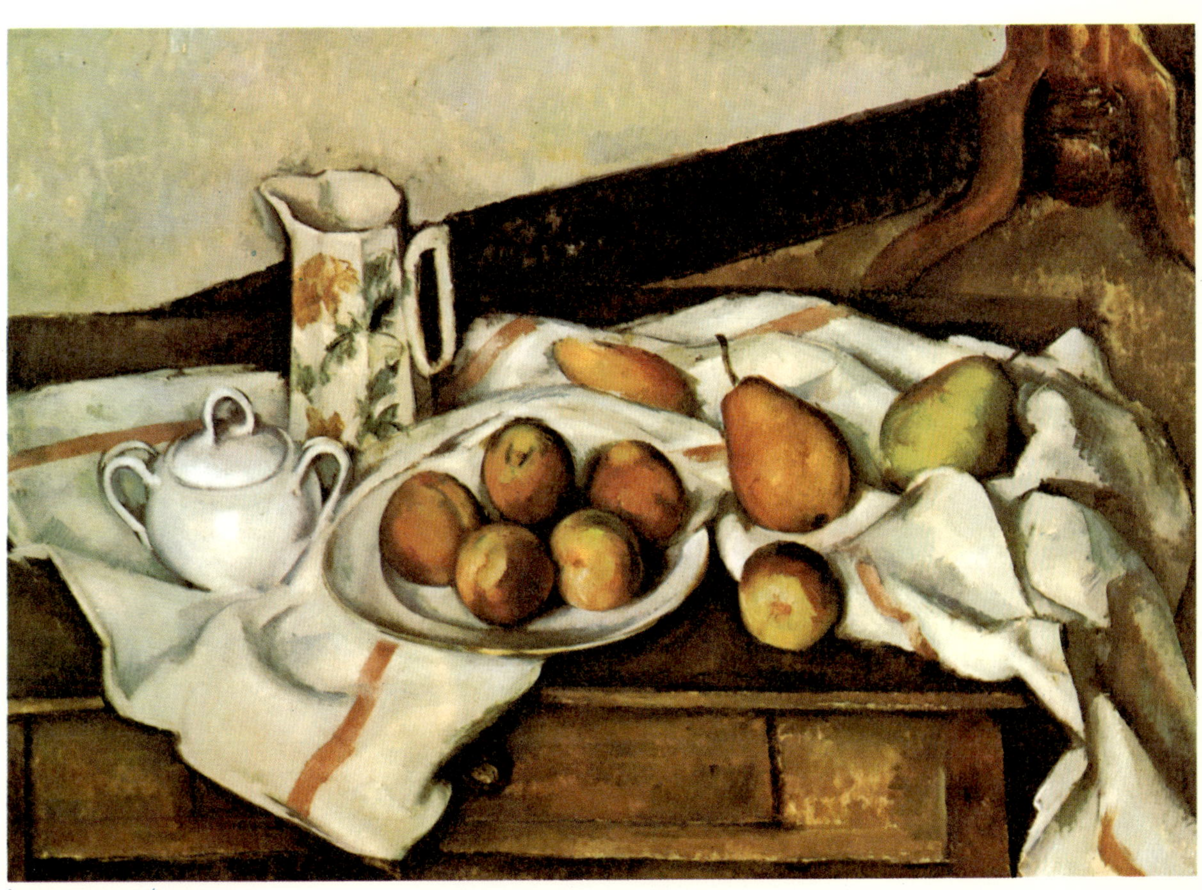

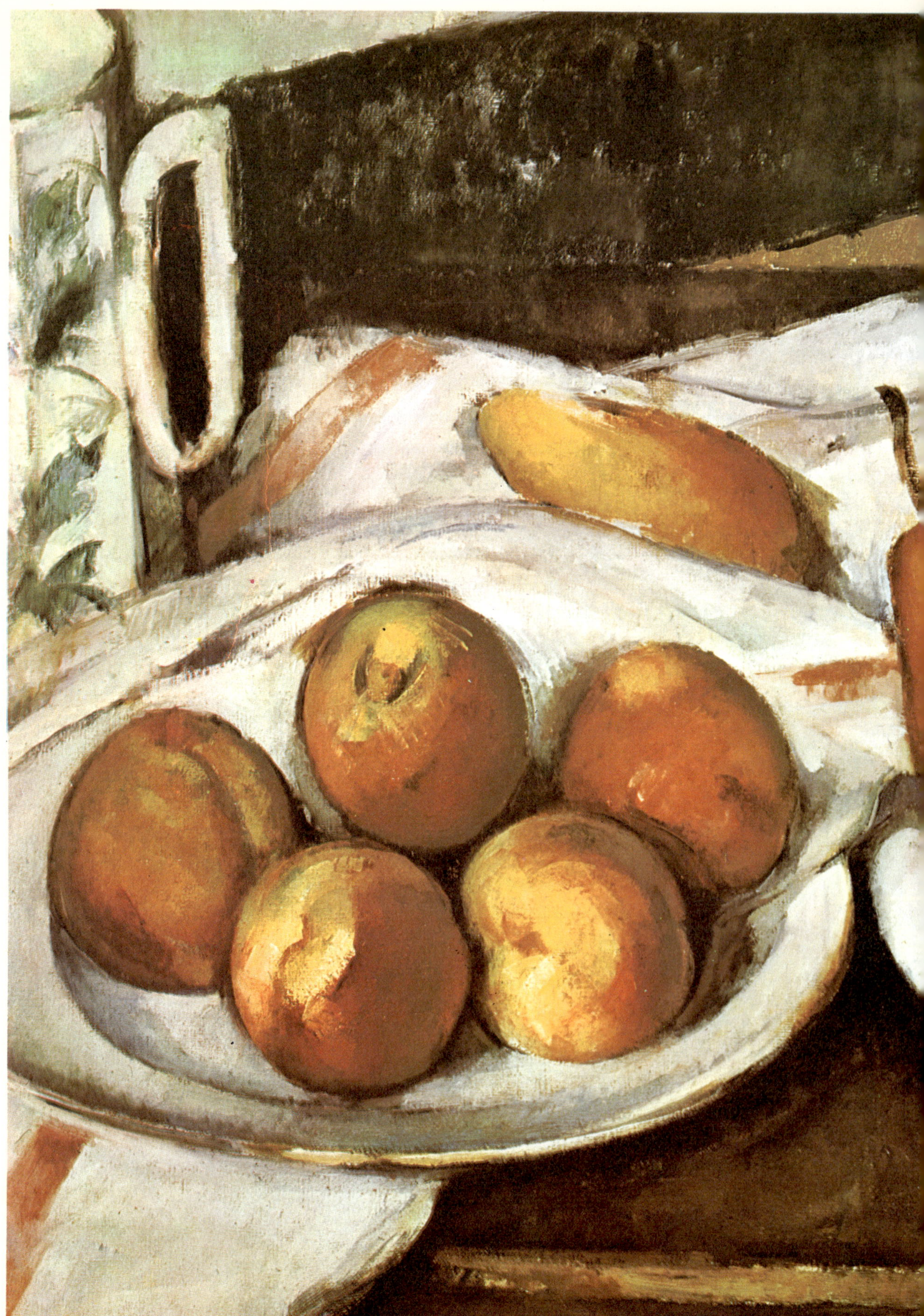

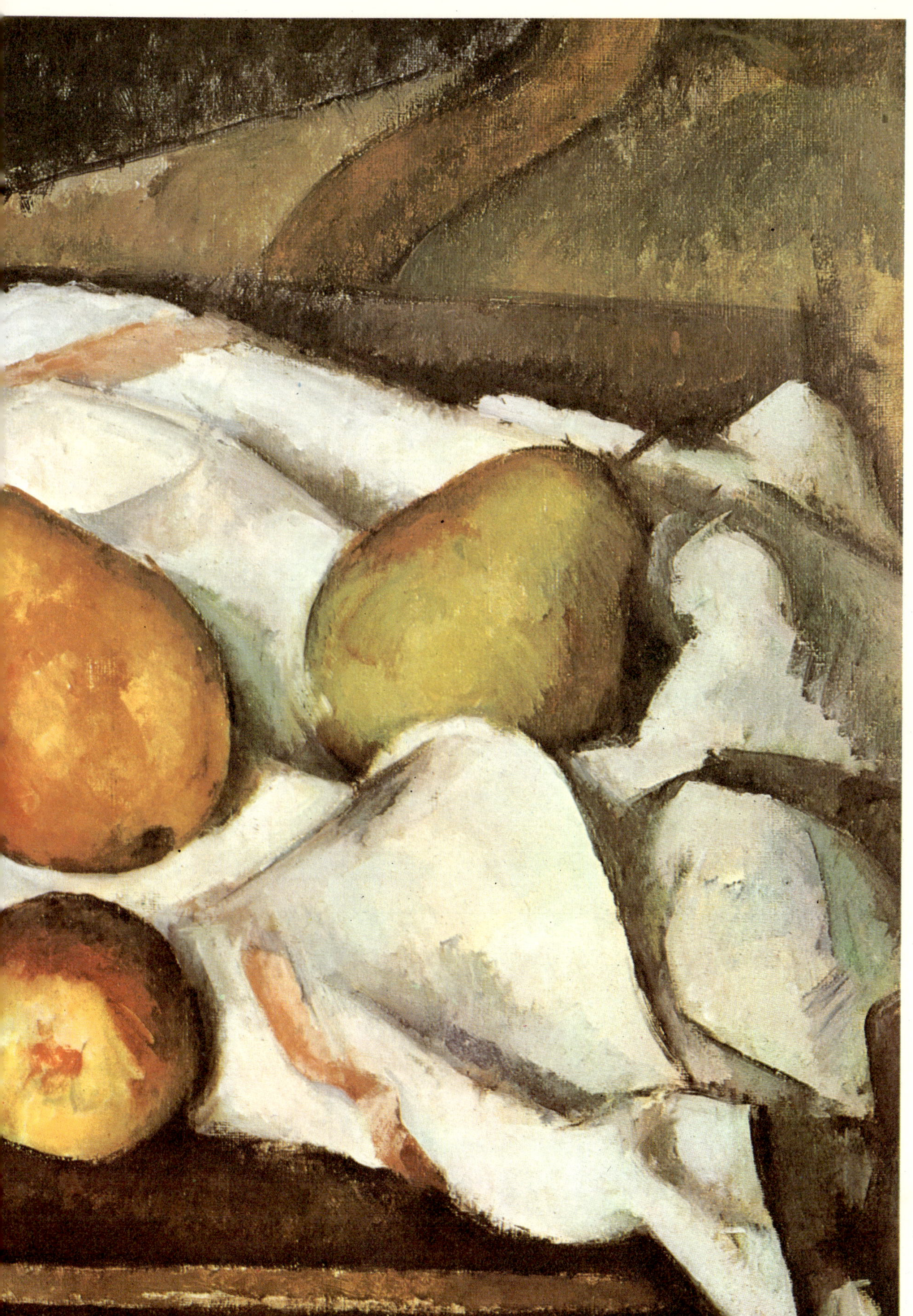

275

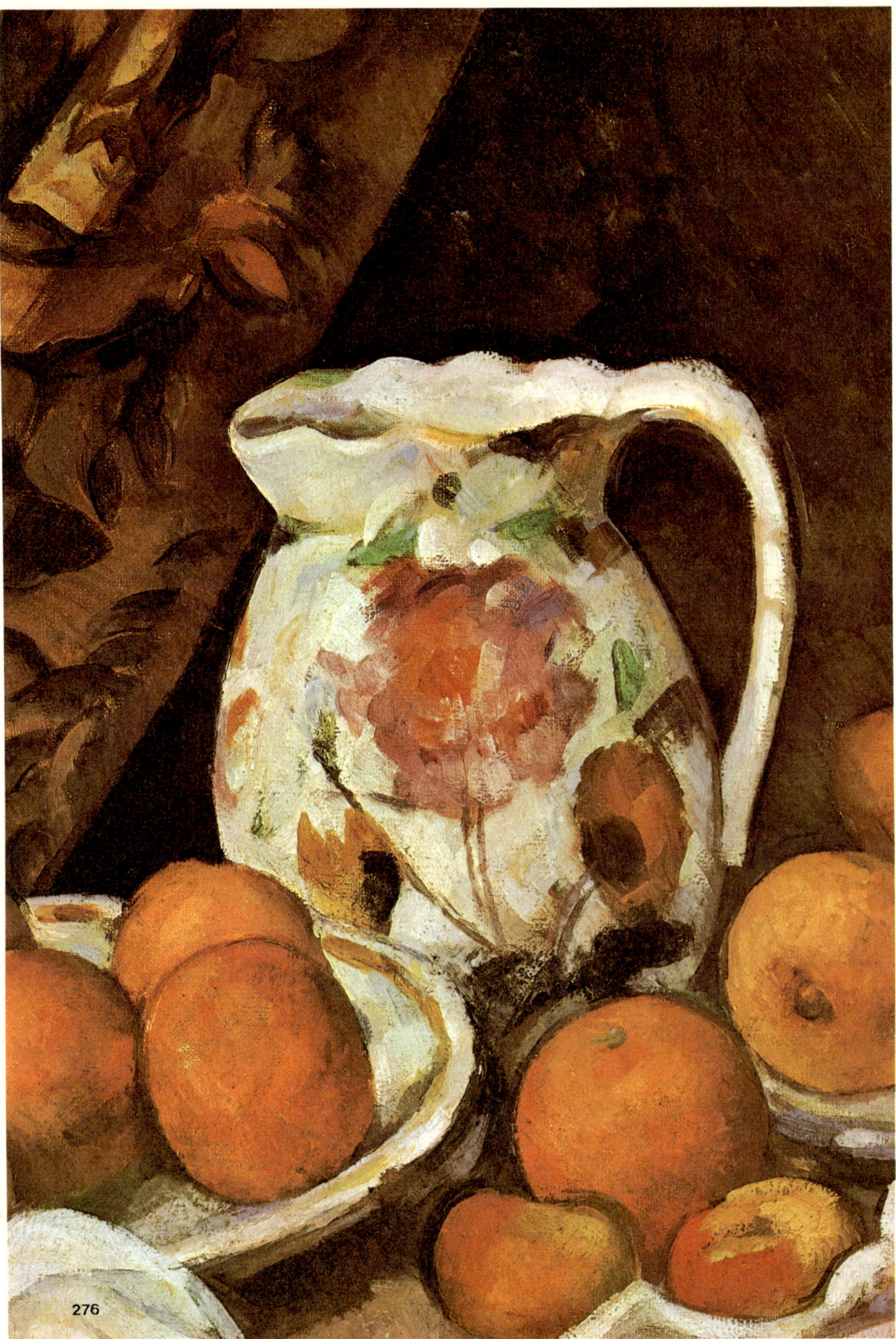
276

returning to the plate in the centre, jumping to the pitcher, to the background, to the foreground and so on. Pierre Bonnard, who was a friend of Cézanne's, said that Cézanne was one of the few artists who could spend a whole evening painting from a model without being taken over by it. In other words, Cézanne stuck to his original interpretation of the model.
Perhaps this method of painting, this rapid moving to and fro over the picture, enabled Cézanne to look at his picture as objectively as he studied his model.

Cézanne's exceptional skill: interpretation

This is very important. Cézanne was one of the few Impressionist painters, possibly the only one, to look carefully at his model, receive a first impression of shape, colour, contrast, light and highlights, begin to paint and be able to hang on to that first impression. Pierre Bonnard has described what happens: "The presence of the model is a fatal temptation: the artist is in danger of being led astray by its closeness, which may drag him away from his initial conception." Bonnard goes on to make his point: "Not long ago I tried to make a direct painting of some roses, with the model in front of me —but I let myself be carried away by details. I was soon out of my depth: I realized I was getting nowhere, that I was lost and could never recapture my initial feelings, that first impression which had dazzled me so!"
Bonnard continued: "It's vital that one discovers a way of fending off the influence of the model." Apparently Cézanne did it like this: before he began to paint, he would gaze at the model for a long time and construct the picture in his mind; he used his creative gift to form the image, drawing inspiration from the model. Then, when he saw his picture in his mind's eye, he began to paint with what the English painter and writer John Berger described as "that heroic self-discipline, that extraordinary capacity for looking at his picture and watching its development just as critically and objectively as he studied his model. It was as if he were all the time saying to himself 'this is it, this is how *I* see it'." Summing up, John Berger wrote: "He makes it look easy. Easy indeed! About as easy as walking on water."

How Cézanne created contrast

Cézanne sought out colour contrast: a green pear beside a red, both pears on a white tablecloth and the cloth on the dark wood of an old table (Fig. 274). Not content with this, when he came to paint, Cézanne used tricks to accentuate contrast. Have a look at pages 110 and 111 where we show a detail, almost actual size, from *Still life with peaches and pears.* You'll notice Cézanne's preoccupation with outline —how he has accentuated the shapes of the peaches on the dish, the lines of the jug and the edges of the tablecloth, using streaks of colour, or a darker colour to bring out shapes and contrast. It's fascinating to see how he "wraps up" the green pear, showing its shape by the direction of his brush strokes. You can see the thickness of the paint very thin at the back, not even covering the canvas completely, but thicker on the pears and peaches. Here's a wonderful example of the rapid painting technique, a picture completed in a single session; notice the zigzag strokes conveying values and shadows in the tablecloth and the constant variation of colour. And that's something worth further discussion.

Cézanne's use of colour diversity

The detail opposite, reproduced almost actual size, is from Cézanne's *Still life with curtain.* The painter has made use of an extraordinarily wide variety of colours and tints —look at just one orange, for example. See how Cézanne applies the orange paint, later adding red, an "orangey" yellow, light red, dark vermilion and sienna. Then the jar. Isn't it amazing? The flower in the centre has an apparently infinite assortment of pinks, creams and lilacs. If you look carefully at the white parts of the jug, you'll notice the remarkably beautiful range of colours. How did he do it? Probably not with the use of any *special* technique —the answer boils down to hard work. Cézanne was a tremendous worker and never satisfied; he worked with ceaseless energy. One of his biographers, the Russian, Barskaya, wrote that: "sometimes he took a palette knife and scraped off a complete hard day's work; on two or three occasions he was so exasperated that he threw the painting out of the window." In August 1906, six weeks before his death, Cézanne wrote to his great friend Émile Bernard: "I continue to study Nature all around me and I think I am making a little progress. I feel very lonely; I am old and sick, but I have vowed that I will die painting."

From theory to practice, 2

Let's go on and actually paint some still lifes in oils. The exercises which follow are based on three still lifes painted for this book by the author. In each case there is an illustrated step-by-step guide to the work, from the preliminary drawing right through to the completed picture. The first painting is on classical lines and, to some extent, reminiscent of Cézanne's work; the second is a still life painted by artificial light; it includes notes on dealing with the problems of glass —how to use oil paints for glass bottles and containers; the third is a still life carried out using the speed-painting technique and painted in a single session, in just over three hours.
We hope that you will find these exercises helpful and enjoyable, as a way of summing up the book as a whole. If you can practise this sort of thing in your spare time, you should soon be able to accomplish a great deal more in the field of oil painting.

step-by-step painting no. 1

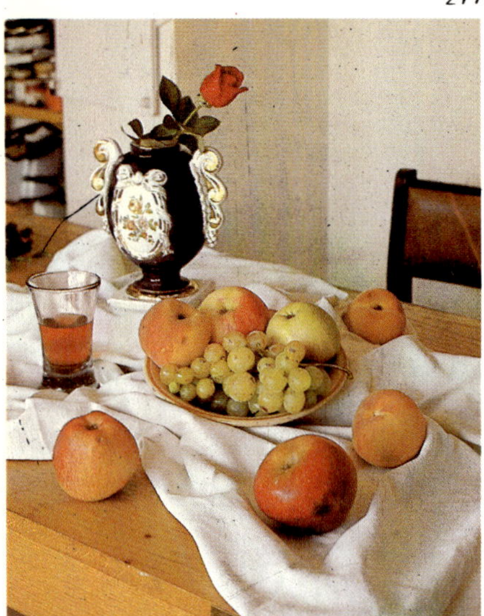

277

Fig. 277. The subject: a red rose in an ornamental porcelain vase, a bowl of fruit, a glass of wine, three peaches and an apple, all arranged about a white tablecloth draped unevenly over a wooden table. The background shows some furniture and a framed picture. This is a Cézanne-type subject. The composition and colours are similar to those in his paintings.

Preliminary drawing (Fig. 278)
This charcoal sketch just indicated the shape and position of each component. If you compare it with Fig. 277 you'll notice two significant changes: (a) the apple in the foreground, on the bare table, has changed in shape and position; it's a different apple; (b) that the peach by the chair at the back has vanished. This is because my subject was originally as sketched here, but I thought I could improve on it by changing the apple in the foreground and adding a peach at the back.

Study of light and shade (Fig. 279)
This sketch is more detailed than the first —the structure is more definitely established now. The various sections of mass (the parts making up the composition) have been studied and one can judge the overall balance of light and shade. When the sketch was completed, a spray fixative was applied to fix the charcoal before painting was begun.

Stage I (Figs. 280 and 285)
The picture's development at the end of the first stage can be seen better in Fig. 285 further on, but it's interesting to have a look at Fig. 280 which shows that I began by painting in the masses at the back, the grey parts of the tablecloth and the dark sienna of the table; this has got rid of the big empty spaces, making it easier to adjust the colour.

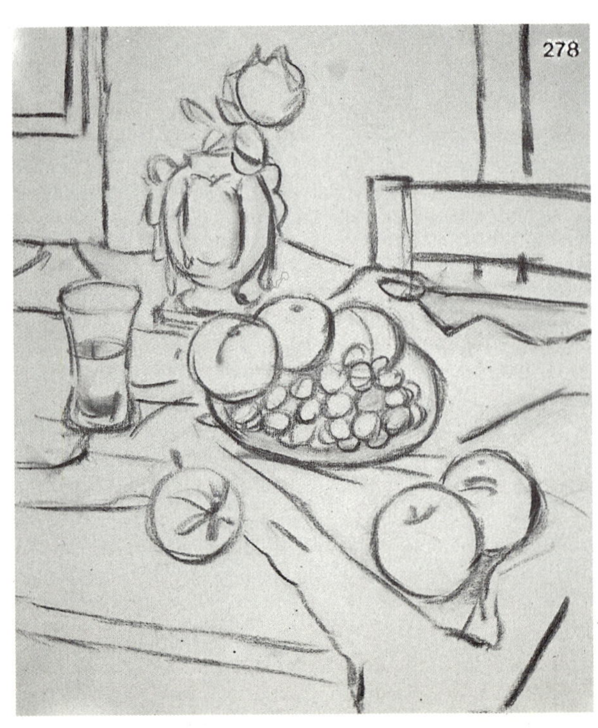

278

step-by-step painting no. 1

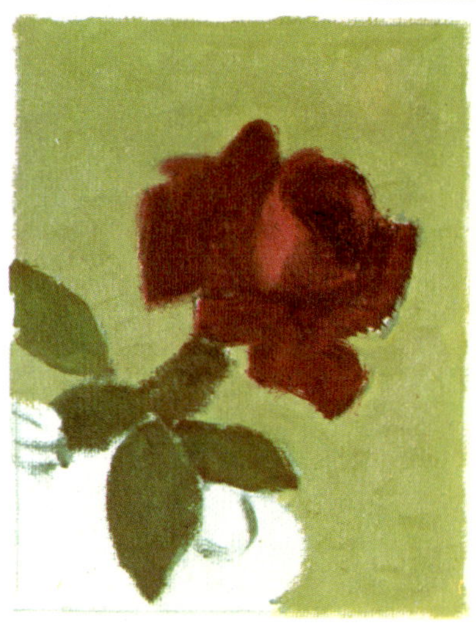

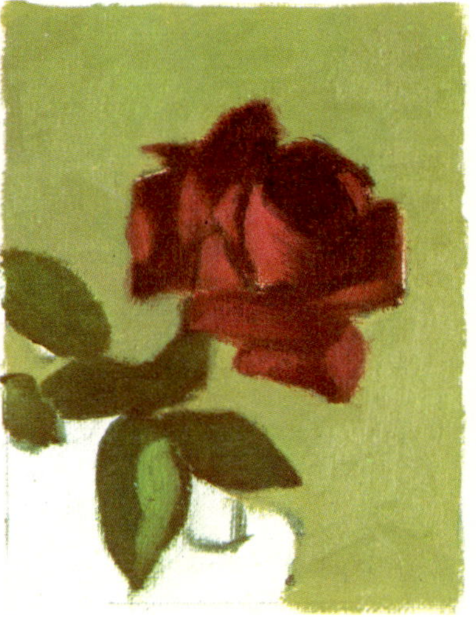

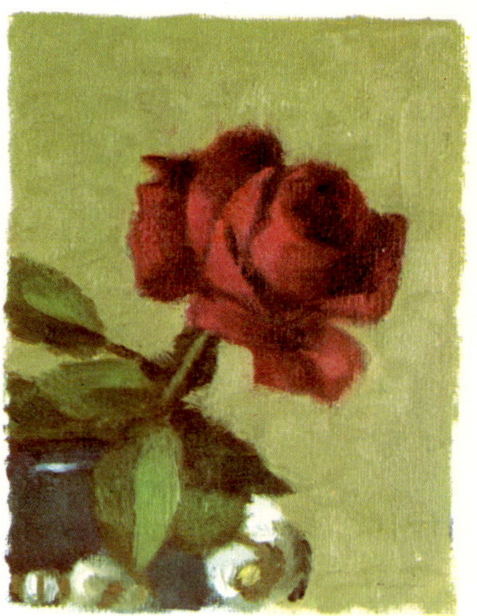

Painting a rose is no more difficult than painting an apple or a bunch of grapes. It's a good idea to draw in the actual shape of the flower first, very carefully. This is how I painted the example above (Fig. 281). The background was painted in first, then I used a dark green for the leaves and finally a fairly standard red (a dark carmine) for the rose. The order may seem illogical, since the initial drawing was immediately covered, but the first sketch really helps one remember the shapes, tones and colours which your memory and the subject itself provide when you are painting and drawing at the same time.

Fig. 282. In the second picture (above) I've used lighter colours on the dark carmine ground and have more-or-less modelled the shape of the petals.

Fig. 283. Finally, the leaves have been modelled in as well. You'll notice a few important details: I've used the background colour again to simplify and blur outlines. The colours used in the rose are: rose madder, red and white, plus a bit of Prussian blue and burnt umber for outlines and the darker areas.

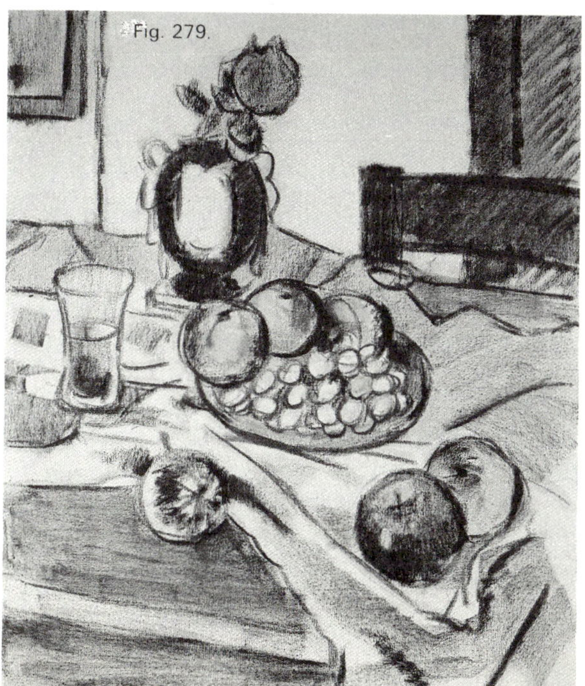

Fig. 279.

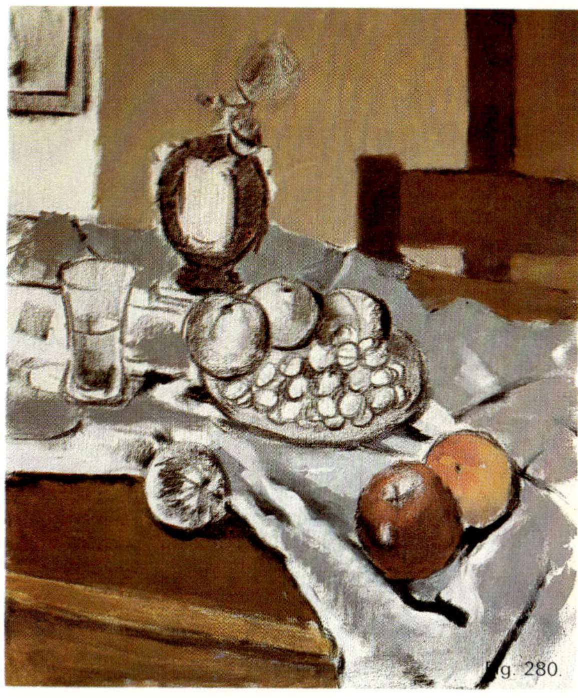

Fig. 280.

step-by-step painting no. 1

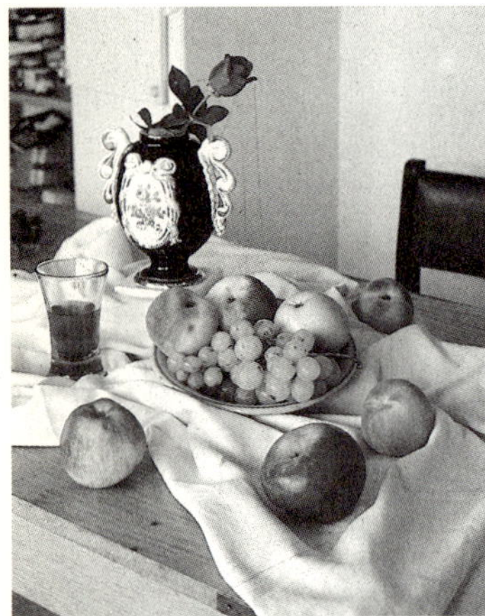

Fig. 284. Reduced photograph of the model, to help you follow the process step by step.

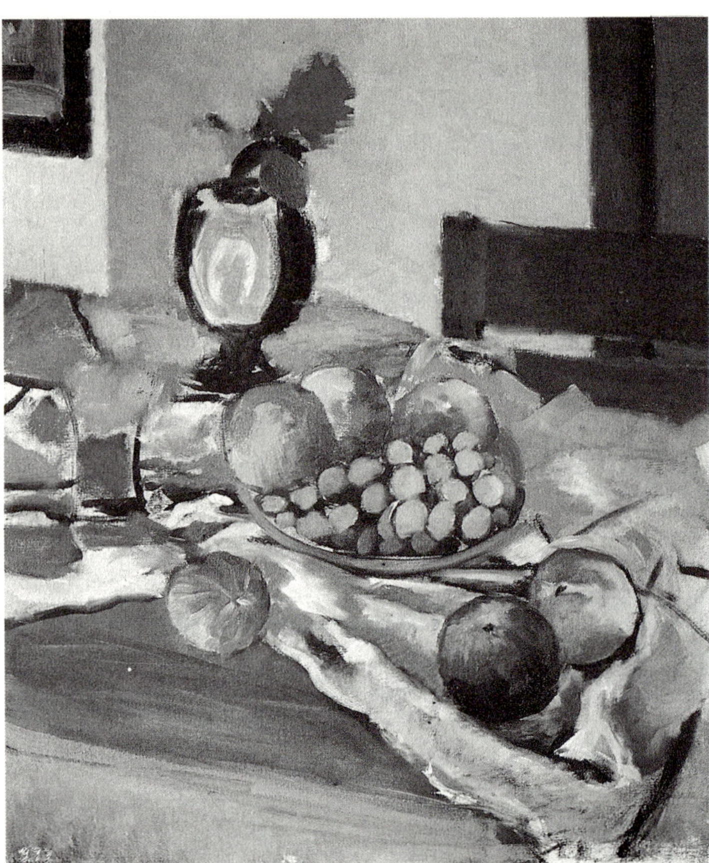

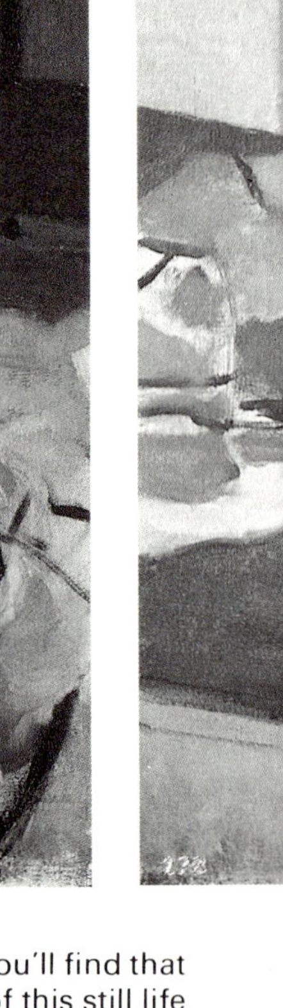

End of Stage I:
Fig. 285 (above) shows the state of the picture after the first stage of colouring, i.e. after all its components have been washed in. I'm still following the original model with no peach at the back and with a different apple on the bit of bare table. There's been no attempt yet to get any clearly-defined shapes, so changes can still be made, as, for example, in the rose: it started off as a bud (Figs. 277 and 284) but I washed it in as an open rose. I've also changed its leaves, as well as altering the arrangement of the grapes and the actual pieces of fruit in the bowl. The shapes of the fruit will be altered later. This doesn't mean that everything here is temporary! You'll find that many components of this still life will be kept just as they are, for example, the background, the chair and the picture behind, together with the basic lines of the tablecloth.

step-by-step painting no. 1

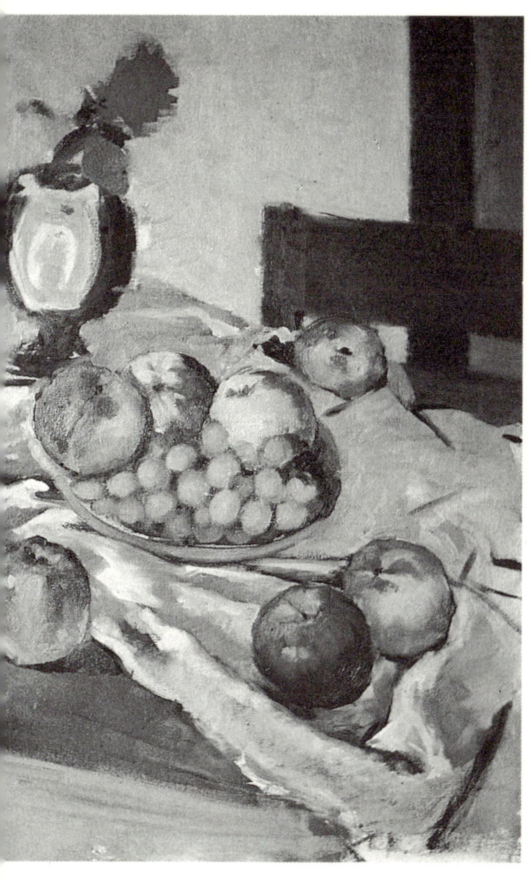

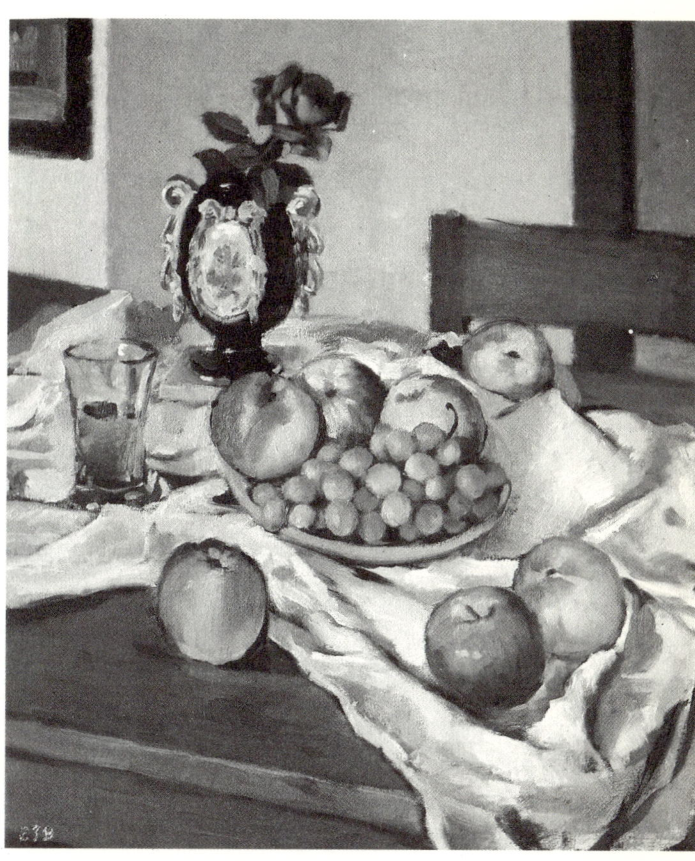

Stage II: shape and colour adjustment (Fig. 286).
At last I've worked out a final version: I've changed the apple in the foreground, added a peach at the back and replaced two of the peaches on the dish by two apples. The idea is to try to get greater variety in shape and, more especially, in colour. Some parts of the picture are now there for good, for instance the peach at the back and the two apples in the dish, also, to some extent, the pieces of fruit in the foreground. But the bunch of grapes will be changed and painted again, as you'll see in Fig. 287. Perhaps the best advice to give at this stage is to try to "move about the picture", i.e. don't hang around over any one component or bit of colouring. It's better to make a quick attempt and go back later, all the while trying to sharpen your creative perception, interpretation and synthesis.

Stage III: completion (Fig. 287)
The picture is completed, but there's still room for improvement; check over a few details, e.g. the highlights on some of the fruit, grapes included; look at the colour of the wooden table and one or two lines and highlights in the tablecloth. The finished work can be judged more easily from the colour reproduction overleaf.

step-by-step painting no. 1

Fig. 288. This reduced photograph of the model should help your study of the still life at its final stage.

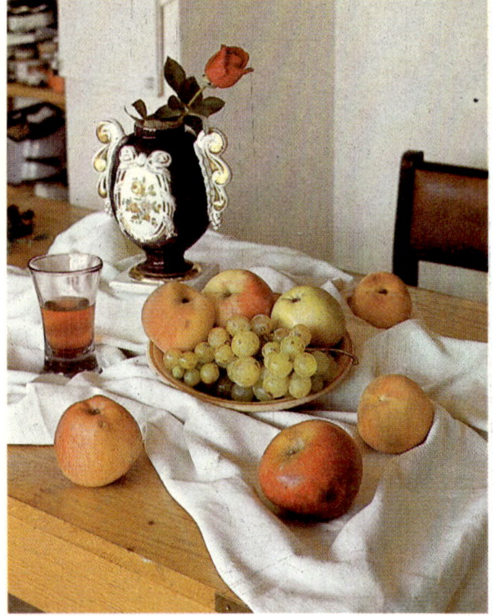

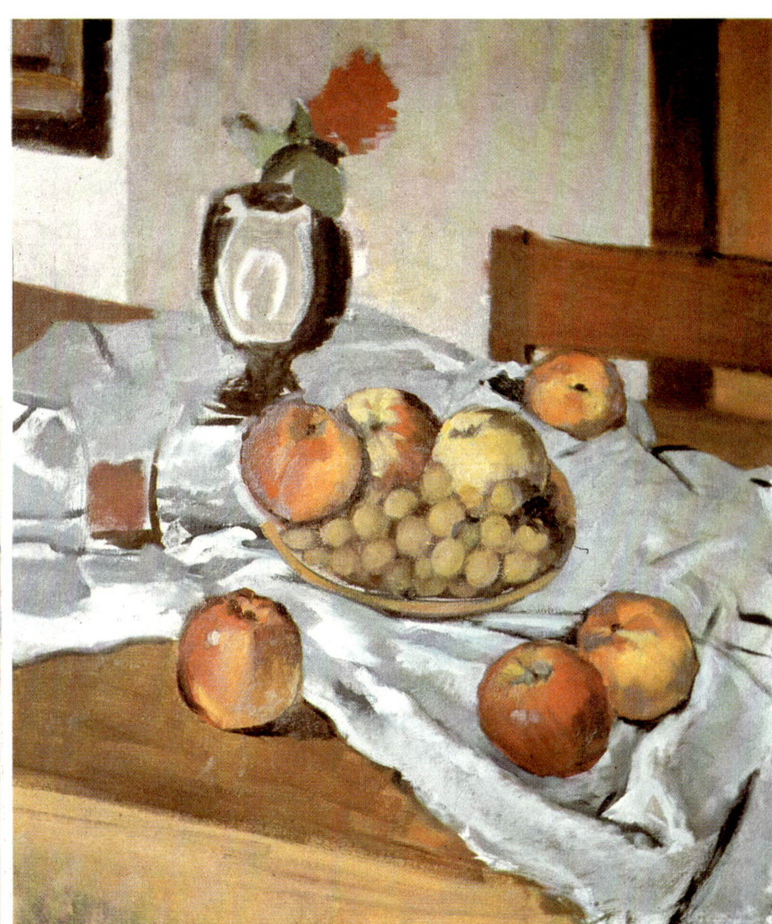

Fig. 289

You may find it simpler to follow through the three stages if you look at Fig. 289 (above) which accompanies Stage II: shape and colour adjustment. Compare Fig. 289 with the reproduction of the finished picture (next page), checking off the alterations in shape and colour made in some parts of the picture, including the complete restructuring of the bunch of grapes, the changes made to the apples in the foreground and the differences made to the construction and colouring of the tablecloth by the use of whites and light greys to emphasize the folds. You'll see the work that has been done on the tumbler and the porcelain vase.

Take a careful look at the progress worked from Fig. 287 (previous page) to the completed picture and notice the finishing touches. If you would like to sum up the suggestions given in this sections, try to paint a still life in this style, in the light of what you now know of Cézanne and his work.

step-by-step painting no. 1

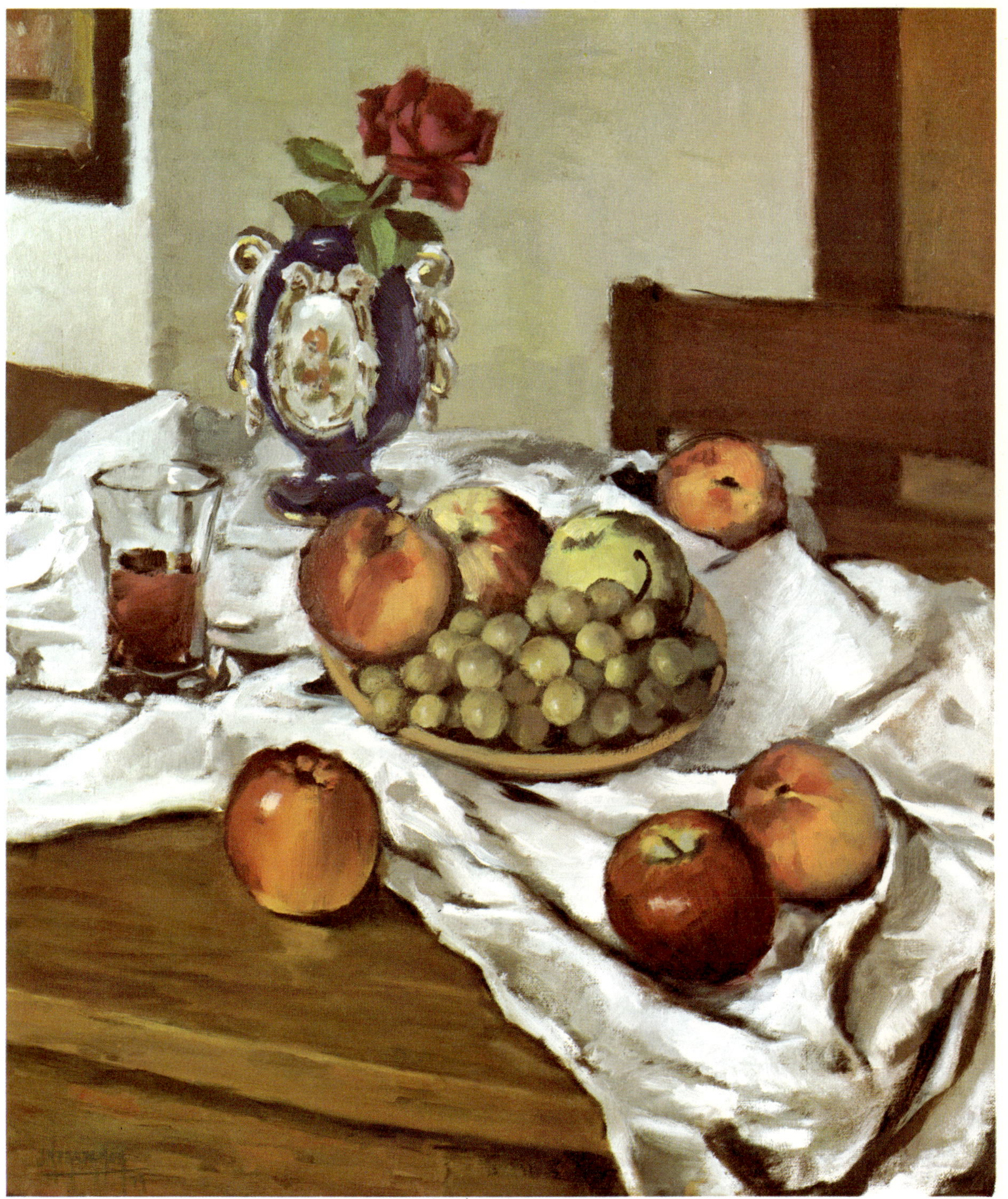

290

step-by-step painting no. 2

The subject

The step-by-step guidance given here includes a couple of very important points about oil painting in general and, in particular, still lifes in oils. The picture in question (p. 123 shows it completed) was painted by artificial light and took two evening sessions of about two-and-a-half hours each. Fig. 291 (right) is a photograph of the subject and the table lamp used for lighting it —it's an ordinary 100 watt bulb. My easel was one-and-a-half metres or less away from my subject; my work was lit by a 100 watt bulb in an adjustable lamp fixed to the easel (see Fig. 70, p. 40). The subject and the kind of lighting are important, since the model consists largely of glass objects against a dark background. Bear in mind three points which follow logically from this: (a) that glass is transparent, so that background colours or objects immediately behind the glass are visible; (b) that shapes seen through glass bottles and so on will appear distorted; (c) that portrayal of glass objects consists mainly of dark outlines, dark and light patches and highlights. We'll bear these points in mind in our step-by-step painting of this still life.

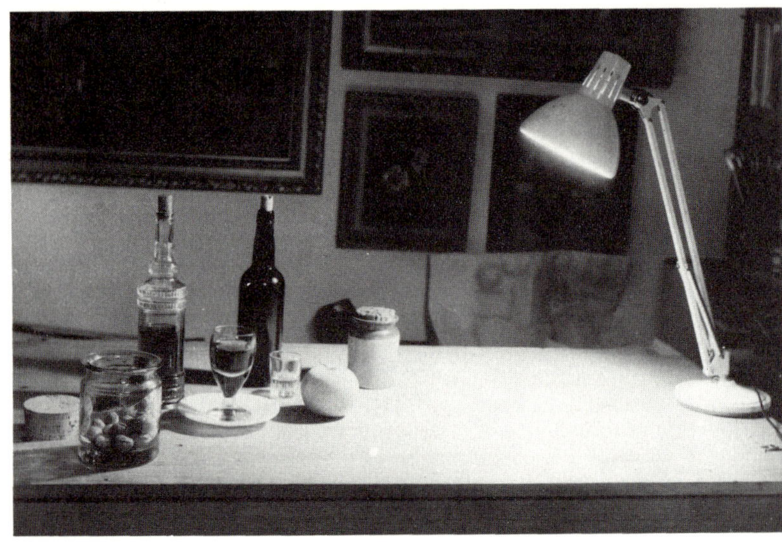

291

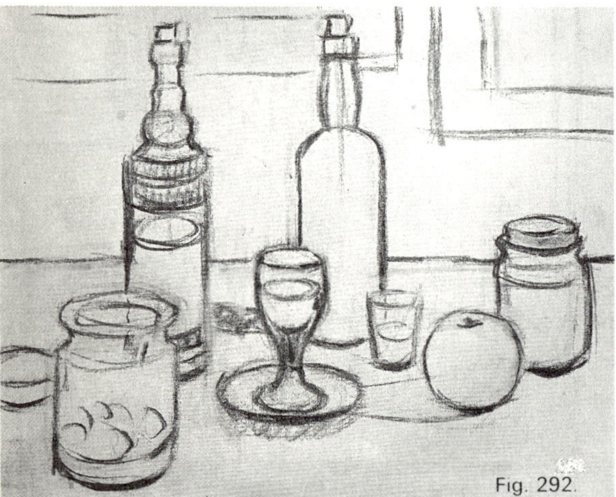

Fig. 292.

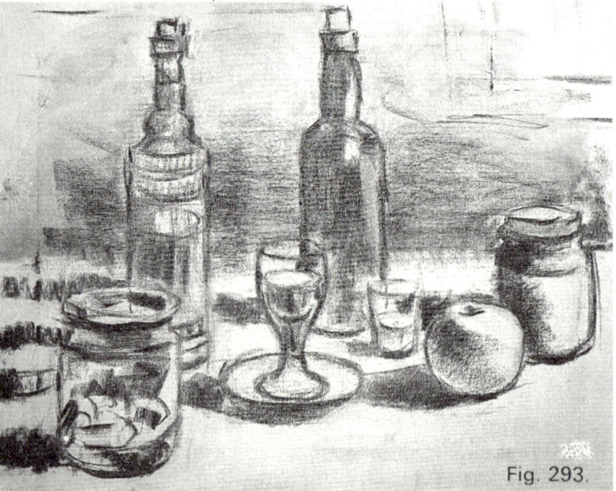

Fig. 293.

Fig. 292. Preliminary charcoal drawing, done after making a few sketches to work out proportions, consider composition and check how the subject fits into the picture.

Fig. 293. Same drawing treated with charcoal in order to sort out volume, shapes and projection of shadows.

step-by-step painting no. 2

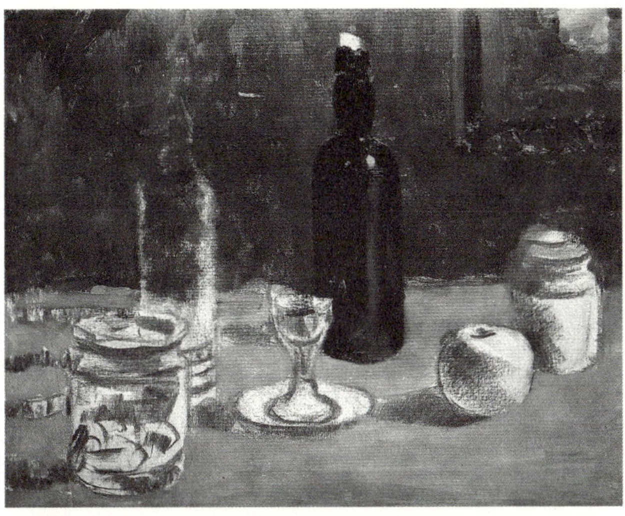

Fig. 294. The dark tones of the background and the light sienna of the table were painted first. The bottle was painted direct with a finish that seems more-or-less final. If you look at the finished picture you'll see that the volume of this bottle is conveyed just by the highlights and reflection of a dim glow from the ochre and yellowish colours of the tabletop and the apple. The dark background blurs the shape of the transparent bottle towards the left and we have merely a hint of its size. The wine glass was not painted at this stage; the cork (left of photograph) has been left out for now. Both seemed to complicate the composition.

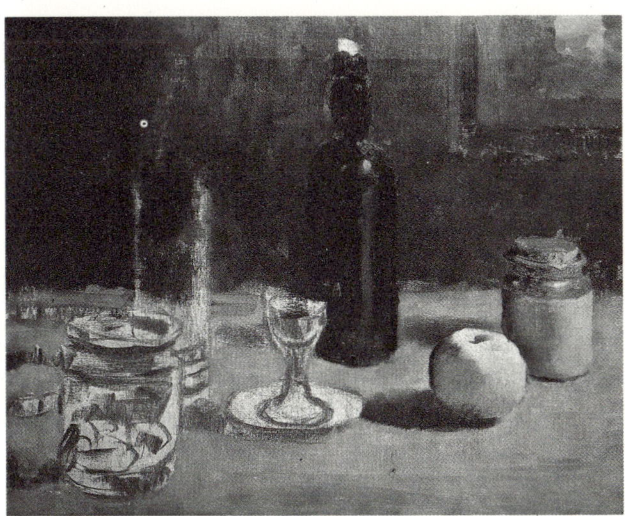

Fig. 295. The apple and the earthenware jar have been painted as they will stay. Look at the finished still life on p. 123 and see how the different objects are positioned so that the apple stands out, presenting a sharp contrast which makes it the focal point it was intended to be.

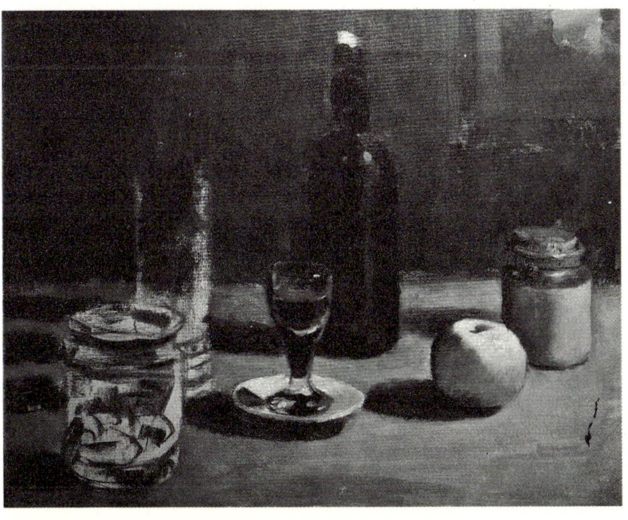

Fig. 296. When I started to compose this still life I put the wineglass where it is now, but left out the white saucer. I realized after the preliminary sketches that the patch of white was needed to provide diversity. In the reproduction of the finished picture you can see how the glass has been synthesized into a few simple strokes of dark greys, light greys and white highlights. This is an example of the law of contrasts: "a light colour becomes paler in proportion to the darkness of its surrounding colour."

step-by-step painting no. 2

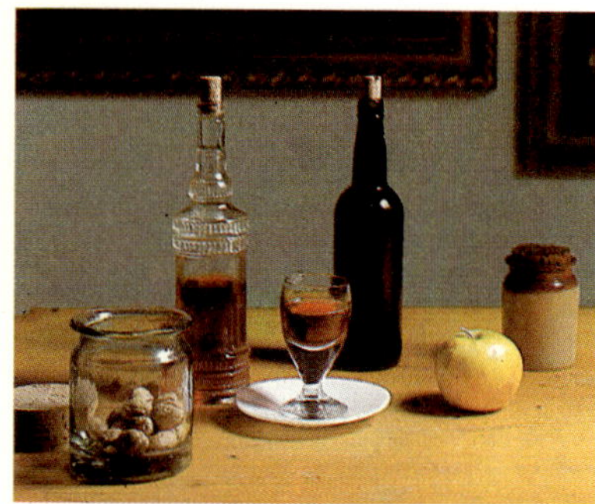

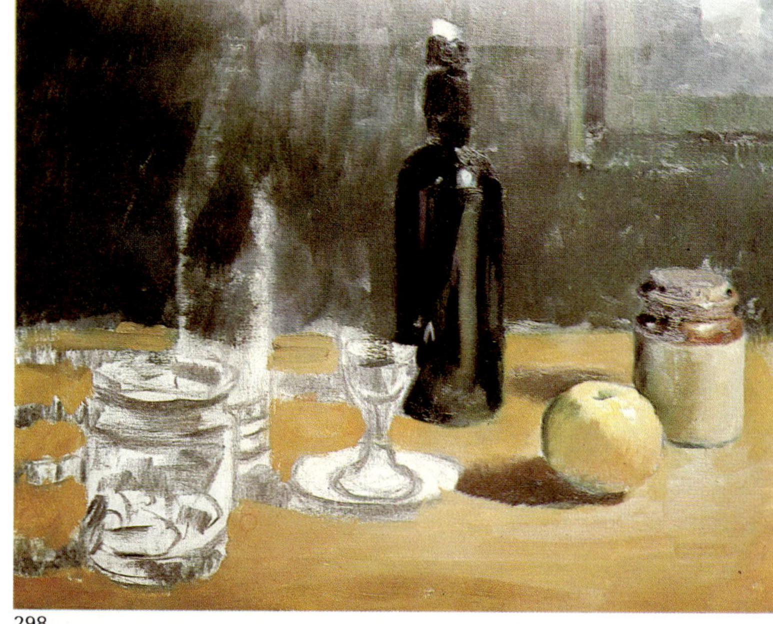

298

Fig. 298. These colour photographs of the picture in various stages were taken in my studio. Although tests were carried out beforehand and the greatest care was taken, it was not always possible to prevent the quality of reproduction being affected by the sheen and reflection from the newly-painted canvas. This is shown clearly in the two photographs on the right, Figs. 298 and 299 and is most marked at the top of each photograph. See how the background colour distorts the top of the glass and the slightly blue-tinged white in the highlights of the darker bottle.

Fig. 299. A glass jar like this at the left foreground of the picture, with odd transparent patches, vague shapes inside —a few nuts— the distortions, uneven chiaroscuro and highlights may look a very complicated and difficult subject.

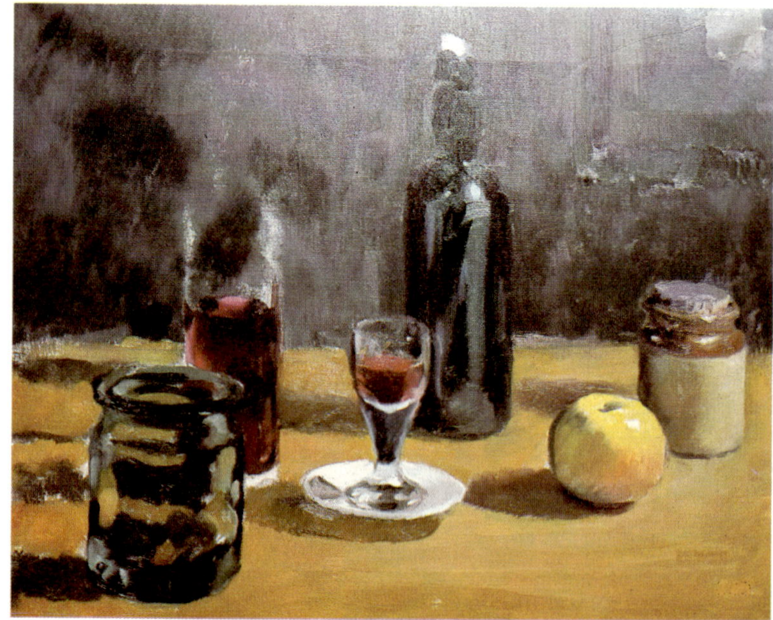

299

step-by-step painting no. 2

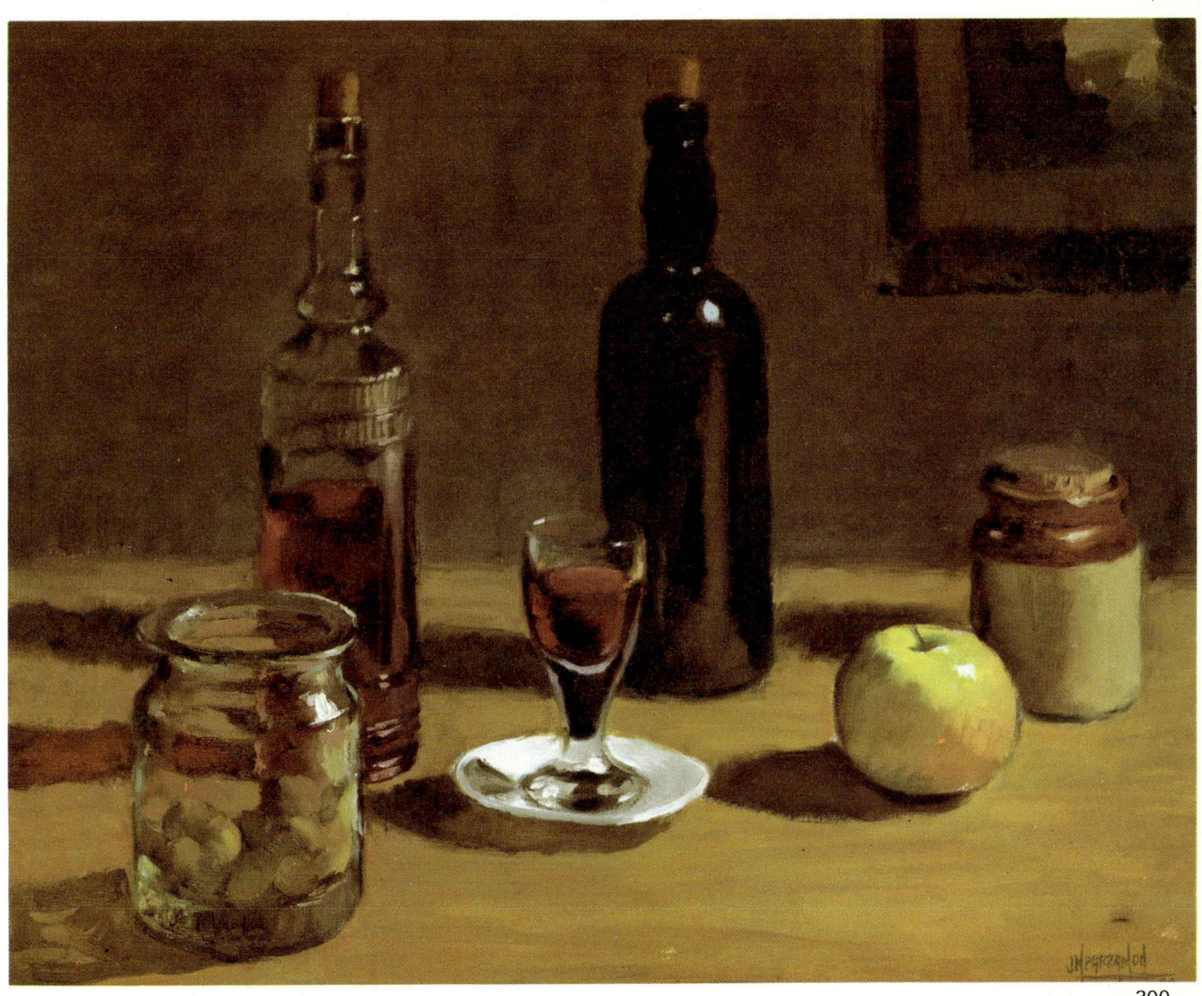

300

But it's no more difficult than anything else and requires no special skill. You have to remember Michelangelo's often-quoted precept: "Draw everything; copy everything." In other words, look at each shape, every patch of colour and every highlight as if it were a subject in its own right, analyzing its contours and size in relation to everything else you draw.· It sounds straightforward enough.

Fig. 300. Here is the final result after a bit of retouching, i.e. making the background and the table paler, reconstructing the top of the glass and finishing the glass jar and the wine bottle. If you look carefully at the wine bottle, you'll see how the effect of volume is conveyed on something that merges with the background. A few carefully placed dark patches and one or two light, almost white, flecks show the highlights. If you look closely at these, you'll find that hardly any are *absolutely* white. Nearly all the highlights are slightly tinged with self-colour. The highlight on the apple is white; on the earthenware jar it's white with a tinge of stone; the small highlight on the left shadowed part has a touch of blue, while the highlights on the darker bottle have a noticeably bluish tone. Some highlights on the clear bottle are very pale grey, some slightly bluish and some pale ochre. And most of the outlines are slightly blurred, especially those at the back of the picture.

You might try to paint something which presents the same problems, spending an evening or two painting by artificial light. It's a helpful and interesting exercise.

HOW *YOU* CAN PAINT A STILL LIFE IN OILS

step-by-step painting no. 3

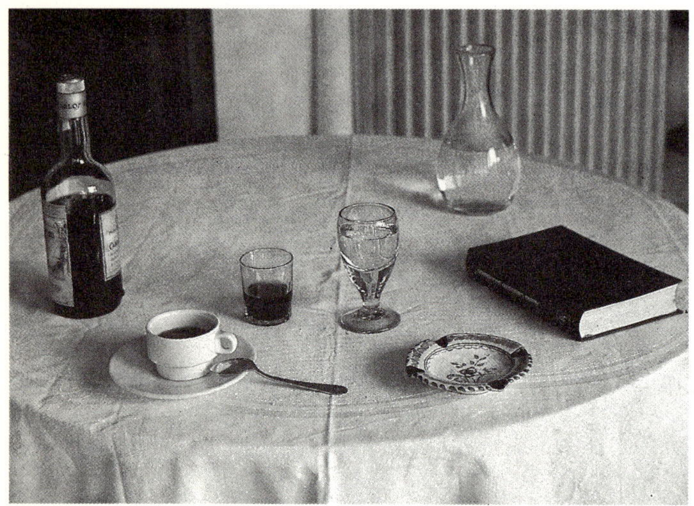

Our final project is a still life in daylight, using the speed-painting technique. The picture is finished in a single session.

The subject (Fig. 301)
This is a simple subject, but attractive and interesting: a round table with a white tablecloth on which stand a carafe, a bottle, a tumbler, a wineglass and so on, as if left on the table after lunch. There's an ashtray with an (imaginary) cigarette end and a book. It is a simpler subject than the other two, but it presents its own challenge —you have to *use* the simplicity.

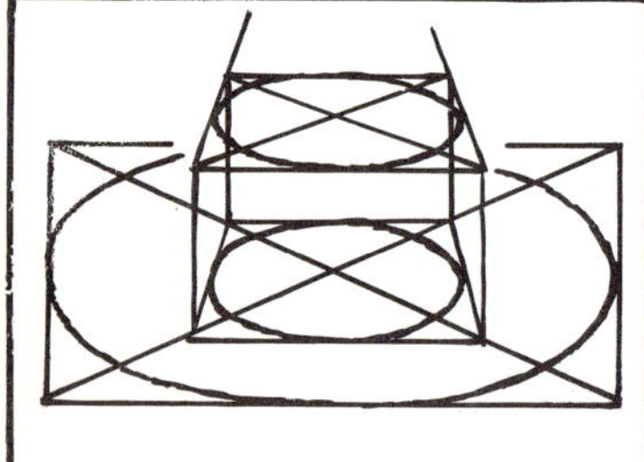

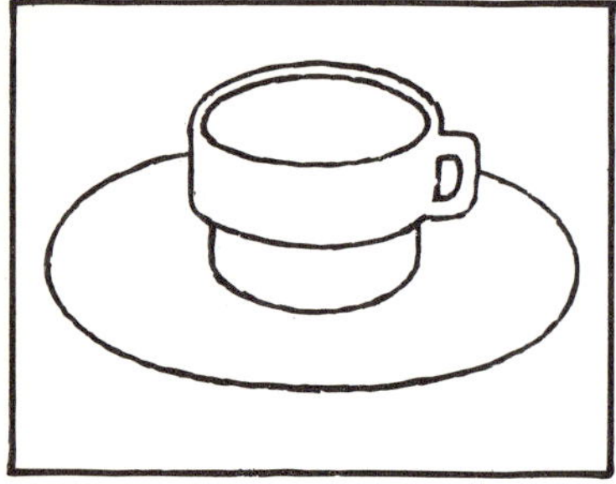

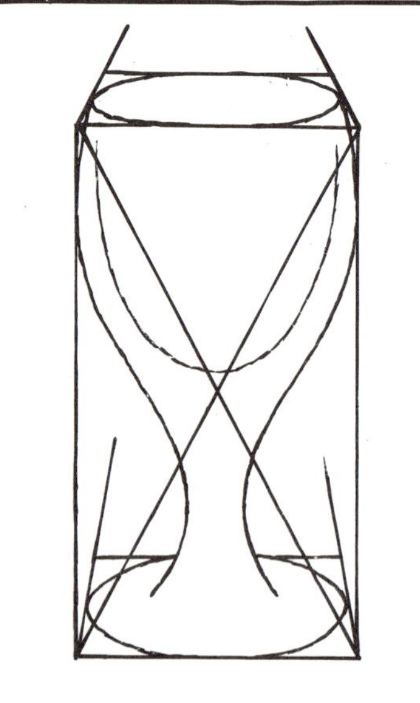

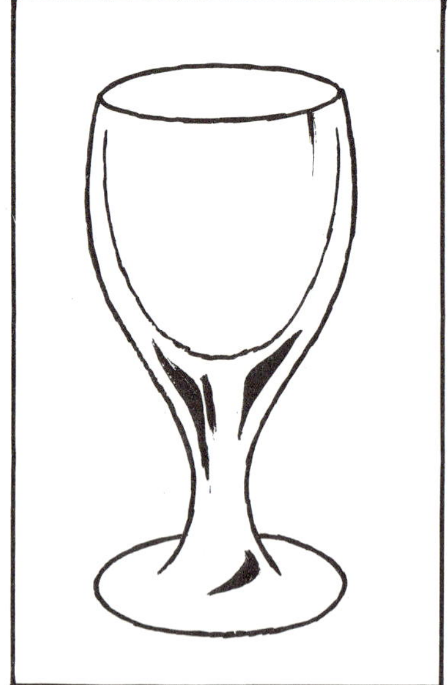

Construction and perspective

Fig. 302. As you will have read earlier on, the still life demands a thorough grounding in the rules of structure and perspective using basic shapes —the cube, the sphere and the cylinder. Here, as in the last still life, the components match those classic shapes. If you think you can manage these shapes without difficulty, in a cup and saucer or a goblet, then go ahead and use colour as well. But, if you're a bit doubtful, you may make a mistake too late. So practise drawing cups, saucers and goblets over and over again. These diagrams should help.

step-by-step painting no. 3

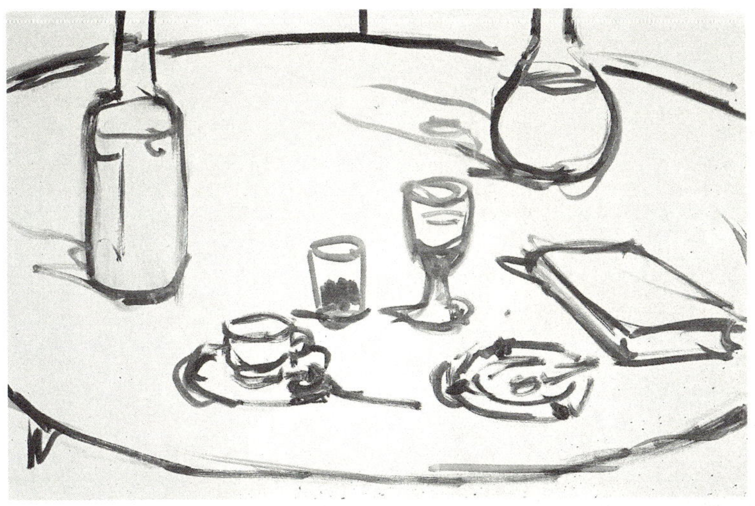

Stage I: construction (Fig. 303). There's no time to spare. The subject must be drawn and painted at the same time. So construction should be rapid, painting direct with Prussian blue and raw umber thinned with plenty of turps, so that the paint is fluid. The construction should be worked out roughly, finding size and proportion of parts and their positions in the picture —you can't stop to draw and construct each shape. I need very simple outlines to start with —that's all.

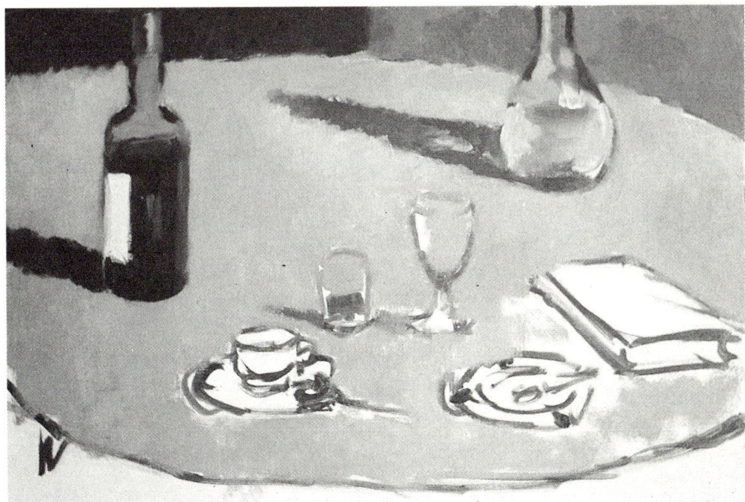

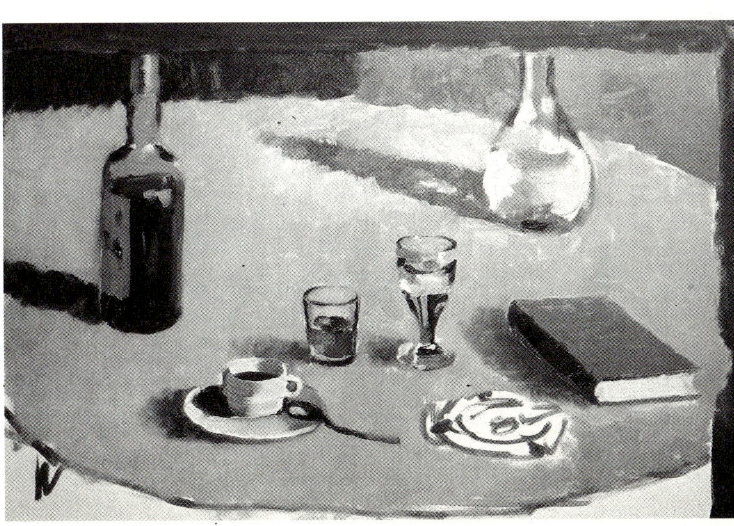

Stage II (Fig. 304.
The first step is to cover up the bare canvas, in this case by painting in the background and the grey of the tablecloth. I used a No. 24 flat brush to apply this grey, mixed from white, raw umber and Prussian blue. (At this general colouring stage all the brushes I used were flat and large, for example 12 and 18.) In Fig. 304 (left) the colour of the tablecloth shows through the transparent shapes of the carafe, the wineglass and the empty part of the brandy glasss. The book, ashtray and cup, which have colours of their own, are set apart; so is the brandy bottle, complete except for painting detail on one of the labels (I've left out the other). I'll show the highlights in the glass. I may come back to some of the painted parts later. I'll need to make the background colouring richer and more varied, but most of the shapes and colours are more-or-less done. I've not cleaned the palette yet, it's still holding the grey mixtures for the tablecloth in case I need to retouch, repaint or correct outlines or contours.

Stage III (Fig. 305).
Now for the book, the wineglass and the small tumbler. I used No.

step-by-step painting no. 3

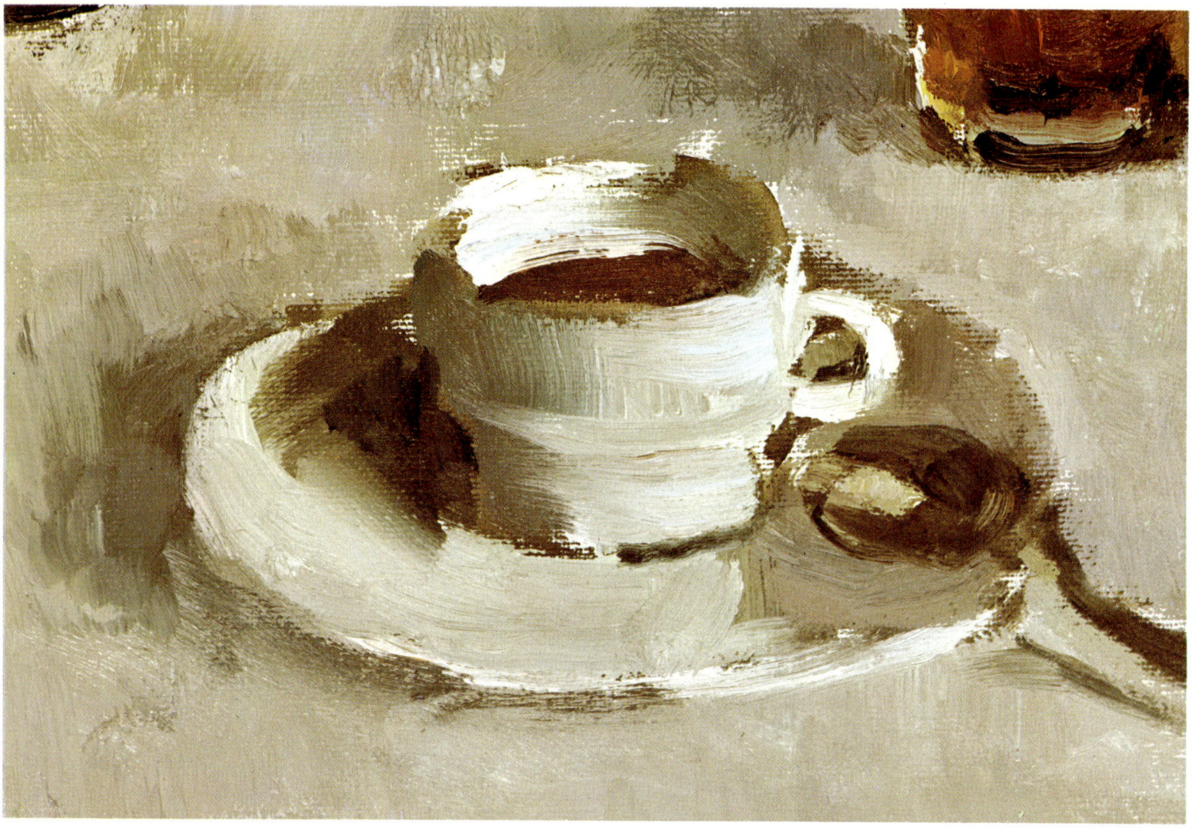

8 and No. 6 brushes to paint the wineglass, the larger brush for the darker greys and the smaller for the medium greys. Here, as in all the components of this still life, the painting and drawing are done at the same time. You need determination for this —a certain boldness and self-confidence is vital if you are going to combine drawing and painting with no hesitation, since construction and, indeed, the whole shape of the work emerges straight from your paintbrush.

I painted the cup, saucer and spoon in just a few minutes, concentrating really hard to get the best possible synthesis of shape and colour. You'll see this more clearly in Fig. 306 (above), a large detail showing the coffee cup with its saucer and spoon.

I found that I had to spend a lot of time —about half-an-hour— on the ashtray with the imaginary cigarette —there wasn't one handy! This called for meticulous treatment and took longer than anything else, because all the other things are easily recognizable shapes, even by the time they've been drastically simplified. The ashtray had to be more clearly defined and painted in more detail.

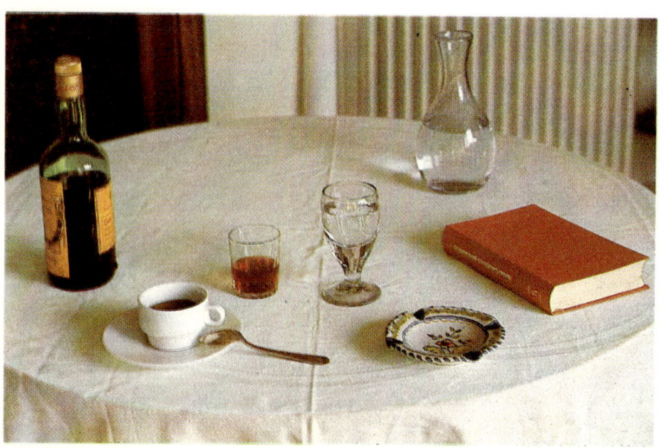

Fig. 308. Use this colour photograph for comparison —you'll notice that I've painted the brandy bottle label white instead of yellow; I've left out some creases in the tablecloth, altered some of the projected shadows and so on.

step-by-step painting no. 3

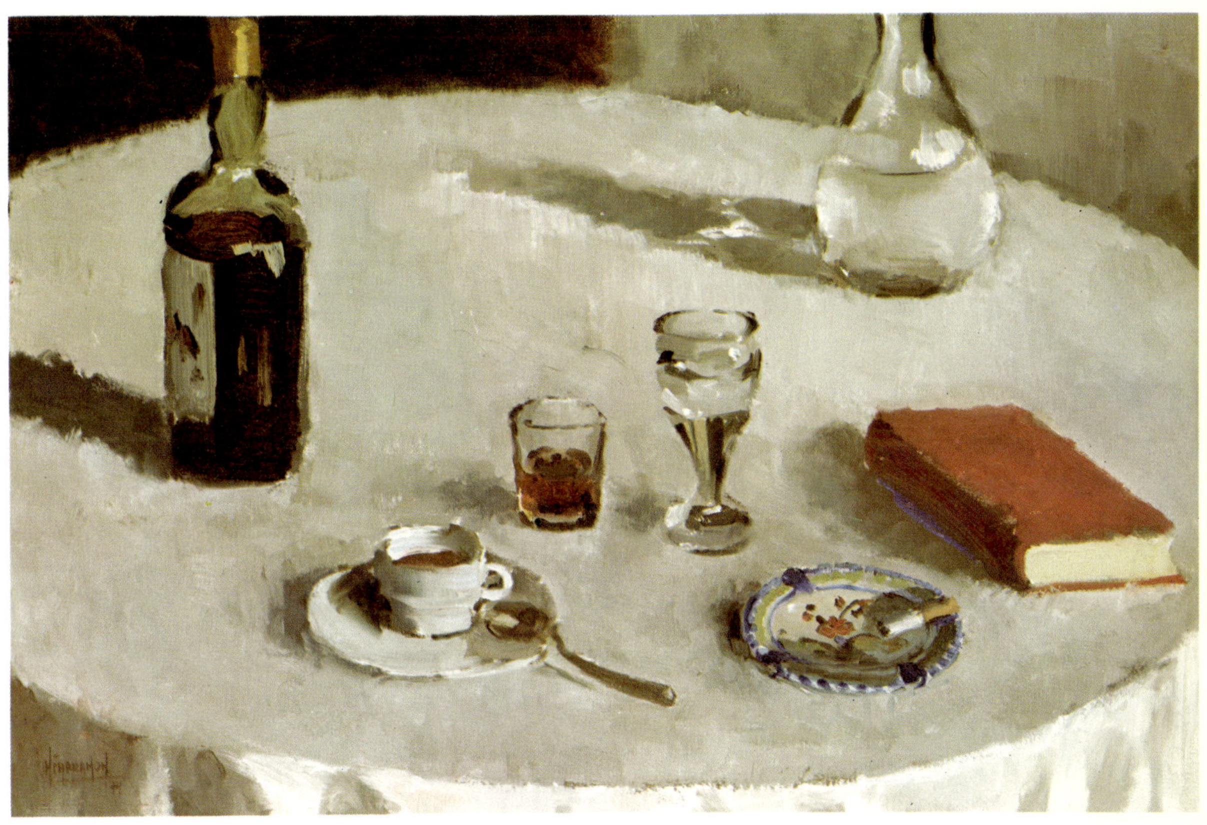

Final stage: finishing off (Fig. 307 above).

Here's the finished picture. There was very little left to do but, when I was completing the painting, I noticed a fault —a lack of symmetry in the outline of the round table. Its shape had to be put right by correcting the curves.

This was done without looking at the model; it was a question of symmetry and geometry. A bit of minor retouching of detail was necessary before I could bring the painting to its final state as shown above.

Total timing: three hours and ten minutes.

the dedicated spirit

"I have vowed that I will die painting."

In August 1906, six weeks before Cézanne died, he wrote to his great friend Émile Bernard: "I still study Nature constantly. I still paint; perhaps I am making a little progress. I feel very lonely and I am old and sick, but I have vowed that I will die painting."

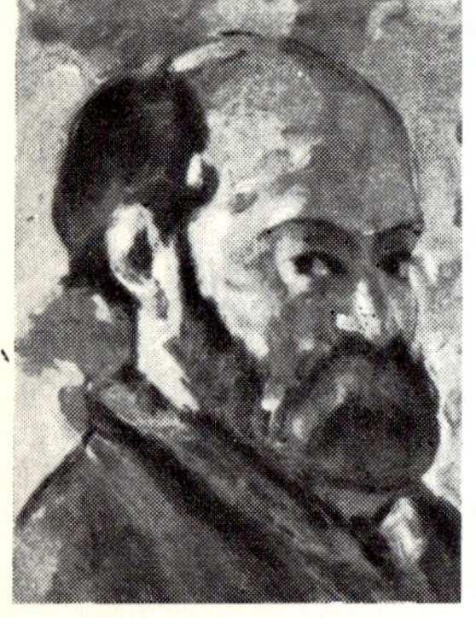

CÉZANNE (1839-1906)

The words are poignant but inspired; they stem from true genius. But genius can be made —it is not always born. Schopenhauer wrote about this: "An individual may possess the quality of genius because of the way he works. He is completely immersed; his art almost swamps him. The thought of inspiration is rejected; his faith in hard work is a lifelong companion."

The achievement of something good in painting or any other art— is based on effort. Real brilliance belongs to a great master like Cézanne. But simple good painting comes from hard work, together with the humble and dedicated spirit of Cézanne himself, of Degas ("I was born to paint") or of Ingres who, at eighty-six, set himself the task of copying a Giotto fragment. Someone asked him —it was a year before his death— *why* he was doing this? Ingres' reply was simple: "I must learn."